Breaking the Fourth Wall

Breaking the Fourth Wall
Direct Address in the Cinema

Tom Brown

EDINBURGH
University Press

© Tom Brown, 2012

Edinburgh University Press Ltd
22 George Square, Edinburgh

www.euppublishing.com

Typeset in 11/13 Ehrhardt by
Servis Filmsetting Ltd, Stockport, Cheshire, and
printed and bound in the United States of America

A CIP record for this book is available from the British Library

ISBN 978 0 7486 4425 4 (hardback)
ISBN 978 0 7486 4426 1 (webready PDF)
ISBN 978 0 7486 6953 0 (epub)
ISBN 978 0 7486 6952 3 (Amazon ebook)

The right of Tom Brown
to be identified as authors of this work
has been asserted in accordance with
the Copyright, Designs and Patents Act 1988.

Contents

Acknowledgements

I would like to thank the staff at Edinburgh University Press for their support throughout the writing of this book and the external readers for their insightful comments on the proposal.

A number of people have had a major impact on the development of this research. My interest in direct address began at the University of Warwick, where MA courses run by Richard Dyer, Ginette Vincendeau and Rachel Moseley directly influenced my thinking about the device. Jon Burrows was also most helpful in suggesting key texts from early cinema. I must also single out Victor Perkins, who originally suggested *La Ronde* to me and who has since been very generous in his exchanges about the topic. Special thanks must go to Charlotte Brunsdon for supervising the dissertation that was the seedbed for this work – our discussions (and her drawings) of the bigger picture have stayed with me.

A number of other people deserve special thanks, including Louis Bayman for his help on things Italian, Bernd Rest for his invaluable musical knowledge, James Walters for a number of stimulating conversations and Robin Brown for his insightful suggestions for Chapter 4. Lucy Fife-Donaldson has also been tremendously helpful, not least in suggesting lots of direct address films – I am only sorry there wasn't the space to discuss more of these films here.

I have had the tremendous good fortune to work in the University of Reading's Department of Film, Theatre and Television, which maintains a long-standing commitment to close analysis. I must single out John Gibbs for special thanks in this respect. The department's close analysis group, the Sewing Circle, was of enormous value in the writing of this book, and separate seminars were devoted to four of the films examined at length below. I thank all the members for their input. I cannot single out individuals because of the collective nature of the experience, except to thank Doug Pye for his extraordi-nary input in those seminars, as well for his editorial guidance on large sections of this work.

Finally, I must thank my wife Mel, whose love and support make all things possible.

List of figures

Preface

He wants realism? I'm a grown man, talking to the camera, in a fucking womb!

Steve Coogan in A Cock and Bull Story (2005)

This study examines characters in movie fictions who appear to acknowledge our presence as spectators; they seem to look at us. It is often assumed that, for narrative filmmaking, this destroys the illusion of the story world and, by acknowledging the technology behind the cinema (i.e. the camera), distances us from the fiction. While this book considers a range of approaches to direct address, I will favour films in which this is not the case: films in which this form of what may be called 'direct address' can be said to intensify our relationship with the fiction.

First a note on terminology. The clumsiness and imprecision of the phrase 'direct address' have become increasingly apparent to me in writing this study and in discussing the topic with others over a number of years. Looking at the film audience is clearly never 'direct' in any material sense; it is also rare that its effect or meaning is as obvious as 'direct' implies. 'Address' is scarcely better, as it implies the communication of some statement (its primarily verbal connotations also sit uneasily with the wordless examples examined here), and follows on so clearly from 'direct' as to risk being tautologous. Such disclaimers aside, I have chosen to continue using 'direct address' for intellectual and more pragmatic reasons – the main pragmatic reason being that, normally, people instinctively understand to what 'direct address' refers. That said, the terms are clearly not absolute. This is my starting point for interrogating the nature of a particular moment's 'address' of its audience, and the extent of its 'directness'.

These questions of terminology were raised most vividly at the 'Continuity and Innovation Conference' at the University of Reading (September 2008) when, in the midst of researching this topic, I was lucky enough to hear Gilberto Perez's keynote paper, entitled 'Looking at the Camera'.[1] Perez's focus is, in a sense, far clearer than mine. 'Looking at the camera' is the material fact behind direct address, our ability to discern it circumscribed only by the extent to which the on-screen performer's eye-line is or is not clear. However, Perez's focus is also broader than mine, as it includes direct address but is not limited to it (he also considers 'axial' shot-reverse-shots, as well as examples in which the camera being looked at is meant to occupy the position of a person or an object within the film world – as, for example, in what some may describe as 'subjective' or optical point-of-view [POV] shots. There are also problems in Perez's seemingly clearer choice of words. Yes, an actor looking at the camera may be a material fact, but when we come to discuss a fictional character looking at the camera, such assurance crumbles. To quote V. F. Perkins and an essay particularly important to the chapter on *La Ronde* (1950):

> I have been more conscious than ever of some problems attached to our use of the word 'camera' to deal with the mobility of frame and viewpoint in movies. There is a gap in our vocabulary here, apparently irreparable since the alternatives to 'camera' are all more misleading or more cumbersome. We seem to be stuck with expressions like 'looking into the camera' to describe some images where that is not what either the character or the actor can be supposed to be doing. (Perkins 2005: 39n4)

Though it is less clear why 'looking at the camera' should be a problem in relation to what *the actor* can be supposed to be doing (the occasional problems of discerning eye-line notwithstanding, surely an actor simply is or is not looking into the camera?[2]), Perkins suggests that one of the terms we most take for granted can also pose a challenge for this particular topic because:

> Though the performers have to be aware of the camera's needs, their playing most often creates the camera's absence and thereby transforms the nature of the space in front of them. It is not that these characters are oblivious to the camera. *There is no camera in their world.* (ibid.: 24; emphasis added)

Perkins describes an aspect of what is 'usual' in the cinema, and provides an account of fictional worlds flexible enough to be able to incorporate instances in which characters might be said to look at the camera. Recognising the inherent slipperiness of the issues, I will risk the apparent naivety of describing actors or characters looking 'at us' in order to evoke the effect sought rather than labouring at each point the complex ontological status of a look that is, in fact, materially impossible.

Implicit in the recourse to Perkins is my treatment of film characters as discrete entities existing within distinct fictional worlds; to say that 'there is no camera in the character's world' is to say that he or she is, fictionally, a real person (see Walton 1990 for a more extended consideration of these questions). This seems to clash with the 'Brechtian' attitude that has been favoured in (the relatively scarce) film scholarship on direct address. I shall tackle these issues head-on in subsequent chapters but, for the moment, suffice it to say that the structure of what follows places greater emphasis on direct address as a facet of essentially unified characterisations because this is what has been most neglected by film scholarship. Each of the films taken as major case studies seems to subscribe to the idea that the eyes are 'windows to the soul' and that therefore eye contact with the camera has the potential to be particularly revealing. However, they each maintain the essential mystery of one's experience of looking into another's eyes: the search for another's subjectivity; the difficulty of ascertaining motives and thoughts outside of one's self. These terms are romantic and this is because romanticism (and romance) is crucial to each of these films. Each, to a greater or lesser extent, articulates as a topic of its fiction the disparity between the apparent clear-sightedness expressed in their protagonists' look towards us and the problems these characters face in understanding the motivations (primarily romantic and / or sexual) of the other inhabitants of their filmic worlds. The key intervention sought in this study is to understand direct address not only as a gesture towards what is outside the film fiction (we, the viewer, the material act of filming and so on), but also as a potentially rich metaphor for the problems of vision (insight, foresight, other kinds of perceptiveness) that are so often the currency internal to movie narratives.

I have already stated that my focus is movie fictions. The delineations of this corpus require some further commentary. I focus solely on cinema because this is the medium whose theorists have often defined it by its 'presence-absence' and by an implied *refusal* of direct address. In contrast with live theatre, whose actors are fully present to its spectators and in which interaction (or inter-acknowledgement, at least) is sometimes expected / encouraged and / or a convention, a film performance was recorded in a place and a time removed from the moment of its spectating. Cinematic direct address can only ever feign the contact between actor and spectator common to theatre. I will not discuss television (where direct address is pervasive in many genres) because that medium also is often defined, in contradistinction to the cinema, in terms of 'immediacy' and 'liveness'. And because my focus is fiction, the genre of documentary is generally elided. The latter omission is perhaps more troubling and, indeed, is only partial. In fact, I treat the documentary aspect of much cinema as crucial to the relative frequency of direct address. Moreover, the films of Jean-Luc Godard, perhaps the director most associated with direct address, are notable for their blurring of the boundaries between fiction and documentary.

As already suggested, unlike Gilberto Perez, my analysis is not focused on camera looks which can be described as seen through 'first-person' or optical point-of-view shots. Though less an omission than a clarification of my object of study, it is worth also underlining that this book does not focus on films (or moments within films) in which direct address is performed to a diegetic camera – a camera that is part of the story world (the 'diegesis').[3] Imagine, for example, a film in which a character keeps a video diary, and their testimony to their camera plays out on our cinema screen. (One does not need to imagine such a film – *The Blair Witch Project* [1999] immediately springs to mind.) Diaries are not (or were not traditionally) intended to be seen by other people and therefore there is no specific diegetic observer to whom the testimony is addressed. Does this make a film like *The Blair Witch Project* a direct address film? I would say not. Here, talking to the camera is explained (explained away) by the *possibility* that other diegetic characters might see this testimony. The absence of a diegetic camera is not a prerequisite to a film's inclusion in this book – many of the films examined are more ambiguous than that – but the ontological strangeness of direct address as moments in which fictional characters seem to look out of their world and into ours is what interests me most.

It may seem that we have moved towards the delineation of a body of films that is so small, so marginal, as to be largely irrelevant to the mass of cinema production. This is not the case. Throughout its history, the cinema has had no problem in producing films in which fictional characters address themselves to viewers who are inaccessible / invisible to them. I believe that ordinary movie-goers also rarely have a problem with the device. Despite the ease of the apparatus and our ease as spectators, film studies has not found it easy to deal with the questions direct address raises (nor even much to pose them). When I was talking about *High Fidelity* (2000) with a friend (a friend perhaps sceptical about scholarly monographs of this nature!), he said to me, 'He [the lead character] talks to us throughout the film . . . It's no big deal.' My friend was little interested in the film's 'ontological strangeness'. To say that I think, in essence, my friend was right could be construed as making this book's project redundant. However, as we shall see, the 'ease' of cinematic direct address will be hard won. Much work needs to be done in order both to understand the complex and varied role direct address may play in different kinds of films, and to enact analyses of its function in individual movies that may still capture its experience as, for many spectators, ontologically speaking, 'no big deal'.

*

Finally, some words on structure. In line with scholarly conventions, the Introduction includes a brief survey of the critical field. The book then proceeds through two chapters that consider the role of direct address in 'counter-cinema', on the one hand, and mainstream comedies and (to a lesser extent) musicals on the other. Then three case studies chapters examine individual films before a concluding chapter brings the analysis to a close with brief recourse to some wider and more recent trends in film production. My central method of investigation is thus the close analysis of individual films. Rather than theorising in the abstract, I will develop understandings of direct address primarily through practice (the practice of close analysis). As an example, while issues such as the influence of Brechtian notions of alienation on our understanding of direct address and the problems some classic film theory represents for grasping the self-consciousness of some 'classical' films are broached in the Introduction and subsequent chapter, these questions also come out in the concrete context of the films chosen for case studies (especially with *La Ronde* in Chapter 6). Also, the somewhat broader scope of Chapters 1 and 2 means that, unfortunately, one risks perpetuating certain binaries (alternative / avant-garde versus mainstream / classical) that my choosing of borderline and difficult-to-pigeonhole films such as *La Ronde* and *Le Notti di Cabiria* seeks to refute. (For example, Federico Fellini's film being on the cusp of a more 'realist' practice and a practice based more on abstractions is a topic of my analysis of it.) Though they have proved necessary for the sake of coverage and focus, separate chapters on 'counter-cinema' and on 'comedies' will, inevitably, rather neglect what may be funny in Godard and polemical in Chaplin. For this and other reasons, readers are welcome to turn first to any of the case studies chapters, where my theorisation of direct address is developed from the 'bottom up' and in which my analysis of individual instances of direct address may speak for itself.

NOTES

1. Perez graciously provided me with the text of his speech. A small section of his analysis appears in a review of two books on Andrei Tarkovsky (Perez 2009).

2. I asked this very question of Perkins and I am grateful for his permission to print his response:

> I take it that we agree that there is a difference between looking in the direction of the camera and looking into the camera, the difference being roughly that one implies paying attention to the camera – seeking to connect one's gaze with it, or being unable

to disconnect one's gaze from it – and the other does not. The
starkest instances result, I suppose, from the use of telephoto
lenses; and these most clearly call into question your sense of the
clarity of the distinction between looking and not looking at it.
An interesting instance is Genevieve's turn away from Robert in
the post-hunt scene out in the marshes in *The Rules of the Game*
(1939). There's a significant ambiguity as Genevieve begins to
speak ruefully / resentfully of Christine's arrival to spoil her
affair with Robert: against common sense the image gives the
feeling that Genevieve may be addressing herself to Christine
and advertising Robert's adultery. Mila Parély here should surely
be described as looking towards camera but not at or into it.
Am I being over-subtle, manufacturing a distinction rather than
observing one?

The answer to the final question is, I think, no, the distinction is real,
not manufactured. Perkins's description of the moment from Renoir's
film underlines that there is still much work to be done in describing the
relationship between performers and the cameras that film them. I am
examining only one, relatively eccentric permutation of that relationship
here. However, the difference between playing to the camera and looking
directly into it resonates with the distinction between more tentative
instances of what I will later describe as 'to-be-watched-ness' and direct
address. For example, the development of Giulietta Masina's performance over the course of *Le Notti di Cabiria* pushes at this distinction – she
only looks directly at the camera and, I suggest, at us in the film's final
shot.

3. The term 'diegetic' is associated primarily with film music. In examining
music's relationship to direct address, I have frequently come up against
the distinction between diegetic and 'non-diegetic' or 'extra-diegetic'. A
distinction familiar to students and scholars of the cinema, these terms
describe music that appears to originate in the story world and that which
comes from outside – these terms indicate the difference between, say,
music accompanying an orchestra we see playing on screen (diegetic) and
an orchestral score that accompanies action in which no musician is present
(non- or extra-diegetic). Claudia Gorbman's work has interrogated this distinction in depth, pointing out the frequency with which it is transgressed,
and positing 'meta-diegetic' as a third category (see especially Gorbman
1987: 3, 20–6). As itself a transgression of the distinction between inside
and outside the immediate story world, direct address forces us to consider
the value of such terminology. However, I have chosen to try to keep terminology simple, to make use, largely, of existing vocabulary, and allow

discussion of such distinctions to emerge out of the films themselves. That said, my preference throughout will be for *extra*-diegetic over *non*-diegetic, because of non's rather unhelpful-sounding finality. I sometimes use the term 'cross-diegetic' to describe direct address itself.

CHAPTER 1

Introduction: direct address in film history, theory and criticism

A unifying theory of direct address is neither possible nor desirable; it is far too varied in its meanings and functions within film fictions. Neither is there the space in this study to offer anything remotely like a full account of its history. Many of the first films were documentaries, and many of their subjects acknowledged the camera; even the earliest fictions often involved direct address, and the device continues to crop up in feature productions around the world to this day. The book may prove more 'comprehensive' in offering a critical approach to the device; I openly favour certain practices over others, but will reflect on the criteria for value judgements at various stages of this book. It is worth, however, introducing the topic and tracing the history of its scholarly neglect by making reference to the categories of film history, theory and criticism. Though these are gross simplifications, film theory can be thought of as posing the question, 'What is "film"?'; film history, 'What has "film" been?'; and film criticism, 'What is *this* film, and what is its relationship to others?' The study of direct address impacts upon all three sets of questions. However, as 'criticism' of direct address has been especially absent (and criticism has endured 'an illicit and ghostly existence' in our field more generally – Clayton and Klevan 2011: 2), 'criticism' is where I shall set out an introductory summary of what I take direct address most usually to 'mean'.

DIRECT ADDRESS IN FILM HISTORY

Direct address is a regular feature of early cinema. Indeed, its frequency in late nineteenth- and early twentieth-century moving images is often seen as evidence of their primitivism and naivety. One of the scholars who has done most to refine this understanding of the early period of motion picture production is Tom Gunning, and his notion of (especially) pre-1906 / 1907 as the 'cinema of attractions' created 'this film studies generation's most quoted watchword' (Altman 2004: 9).[1] The cinema of attractions is partly defined by the directness of its address to its audience:

> The performers in the cinema of attractions greeted the camera's gaze with gusto, employing glances, winks and nods. With the establishment of a coherent diegesis, any acknowledgment of the camera became taboo, condemned by critics as destructive of the psychological effect essential for an involved spectator. (Gunning 1991: 261)

With Gunning's second sentence, he describes the transition from an attractions-based cinema to the 'cinema of narrative integration', a style whose development is associated primarily with D. W. Griffith. The cinema of attractions prior to Griffith and the practice he represents was frequently more concerned with what might be called a 'vaudevillian' engagement with its audience than with a more rigorous creation of a unified fictional world. (The allusion to vaudeville reminds us of the limitations of contrasting cinema with 'theatre' in any straightforward way. The fourth wall was, of course, first a theatrical convention but its absence is one thing that distinguishes vaudeville – where many early cinema screens were placed – from legitimate theatre.) This is not to suggest that the cinema of attractions was entirely non-narrative but, rather, that narrative 'immersion' might often be put aside in favour of a direct assault on the spectator's more physical reactions, their emotions, sense of humour and so on. For example, one of the most important films in histories of the development of early film narrative is also famous for a very 'attractions' kind of direct address. As well as for its cross-cutting, Edwin S. Porter's *The Great Train Robbery* (1903) is famed for the shot of George Barnes, playing one of the film's outlaws, aiming and firing his pistol directly at the camera (see Figure 1.1). The shot was provided separate from the main body of the film and could be inserted at an appropriate time by the projectionist / exhibitor. Edison's strange but revealing classification of the shot (it is simply listed in his catalogue as 'REALISM' – see Pratt 1973: 36) hints at a conscious use of direct address of the camera as a means to put the viewer perceptually in the firing line – myth has it that this 'shot' had early cinema spectators fleeing from the screen, as they (also perhaps apocryphally) did from the Lumière brothers' *Arrival of a Train at La Ciotat* (1896).

A less famous but no less fascinating use of direct address provides the punch line to another film shot by Porter (and George S. Fleming), *Burlesque Suicide, no. 2* (1902; I can find no evidence of a version number one). The film, now viewable in its entire sixty seconds on YouTube, comprises a single shot of an apparently drunk man facing towards the camera. He is sitting at a table on which there is placed a revolver, a decanter and glass of drink. The

Figure 1.1 *The Great Train Robbery* (Edison Manufacturing Company, 1903): George Barnes shoots at the audience.

man, clearly intoxicated and in great distress, wipes his brow, takes a number of sips and holds the gun to his head. He appears to think better of it, pushes the gun away and instead goes to take another drink. As the glass comes close to his lips, a smile begins to crack across his face, but this is the smile of the sober actor, not the drunk character – the smile would be called 'corpsing' in a performance where it was not intended – and the man suddenly lowers the drink and points at the camera and at us, laughing hysterically. This final gesture exemplifies the way performers in the cinema of attractions 'greeted the camera's gaze with gusto'. However, what is noteworthy is that the gesturing towards the viewer only makes sense as the punch line to a film that, until that moment, has constructed the audience as absent to its fictional character. The action (the man's suicidal despair) could hardly be more 'private' and, until the final moment of direct address, the actor scrupulously avoids making eye contact with the camera. A cinematic 'fourth wall' was obviously available to 1902 filmmakers. Otherwise, its breaking could not be so pointed, nor so funny.

A whistle-stop tour through the device's early history could take in major silent- into sound-era cinema practitioners (such as Charlie Chaplin and Laurel and Hardy), who are discussed at later points of this book. Other less widely known silent stars such as Harry Langdon have been noted for the frequency with which they address their audiences,[2] and the eyes of other major performers of the period – for example, those of Roscoe 'Fatty' Arbuckle – are in frequent, mischievous contact with the camera. A focus on performers is useful, given the topic under consideration here. However, Gunning's concept of the cinema of attractions is more valuable in suggesting the spectatorial logic behind direct address. Usefully, Gunning also suggests ways in which attractions continue beyond 1907 and, even, into the contemporary cinema:

> Even with the introduction of editing and more complex narratives,
> the aesthetic of attractions can be still be sensed in periodic doses of
> non-narrative spectacle given to audiences (musicals and slapstick
> comedy provide clear examples). The cinema of attractions persists in
> later cinema . . . It provides an underground current floating beneath
> narrative logic and diegetic realism. (Gunning 1999: 826)

Gunning's concept of the cinema of attractions perhaps too often provides a short-cut historicisation of contemporary cinematic spectacle and special effects. However, as a short cut, it is useful and Gunning's suggestion of the continuation of an aesthetic of attractions into musicals and slapstick is borne out by my focus on these genres in Chapter 3. However, as we shall see, the continuation of direct address throughout cinema history need not be explained by the logic of 'attractions'; direct address may enhance a 'coherent diegesis', rather than be opposed to it.

Far from being absent from the actual history of film, direct address has been neglected by its historiography, scholarship and journalistic commentary. The process of its marginalisation started early. In his book on Griffith, Gunning quotes an early film critic, Frank Woods of the *Dramatic Mirror*, whose contemporaneous reviews celebrated D. W. Griffith and what he saw as the necessary maturation of film style and performance away from histrionics and direct address:

> 'The good director,' Woods had intoned in his weekly column on films,
> 'is constant and persistent in his instruction to his players to keep
> their eyes away from the camera and the good players try to obey this
> injunction'. The actor must not greet the camera's gaze because that act
> would not only make the spectator aware of the camera, but also aware
> of the actor acting and aware of the act of watching. As Woods put it;
> 'When the movement or attitude of the player is obviously unnatural in
> turning his face towards the camera, he betrays by the act the fact that
> he is acting – that there is someone in front unseen by the spectators to
> whom the actor is addressing himself. Immediately, the sense of reality

is destroyed and the hypnotic illusion that has taken possession of the spectator's mind, holding him by the power of visual suggestion, is gone.' (Gunning 1991: 262)

Though Woods seems to suggest the spectator may become aware of the presence of the *director* ('someone in front unseen by the spectators to whom the actor is addressing himself') rather than being troubled by an awareness of their own 'presence' as spectators, this statement, written in 1910, about direct address destroying the 'sense of reality', might well be an article of faith for some modern film critics. Importantly, however, the 'cinema of narrative integration' produced by Griffith is not quite of the concealed illusionism that a simple binary might make it. (The 'cinema of attractions' versus the 'cinema of narrative integration' is a binary but Gunning's is not a simple one.) Gunning describes Griffith's filming style in terms of 'voyeurism'. The notion of film spectatorship as voyeuristic (because we as unseen spectators watch oblivious figures from our darkened auditoria) is, arguably, one of the pre-eminent clichés of film studies. However, Griffith's 'voyeurism' is not self-concealing in the way that term implies:

> The powerful voyeur camera, stripping away both presence and
> pretense, destroyed the histrionic style as much as any other factor . . .
> The voyeur camera empowers the spectator as it seemingly catches
> the actor in a moment of self-revelation. The extreme development
> of the powerful camera comes – paradoxically – in moments in which
> Biograph actors actually do acknowledge the presence of the camera,
> but in a diametrically different manner than the cocky salutes and
> saucy winks shared with the camera by performers in the cinema of
> attractions. Rather than exhibiting themselves, Griffith's actors seem
> at these moments to hide from the camera, as if from a sense of shame.
> (Gunning 1991: 262–3)

There is some slippage here: surely Gunning means the spectator catches the *character* 'in a moment of self-revelation'? (Unless, of course, he means that the documentary aspect of all filmmaking is revealing something of the actor's essence?) This aside, this sense of the camera's presence being active in the actor's playing and therefore in our experience of that performance, is fascinating and so often forgotten in accounts of the film apparatus that regularly assume Griffith to stand for a certain notion of 'classical' (thus self-effacing) film illusionism. While, as Gunning shows, Griffith's style does not quite make his camera absent to his characters, an even more obvious example that puts into question the 'voyeurism' of mainstream cinema would be Charlie Chaplin, whose career flourished after the development of the 'cinema of narrative integration', and who continued to acknowledge the camera actively in his performances of both pathos and comedy: '[Chaplin would look at the camera] throughout his career, using the instrument as a means of establishing a direct and openly acknowledged relationship between himself and his audience' (Robinson [year unknown]).[3]

As a concluding note to this discussion of direct address and film history, I shall quote from one of the few previously published discussions of the device as a way of clarifying my own aims. Jane Feuer notes the following while situating Maurice Chevalier's direct address within traditions of live theatre and a broader entertainment tradition: 'It is absolutely essential to see a technique such as direct address in this historical context. Otherwise one may argue that direct address is inherently subversive or radical. It is not' (Feuer 1993: 39). Feuer's final point is one I wholly subscribe to and she is right to suggest that historical contextualisation can offer one kind of proof that this is so. Such historical contextualisation does enter into my later analyses to the extent, for example, that a film such as *Le Notti di Cabiria* is related to the traditions of national filmmaking that preceded it and, more obliquely, aspects of those films' aesthetic treatment of the material deprivation felt in the country at the time. However, my focus in this book is more 'theoretical' and more 'critical' than 'historical' for practical and more polemic reasons: they are practical because a thorough international history of the device from cinema's birth to the present day is impossible in a form such as this; polemic because certain theoretical positions on the medium are what has prevented enquiry into the device. Moreover, 'history' first needs 'theory' in order to make sense of its object of analysis. I shall turn to 'theory' and 'criticism' now.

DIRECT ADDRESS AND FILM THEORY

The terms by which Frank Woods condemns direct address make it scarcely surprising that it should be advocated by the politicised film theory of the 1970s. What Woods and others like him wished into being, Marxist, radical and oppositional critics would later identify as the model to be resisted; what Woods would lovingly refer to as the 'hypnotic illusion' (Gunning 1991: 262), Bertolt Brecht would denounce as cinema's 'witchcraft' (quoted in *Screen* 1975 / 1976: 48 – a special Brecht-themed issue of the journal most associated with the application of his theories on to cinema). In the 1970s and into the 1980s, direct address came to be held up by important strands of film theory and advocated on behalf of an avant-garde 'counter-cinema' resistant to the manipulative mainstream. This association between direct address and the avant-garde had historical roots. To continue, for the moment, an equivalence between 'attractions' and direct address, it is worth noting that perhaps

Gunning's best-known essay on the cinema of attractions (1990) links the practices of early cinema to the avant-garde.

The body of work in which direct address most frequently crops up as a subject of discussion is often referred to as '1970s *Screen* Theory'. It is a moment in film studies susceptible to caricature and one must be careful of lumping together a wide collection of books and essays into an easy category.[4] However, as the dominant strand of film theory of the period, '*Screen* Theory' developed a *relatively* coherent model for the mainstream and / or 'classical' cinema in which direct address is not only absent but is, in fact, structurally incompatible. Direct address was, rather, appropriated by critics and theorists within *Screen* Theory on behalf of filmmakers resistant to the hegemony of Hollywood.

Working at the intersections of psychoanalysis, semiotics, Marxism and an extolling of Brechtian formal strategies in the cinema (as in television), this body of work aimed to offer a means of revealing, and thus resisting, the conservative structures of conventional cinematic representation. The latter was seen as repressive because it leaves the viewer in a passive, inert position, merely indulged in their escapist voyeurism. Perhaps the most famous essay from this period (and still, perhaps, film studies most cited) is Laura Mulvey's 'Visual Pleasure and Narrative Cinema' (originally published in *Screen* in 1975). Laying the foundations for a particular method of feminist film analysis, Mulvey attacks the dominant discourses of patriarchal society at work in 'its favourite cinematic form – illusionistic narrative film' (1992: 32). Having at its heart a polemical aim to reveal woman's consistent objectification within popular cinema, Mulvey uses a vocabulary noticeably coloured by Brechtian perspectives:

> the mass of mainstream film, and the conventions within which it has consciously evolved portray a hermetically sealed world which unwinds magically, indifferent to the presence of the audience, producing for them a sense of separation and playing on their voyeuristic phantasy.
> (1992: 25)

In this context, the use of 'magically' echoes Brecht's own description of cinema's 'witchcraft'. The easy separation between text and spectator is precisely what Brecht sought to counter in his epic theatre, via direct address and distanciation (very different from 'separation') strategies. However, what is at issue in this discussion is indicated by 'hermetically sealed' and 'indifferent to the presence of the audience' – direct address is a clear challenge to this account of cinema's 'voyeuristic phantasies' and separation from its audience. Moreover, the coupling of a supposedly passive viewer (one unable to construct meaning independent of the dominant ideologies behind the film-text's construction) with a 'satisfying sense of omnipotence' (Mulvey 1992: 28) cannot account for the complex text–viewer relationship encouraged by the direct address of many of the examples examined in this book.

Of course, we must keep in mind that Mulvey's aims are polemical, as she sets up a basic cinematic model (mainstream narrative film) and begins to propose an alternative resistant to female objectification. However, her formulation of the mainstream is worth citing for its incompatibility with direct address:

> There are three different looks associated with the cinema: that of the camera as it records the profilmic event, that of the audience as it watches the final product, and that of the characters at each other within the screen illusion. The conventions of narrative film deny the first two and subordinate them to the third, the conscious aim being always to eliminate intrusive camera presence and prevent a distancing awareness in the audience . . .
>
> The first blow against the monolithic accumulation of traditional film conventions (already undertaken by radical filmmakers) is to free the look of the camera into its materiality in time and space and the look of the audience into dialectics, passionate detachment. (1992: 33)

The latter point is a clear call for Brechtian distanciation techniques for presenting a socio-political problem or contradiction, such as those employed by the likes of Godard, Gorin and Straub-Huillet. The emphasis on freeing the camera and audiences' looks from their subordination to the realist, coherent and thus 'illusionist' intra-diegetic looks, hints at the enormous stock potentially put into looks which break the 'fourth wall'. Mulvey sees mainstream film as working to prevent the fetishisation of the female figure from appearing 'directly (without mediation) to the spectator', leaving the spectator no space in which to achieve 'any distance from the image in front of him' (1992: 33). Not only a formal strategy, direct address in Godard is thus celebrated for its thematic and political 'directness'.

Around the same time, Paul Willemen built on Mulvey's model by positing a 'fourth look', one at the viewer: 'it must be stressed that the fourth look is not of the same order as the other three, precisely because the subject of the look is an imaginary other, but this doesn't make the presence of the look any less real' (1976: 48). Willemen's analysis centres on the avant-garde work of Stephen Dwoskin, a filmmaker who frequently employs the look at the camera to implicate the voyeurism of the viewer and precisely the cinematic fetishisation of woman that Mulvey discusses (though, arguably, this sometimes becomes another order of fetishisation/victimisation, in Dwoskin's case). Willemen's attention to the avant-gardist use of direct address ties in with *Screen* Theory's principal areas of concern. However, Willemen's view of the mainstream is more open to the potential role of direct address therein:

> In Hollywood cinema, as Metz correctly points out, the spectator is inscribed as 'invisible', but that does not mean that he / she is not also subjected to a look, merely that the look is effaced through a series of aesthetic strategies. (1976: 42)

Willemen's addition to Mulvey's structure of looks begins to open up a space in which one might envisage a place for direct address within what are otherwise monolithic conceptualisations of mainstream cinematic practice. However, where Willemen uses 'imaginary' in its Lacanian sense to designate the subject of the look *at* the audience, I would prefer 'symbolic'; it is symbolic of the film-text or filmmaker's attitude towards the viewer's role. As V. F. Perkins tells us, 'Attitudes towards the audience contribute as much to a movie's effect, and therefore its significance, as attitudes towards its more immediate subject matter' (1993: 134).

Stephen Heath is another '*Screen* Theorist' relevant to situating direct address within these discourses. Heath writes, 'a broad conception is emerging of what might be a critical role of art, of a practice of cinema, and in terms of a production of contradictions against the fictions of stasis which contain and mask structuring work' (1981: 7). This formulation prescribes a Brechtian approach to filmmaking, almost identical to the one extolled in other *Screen* articles (see especially Colin MacCabe 1974 and 1975 / 1976: 48). Heath sees 'suture' as the process by which such 'fictions of stasis . . . contain and mask structuring work'. Suture is a concept oriented around psychoanalytical understandings of the workings of dominant ideology – it often draws upon Lacan's notion of the 'symbolic', Heath, for one, drawing much on Lacanian as well as Brechtian theory. 'Suture' denotes the structural work which moulds and contains the illusory world of the screen. We can see a shared emphasis on this notion of suture in Pascal Bonitzer's article on direct address in *Cahiers du cinéma*.[5] Bonitzer describes how the intra-diegetic looks and 'suture narrative' block the desire for '*l'Autre réel*' that direct address embodies (1977: 42). This illustrates how the rare evaluations of the device which do exist remain couched in psychoanalytic terms. (This said, Bonitzer's descriptions of an *auteur*-oriented and 'abject' 'contre-regard' [1977: 45–6] will be worth returning to.) The notion of 'suture' has been largely expunged from the discourses of contemporary film studies, and, where writers such as Stephen Heath talk about suture, the symbolic and the discourses of ideology, I shall discuss editing, structure and broadly generic practices, allowing for the way these mould, contain or 'let escape' the power of direct address.

Heath, with his support for the 'Brechtian' and the practice exemplified by Jean-Luc Godard, appears to share Brecht's view of cinema as, in essence, regressive: 'the public no longer has any opportunity to modify the actor's performance, it is confronted not with a production, but with the result of a production produced in its absence' (Heath 1981: 9). Certainly, some radical filmmakers of the period used direct address in order to counter this limitation on the medium's capacities. For, example, the Marxist–Brechtian use of direct address employed in *Tout va bien* (1972) confronts the audience with a moment of production or, at least, the recording of a moment of production. As with a Brechtian aside in the theatre, this seeks to enable audiences to see the forces of artistic and ideological construction behind the work, rather than being driven 'blindly' by them. However, Heath warns against equating the self-referential foregrounding of illusionistic cinematic devices (he cites Resnais as an example), which are 'merely' another form of illusionism, with Brechtian distanciation and anti–illusionism (1974: 106). With this in mind, it is worth stressing that my analysis of a series of highly self-conscious texts does not seek to equate reflexivity with the politically progressive.

Tom Gunning makes a link between Frank Woods's writing during the early years of the film medium and another theorist strongly associated with 1970s *Screen* Theory:

> Woods describes an essential aspect of classical cinema which Christian Metz has described as the voyeuristic position of the film spectator: 'The cinema's voyeurism must (of necessity) do without any very clear mark of consent on the part of the object.' For Metz, and this accords with Woods's description of the process, the relation between film and spectator is founded upon a spectacle which '*lets* itself be seen without *presenting* itself to be seen.' (Gunning 1991: 262)

Quoting from Metz's *The Imaginary Signifier* (published in a shortened form in *Screen* in 1975 – a special issue devoted to his work), Gunning cites a notion of mainstream, classical cinema's 'voyeurism' that was widespread at the time and persists still. It more or less explicitly excludes direct address because direct address is a marker of the filmed object / subject's consent; direct address is, moreover, presentational rather than 'only' representational. Though extremely influential in the 1970s and 1980s, Metz's theoretical writing has gone much out of favour. However, it is worth pointing to the persistence of quite similar theoretical positions on the classical cinema that remain highly influential. For example, the notion of Hollywood's classicism advanced by Bordwell, Staiger and Thompson (1985) and widely disseminated in Bordwell and Thompson's text book, *Film Art: An Introduction* (now in its ninth edition – 2010), is rather similar to the formal model offered by Metz; both see classical cinema style as essentially self-effacing and designed to prevent the audience from reflecting on the fact that they are watching a film.[6] The formalist model laid out in *The Classical Hollywood Cinema* (Bordwell et al. 1985), which is an account of 'the world's mainstream film style' (ibid.: 4), is also incompatible with direct address.

To isolate the formal arguments from the political exigencies of 1970s *Screen* Theory risks creating a straw man for my analysis. The politically justified attack on cinematic pleasure (articulated most forcefully by Laura Mulvey) will prove informative to our understanding of the films examined in the next chapter but, it must be said, it is ill served in its application to many of the other films examined in this book. Though the preceding critiques of *Screen* Theory are well rehearsed, they have been necessary because the trajectory of film theory since the 1970s explains why direct address is little discussed and, more importantly, why it is difficult *to* discuss within the theoretical frameworks that have dominated the field. Crucially, in highlighting the appropriation of direct address for counter-cinema, I wish to make the simple point that the other to which one opposes oneself must be better or more fully conceived before one prescribes supposedly oppositional formal strategies and determines their effect.

DIRECT ADDRESS AND CRITICISM

In the old days they'd have special little lights on a character's eyes. But sometimes you don't want to see the eyes. It's a question of looking *in* at a movie, rather than have it look *out* at you: the audience has to come to a film, be part of it. It's like acting. I've seen a lot of actors throw themselves at the audience, whereas with others you have to go to them a little, put yourselves into them. That makes for a more thoughtful movie. (Clint Eastwood talking to Geoff Andrew – 2008: 22)

I quote the above in order to reflect upon a dimension of this neglected topic that is especially neglected: how one evaluates particular instances of direct address. Here, I use the term 'criticism' to denote film analysis that engages directly with issues of value (see Brown and Walters 2010: 1–4 and Clayton and Klevan 2011: 3–26 for discussions of 'critical' approaches to film analysis). Value judgements have entered into prior discussions of the device largely to the extent that direct address, as we have seen, has been equated with radical or alternative filmmaking practices, which have been presented as the good alternative to the bad object (conventional narrative filmmaking). In the context of the mainstream, evaluation enters only in that direct address might be considered inappropriate or, when it does appear, it is noted as a novelty or a quirk that differentiates that film from others – this is the extent, generally, of its critical appraisal. One issue is that when, as Clint Eastwood clearly does, one values restraint and subtlety in film style (in which I include styles of performance), direct address may be said to alienate the viewer – not necessarily alienation in the Brechtian sense, but that this projecting 'out' from the movie might be incompatible with us being drawn 'into' it. Such issues can only be answered by close attention to individual films and the patterns and systems in which their direct address is embedded.

In such a context, close analysis may enable more precision about the functions of the device and, at the same time, problematise the boundaries between 'theory' and 'criticism' suggested above. To illustrate this, here is an extended quotation from Andrew Klevan who, in closely analysing a series of performances from a range of Hollywood movies, considers a moment of direct address performed by Oliver Hardy:

> Ollie does not talk to the camera in the manner of Groucho Marx: this would presume too much confidence, and permit a communication with the audience that was blunt and unambiguous. The effect is one of incompleteness; it differs from the smart performer sealing a moment by addressing a sneaky word in our direction, indulging the audience with a clever aside. The film uses Ollie's look to take mature advantage of the camera's status and of the possibilities offered by its ontology – an instrument that is always ambivalently straddling their world and ours – to present the problems of forming new unions. Ollie is permitted to address us, but it cannot bring him into our world (just as we cannot be brought into his). The camera is not even able, necessarily, to give him a view of us, although it does indeed present us with another view of him. The view presented is one of Ollie alone in the frame, stuck, unable to overcome the physical separation between performer and viewer. He must resume contact with his companion, despite their continual failings. Only then will he receive unfailing confirmation – 'didn't we Stanley?' (2005: 32)

Klevan identifies aspects of the dramatic situation ('the problem of forming new unions' and, then, Ollie's move towards being 'stuck', alone) and identifies means by which the film expresses them. Evaluative terms are called upon in order to contrast the subtlety of Ollie's direct address to alternatives that are 'blunt and unambiguous'. It is not subtlety for subtlety's sake that is valued, however, because Klevan shows how the filmmakers have found, for Ollie, a means of communication in synthesis with the character's personality or, rather, in synthesis with the way the film seeks to frame that personality – the alternatives would 'presume too much confidence'. Crucially, there is, in the passage quoted above, no conflict between critical evaluation and 'theoretical' enquiry. Indeed, the two are inextricably linked when Klevan writes that the film 'take[s] *mature advantage* of the camera's status and of the possibilities offered by its ontology' [emphasis added]. This leads to an aside of theoretical import to mature appreciation of many of the films examined in this book: that the camera is 'an instrument that is always ambivalently straddling their world and ours'.

Like Klevan, I will value uses of direct address that are in synthesis with underlying themes. I am also sympathetic to the reticence expressed in Eastwood's quotation about on-screen figures throwing themselves out at the audience. A range of examples will be surveyed below and we shall see that direct address can be more than just the blunt, verbal communication of themes and feelings. Direct address encompasses wordless examples, where eye-line, gesture and the performer's bearing combine with other elements to express unsayable things; in other examples, there is a complex, ambiguous relationship between what is said and what the direct address *performs*. Before beginning this analysis and as a conclusion to this introduction, I wish to set out, in a series of short sections, what I take to be the most common functions and significations of direct address in film fictions. An initial, simple summary that separates these functions will prove instructive but it will be the job of the close analysis (particularly in the case studies chapters) to probe the interlinking of these themes better and to qualify and complicate their relationships.

Intimacy

It is clear that having a character address the audience directly is a very particular gesture towards intimacy with that audience. This intimacy can be threatening (*Funny Games*, 1997 and 2007) or it can, more commonly, be performed for the sake of encouraging our sympathy or some other kind of special connection with a character. The intimacy of direct address might, in more exceptional cases, even be used to make us feel we are 'intruding' on the fiction's private sphere (*Make Way for Tomorrow*, 1937) – in such cases, it might be offered as *too* intimate.

Agency

Linked to the categories immediately above and below is the fact that, generally, direct address will be the province of a single character and that character is often the protagonist or the principal agent of the narrative. The clearest examples are those films where direct address is the means by which a character narrates the intimate details of their own life; *Alfie* (both 1966 and 2004 versions) and *High Fidelity* are very similar in this regard. Moreover, direct address is often a marker of the character's particular power within the fiction. An example of this is the recurrence in horror films (to the point where it perhaps approaches cliché) of the principal antagonist and / or villain looking at the camera (often at the end of the film). The boy Damien (Harvey Stephens) in *The Omen* (1976), who ends the film looking at us, would be the canonic example of this because the anti-Christ is as powerful an agent as horror cinema is likely to give us. (See also the final image of 1997's *The Devil's Advocate*.) The peculiar agency of direct address is also key to its use in a film examined in the next chapter, *Funny Games*. Here:

> Paul is the only character who acknowledges the presence of the camera / audience, a fact which leads Mark Kermode, in his review of the film . . . to claim that the killers and victims 'seem to be in different movies, with [Arno] Frisch [playing Paul] nipping merrily back and forth between the film's world and ours, while [Suzanne] Lothar [as Anna] remains resolutely locked within Haneke's narrative. (Wheatley 2009: 96)

Wheatley relates this sense of *Funny Games* being made up of 'different movies' to the presence of at least two different modernist traditions existing within the film (ibid.: 96). However, focusing purely on direct address, we can see that the logic whereby Paul addresses the audience while the other characters seem oblivious both to our 'presence' and to his breaking of the fiction's boundaries has a lineage within mainstream practice also. For example, *High Fidelity*'s hero is similarly alone in being able to address us without that film being 'modernist' in anything like Wheatley's sense. Paul's particular agency within *Funny Games* makes his direct address feel almost 'natural'. The question of agency is, however, complicated by the tension in such 'counter-cinematic' uses of direct address, whereby a character's agency is somewhat negated in favour of a dramatisation of authorial presence and 'message'.

Superior epistemic position within the fictional world

This is another way of saying that the characters who perform direct address generally know more – or are in a position of greater knowledge within the fiction – than other characters. (See the examples of the devil / anti-Christ cited above.) In the preface, I already suggested that direct address often provides a metaphor for a character's vision and, indeed, it is often used to mark a moment of realisation or a coming-to-consciousness for that character. This relates to epistemology as an issue for fictional characters within the diegesis. However, as direct address inevitably questions the bounded-ness of the fictional world (we – who are exterior to it – are acknowledged after all), it is

Figure 1.2 *Vanilla Sky* (Paramount Pictures et al., 2001): Rebecca Dearborn (Tilda Swinton) abruptly turns to the camera.

unsurprising that the character's knowledge may extend beyond or, at least, question that fiction's bounds. An example of this would be the otherwise completely unanchored direct address of a minor character, Rebecca Dearborn (Tilda Swinton), in *Vanilla Sky* (2001). As the film's twist unwinds, Dearborn, who is an executive in the company that produces the artificial reality that is supposedly responsible for much of what we see on screen, abruptly and briefly turns to look at the camera (see Figure 1.2).[7] Another aspect of this epistemological issue is the relationship of direct address to music, a facet of film form that much more regularly blurs the boundaries of the diegesis. In all three case studies (but especially strikingly in *Le Notti di Cabiria*), a character's awareness of music that is 'cross-diegetic' relates to the knowledge they express via direct address.[8]

Honesty

When direct address is used primarily to express something internal to the character's fictional world (that is, their own personal thoughts and feelings), it is often a gesture of open and 'honest' expression. The 'honesty' of direct address is one of its most powerful expressive qualities. However, inverted commas are required because this can often be inflected ironically. Indeed, were direct address used only when a character is telling the truth, its impact on the concerns of many dramas would be rather deadening – many films are clearly about the limitations of characters' abilities to be honest with themselves and / or with others. Direct address may sometimes, rather, be a gesture of ingenuousness.

Instantiation

While 'distanciation' in the Brechtian sense is more commonly thought to be direct address's chief function in the cinema (I shall discuss this at greater length in the next chapter), most of the effects I am listing here contrast with what that term typically implies. I would suggest 'instantiation' as a more apt word to stress the impact of many examples of the device. I do not use 'instantiation' in its common sense to mean simply an instance of something, but employ it as a term that suggests the present-ness and immediacy of direct address. The temporality of direct address is perhaps the most difficult thing to define and one should acknowledge that the device often features in films in which time is visibly and consciously manipulated (*Hellzapoppin'* [1941] *Fight Club* [1999], *Funny Games*). However, though, like temporal manipulation, direct address is inherently reflexive, it actually derives its force from its present-ness and (I would suggest more tentatively) present tense-ness. This is perhaps the theatrical aspiration of direct address – in theatre, direct address is a facet of the way that medium is dramatically 'there in front of us in this moment'. Clearly, in cinema, where this present-ness is literally impossible, this illusory instantiation might also be used ironically.

Alienation (if that term is reconsidered)

'Direct address is an "alienation effect" in the Brechtian sense, but it does not "alienate" us in the everyday sense of the term' (Feuer 1993: 41). I would fully subscribe to Feuer's second point but the equation of direct address with Brechtian alienation is more problematic. Within film studies, considerably more care needs to be taken with what the term 'Brechtian' is considered to mean. As Gilberto Perez suggested in the conference paper cited in the preface (2008), 'Brecht may not have been quite as "Brechtian" as some have assumed.' One could admit that direct address is a device for 'Brechtian' alienation if we restore Brecht's proper relationship with long-established entertainment strategies and see 'alienation' as consistent with the influences he drew from popular culture.[9] Film scholars have greatly underestimated the extent to which Brecht's own practices encouraged a sense of connection to fictional characters, how his plays were often 'entertaining', while nevertheless questioning and resisting the conventions of 'bourgeois realism'. Redefining Brecht for film scholars could be a project in itself and I shall, rather, limit myself to discussing Brecht (and classic film theory's 'Brecht') within the specific context of certain films and film practitioners (such as Godard).

(Sometimes) stillness

Another abstract quality of direct address (and one linked to its temporality) is its stillness: that is, it may occur as a narrative pause, a moment of reflection that arrests or stands apart from the forward motion of the narrative. There is also something about eye contact with the camera that, even when the figure may be speaking frantically to us, can still have a stillness about it – such is the striking effect of an on-screen figure looking into the lens within a filmed fiction. Linked to this is the fact that, at least since the rise of 'European art cinema' in the 1950s, direct address features more often at the end of films than at any other point.[10] It perhaps symbolises the kind of reflective, meditative engagement certain kinds of films seem to hope for from their audience and which they hope their audience will take with them as they leave the auditorium. The final image of *Les Quatre cents coups* (1959) is the best-known example of this and, though I am unsure whether I would consider it strictly an instance of direct address, its influence on other films is clear.[11] For example, *This is England* (2006), which, like Truffaut's film, ends on a beach, has its young male protagonist (Thomas Turgoose) look at us as a culmination of his journey towards a kind of tentative enlightenment and maturity (see Figure 1.3). Moreover, the direct address at the end of *Le Notti di Cabiria*, which, made two years before *Les Quatre cents coups*, has a stronger claim on launching this (I would hesitate to call it) 'trend' of ending films with a moment of direct address, has, I will suggest, the quality of a 'sigh' or a 'gentle intake of breath'.

The preceding begs the final question: what is the significance of direct address to wider film form? One response might have been to construct a model for the way films 'typically work' which is more compatible with direct address. However, it is in the nature of such models to stress certain features to the detriment of others. In actuality, film is too mongrel a form for this to feel appropriate. Moreover, because my dissatisfaction with such models (particularly with prevailing notions of 'classical' film form) proved an initial motivation for this study, I feel it would be inappropriate to suggest another model, even if another were possible. The conclusions of this study (which looks at an eccentric but undervalued feature of film form) must necessarily be much more tentative and this book will certainly not refute the widespread notion that, in order for spectators to be caught up in the dramas of the screen, they must not become too aware of the events on screen as an artificial construct (this is, basically, what is behind the notion of mainstream film styles as largely 'transparent'). However, what much film theory has greatly underestimated is the extent to which many films are manifestly constructed objects that address their spectators as such. Refuting this is too broad to be taken as this book's ultimate goal. If the following is all that this book can 'prove', then

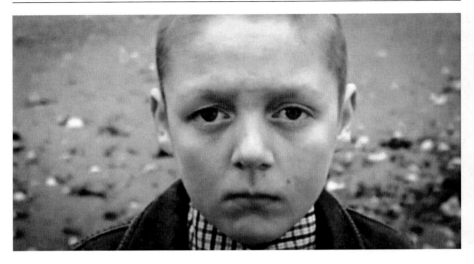

Figure 1.3 *This is England* (Big Arty Productions et al., 2006): Shaun (Thomas Turgoose) looks at us in the film's final image.

it will be enough: there is no contradiction between our emotional involvement with fictional characters and their addressing us through the apparatus of the camera. Precisely the opposite: direct address may enrich our appreciation of the fiction and its characters.

NOTES

1. The origins of 'the cinema of attractions' lie in collaboration between Gunning and André Gaudreault (see Gunning 1990). However, due to his greater prominence in the subsequent literature, and recent individual work on the concept, I will refer to Gunning as the author.
2. Richard Brody, as quoted by Gilberto Perez in his Reading plenary paper (2008), writes that Langdon 'looks frequently and rapidly into the camera as a kind of ongoing aside to the audience'.
3. As a further cautionary note about the biases of the historiography of film form that have banished direct address largely from sight, it is also worth saying something of the emphasis placed on Griffith as an early film practitioner. Woods had a vested interest in exalting Griffith's practice (or a certain version of it that stressed his radical difference from prevailing fashions): not only was he a film critic, but he was also a sometime employee of the director. Also, some have suggested that Griffith's significance to the development of a 'cinema of narrative integration' is apt to be over-emphasised by film historians because all of Griffith's Biograph

work survived, while other production companies failed to preserve their stock. Nevertheless, it is significant that Woods and (it seems through him) Griffith perceived that there was another practice that needed to be resisted in the first place. Though one should be careful not to exaggerate the significance of direct address to cinema as a whole – it remains a relatively eccentric gesture to have one's film characters address the audience – I would certainly contend that classic film theory's blindness to the significant role direct address plays has helped distort some common assumptions about the medium.

4. I am aware that this extraordinarily rich moment in the history of film scholarship is far more varied than is often assumed. However, the extent of the exposition of *Screen* Theory offered here is necessary because some of its fundamental precepts remain influential for contemporary films scholarship even if this influence is primarily latent – the passivity ascribed to the mainstream film spectator by classic film theory of the 1970s has been regularly and explicitly critiqued, though there have remained tremendous disagreements concerning the kind of viewer activity one should put in its place. Even if '1970s *Screen* Theory' is a rhetorical construct distanced from the reality of a fraught and hotly contended period of debate, this construct and, more specifically, a distorted sense of what the 'Brechtian' means, has persisted and perhaps helps explain the striking rarity with which direct address has even been acknowledged, let alone examined.

5. The French publication developed support for Brechtian techniques in parallel with *Screen* (Lellis 1982), and the influence of *Cahiers du cinéma* and other French publications and writers was considerable. Indeed, this broad body of work is sometimes referred to as 'French theory' – Barry Salt, for one, offered a notorious attack on 'French theory' (1992: 4–14). Andrew Britton (1978 / 1979) offers a more measured critique of *Screen* within a journal, *Movie*, often seen in opposition to 1970s *Screen*.

6. E. Ann Kaplan has talked of the irony of the resemblances between Bordwell's notion of classicism and the 'French theory' (of which Metz is a part) that dominated the field in the 1970s (Kaplan 1998: 276). Bordwell (and the narrative theory is primarily associated with him) does stress spectatorial activity in explicit contra-distinction to theorists such as Metz. However, I would contend that the kind of activity he foresees for the spectator is far too mechanical to be consistent with the kind of involved spectator my analysis would imagine. I touch upon these issues in previous published work (Brown 2011). There, I focus primarily on film 'spectacle' within so-called classical cinema. Spectacle is by no means an antonym for direct address. However, like direct address, my analysis of spectacle seeks to uncover its role both as something that draws attention

to itself (both are the opposite of self-effacing) and as a potentially rich expressive device within film narration and its rhetoric.

7. Swinton's previous history with direct address (1992's *Orlando*) might also help explain Cameron Crowe's choice for this moment in *Vanilla Sky*.

8. Another example that is not examined elsewhere in this study comes from the popular 1980s teen movie, *Ferris Bueller's Day Off* (1986). Until the very end of the film (in fact, over the credits), when the hero's antagonist, his high-school principle (Jeffrey Jones), is brought so low that he gives a final, resigned look at the camera that seems to admit Ferris's victory, the lead character (played by Matthew Broderick) is alone in addressing the audience. Ferris is celebrated by the film (in letting him talk to us directly) and within the film's world (he is legendary amongst his on-screen peers) for his 'coolness' and command. This extends to his relationship with music, the most obvious example being the musical number he performs in one of the film's major set pieces. Interestingly, his sister (Jennifer Grey), who is his antithesis in being 'up-tight', appears to hear extra-diegetic music when she finally loosens up – in a moment in the police station late in the film, this is hinted to be a moment of enlightenment. This further example is worth citing to underline that the focus on direct address enables one to note other 'ontologically strange' filmmaking strategies such as allowing characters to seem to 'hear' music not of the diegesis.

9. Masao Yamaguchi's essay (1978) on the intersections between Max Ophuls's practice and Brecht's through the intermediary of the popular clown Karl Valentin suggests aspects of this relationship. More broadly, we might look to Brecht's use of popular song and various folk traditions. See Brecht (1978) for a thorough introduction to his practice and theory (as set out in his various writings on the theatre).

10. Though the effect is very different, silent comedies also often involved a closing moment of direct address. For example, *The Butcher Boy* (1917) has the hero (Roscoe Arbuckle) and his sweetheart (Josephine Stevens) turn and wink at the camera as the film closes with an iris effect. However, I would contextualise the use of direct address at the end of more recent films in relation to other kinds of practice because, in early comedies such as *The Butcher Boy*, direct address is intermittent throughout the course of the entire film.

Another reason it is perhaps found more fitting for films to use direct address in their final shots than at other points was suggested to me by Gilberto Perez, who commented that, if a look at the camera takes you out of the fiction, it is appropriate that it comes at a film's end. He also pointed out that, for similar reasons, camera looks might come at the start of a film (1994's *Through the Olive Trees* was his example). This is consistent with

David Bordwell's observation (though admittedly of a different kind of film practice) that 'a high degree of narrational presence is conventional in the opening of the classical film . . . and of course at the end' (Bordwell et al. 1985: 166). Though Bordwell's formalism identifies the same thing as Perez's more 'interpretative' approach (and, more generally, Bordwell's account of the basic mechanics of classical narration is indispensable), their approaches and views of cinematic narration are very different and I find Bordwell's approach less useful for my aim to analyse direct address as a facet of film's wider rhetorical arsenal (see Brown 2011 for a discussion of related issues).

11. I hesitate over its inclusion because the freeze frame and the zoom achieved in the film's printing arrest Antoine Doinel / Jean-Pierre Léaud's gaze. Thus, I would suggest that the film creates a moment of quasi-direct address rather than have the character address us. Moreover, direct address as a phenomenon of cinema's moving image is clearly of primary concern to this book and the way figures in still photographs often look at the camera – and the freeze frame in Truffaut's films has something of this about it – is another large and separate area of enquiry (see, for example, Wolfe 1987).

CHAPTER 2

Counter-looks: direct address and counter-cinema

Pascal Bonitzer's essay, 'The Two Looks' (1977; my translation) is the most substantial published work on direct address.[1] His division of direct address in two suggested the broad schema that divides this from the next chapter: the idea that, on the one hand, there are looks at the audience that encourage a sense of proximity and, on the other, more 'confrontational' looks that exemplify the attitudes of 'alternative' film practices towards their viewers. While Bonitzer's schema is less pertinent to the analysis of the mainstream,[2] his account merits close attention in relation to the category of 'counter-cinema'.

Bonitzer calls the first of his two looks, somewhat strangely, 'the hidden look' [*le regard caché*]. It is a look at the lens and, via the lens, the off-screen figure of the director. He calls the second look the 'counter-look' [*le contre-regard*], so as to describe the 'exhibitionist provocation of actresses who . . . give themselves to be seen' (1977: 45). Much of the argument is couched in psychoanalytic terms, and Bonitzer seems to mean that the first 'hidden look' is hidden because we, as spectators, imagine ourselves into the position of the hidden filmmaker:

> One must therefore distinguish between two looks into the lens, when the counter-shot is not given in the film, that is to say when the face of one of the partners remains hidden: a 'feminine' look, which addresses the other as if master, director [*metteur en scène*], and places the spectator in this imaginary position . . .
>
> As for the other look – which I have pointed to in *Vent d'Est* [1970], but which one finds in other Godard films and also in Straub's work and that of some other cineastes of the avant-garde – it is precisely the 'order of the cinema' [*ordre du cinéma*] which it threatens and puts into question. It no longer addresses, through the lens, a director or

a master, but the collectivity of spectators addressed [*interpelés*] as such. Such a look is the sign, not of a suspense, but of a rupture of the fabric of the cinematic fiction or rather – because this rupture is in fact impossible – an attempt at its rupture. The actor is there only the intermediary for the auteur, who is suddenly speaking, almost, in the first person. (1977: 45–6)

The opening sentence of the above quotation is at pains to define the camera looks with reference to what is absent (a counter-shot that would make the look at the camera an axial shot-reverse-shot or optical point of view) rather than acknowledge their presence as direct address. In fact, neither look seems to be direct address as I defined it in the opening lines of this book, because neither designation imagines that the fictional character looks at us; the first look seems to require that we identify with the filmmaker and, while the 'counter-look' addresses us as spectators, it is by the actor. This gap in Bonitzer's schema is easily explained because the notion of direct address I am favouring seems tolerant of the cinematic 'illusionism' whose rejection was an article of faith in much film theory of the 1970s. Bonitzer's choice of terms is then problematic for many of the films analysed later in this book. As suggested, 'hidden look' is a strange designation because my analysis will contend that the 'looks of union' favoured from the next chapter onwards are able to make a character's subjectivity peculiarly and specially visible. Also, while Bonitzer makes the extremely valuable point (with reference to Bergman's *Summer with Monika* [1953]) that some looks may 'redouble' (that is, enrich) the fiction (1977: 44), his schema unfortunately stresses the subjectivity of the *auteur* (which, one might add, is no less 'imaginary' in this context than that of the character), to the detriment of other ways of understanding its impact.

However, Bonitzer offers a number of acute observations. Helpfully, the above quotation underlines the fact that the counter-look's 'rupture of the cinematic fiction' can only ever be tentative, a useful corollary to the more obvious point that direct address within more mainstream practice can only ever gesture towards the *illusion* of union between character and the world of the spectator. He also captures an irony at the heart of a number of instances of direct address in what may be called 'counter-cinema'; the 'counter-look' suggests the on-screen figure's special subjectivity while making them subservient to an authorial message. While I will suggest that the device is actually more varied and / or complex in Godard's practice than, ironically, much radical film theory of the 1970s and 1980s gave him credit for, Bonitzer's counter-look can be illustrated and developed with reference to a more recent film.

A CINEMA OF REPULSIONS: FUNNY GAMES (1997 / 2007)

The original Austrian version of Michael Haneke's *Funny Games* was released in 1997 and was then remade by Haneke almost shot-for-shot as *Funny Games U.S.* in 2007. I shall focus on the 1997 film. Both films feature a central character we shall call 'Paul'[3] (played by Arno Frisch in the original), whose aggressively presentational stance involves direct appeals to our involvement in the fiction. Despite my previous assertions of the presence of direct address in many guises throughout cinema history, in the context of so oppositional a film as *Funny Games* the device can nevertheless be seen as a clear declaration of intent to flout certain 'rules'. To understand this, we must examine some of the manifold ways in which the film defines itself in opposition to mainstream filmmaking, and particularly its representation of violence. It does this thematically, structurally and formally. No clear separation of these elements is possible, for the film possesses a unity of purpose and form that is nothing if not direct: 'For such a simple tale of unmotivated torture, [*Funny Games*] is extraordinarily complex in its mode of audience address. It is extremely successful in its aim of producing a near intolerable complicity in the process of inexorable victimisation' (Falcon 1998: 11). Before we turn to the complexities of audience address in *Funny Games*, let us say a little about the 'simple tale' itself, for it is revealing of the film's oppositional status.

The narrative begins with a bourgeois family's arrival at their lakeside holiday home. They greet their neighbours, who are accompanied by two polite young men, both dressed in white polo-shirts, shorts and gloves. The youths then enter the family's home, on the pretext of borrowing some eggs. There begins the 'process of inexorable victimisation'. The father's (Ulrich Mühe) leg is broken so he cannot resist. The son (uncredited) briefly escapes but is recaptured and shot. The intruders leave, only to return about half an hour (of screen time) later. After some more sadistic games, the young men shoot the father and drown the mother (Susanne Lothar) in the lake. The film ends with Paul having entered the home of the dead family's friends. Even this sketch of a story indicates its distance from most film narratives. No three-act structure is evident; the film does not set up a series of obstacles to be overcome; it moves 'inexorably' towards a horrific conclusion. The film maintains throughout a very flat, realist style, with significant long takes and minimal camera movement. Subsequently, the temporary disappearance of the torturers does not mark a shift in tone or style or narrative progression. The family's attempts to escape thus feel futile and the youths' return inevitable. What is more, about one-third of the killers' period of absence is taken up by a single shot of the aftermath of the son's murder – here, not only does their disappearance offer no relief, it actually intensifies the viewer's discomfort. Perhaps most 'radically', the ending gives no resolution. In the film's final shot, the image freezes on Paul as, for the last time, he looks at us. The final image is indicative of the function of direct address in *Funny Games*' strategies of 'opening out' its textual boundaries. Though I will suggest that the viewer activity this presumes is circumscribed to the point of not being very 'open' at all, it does ask the audience to imagine further narrative progression and, as part of a wider schema, encourages us to reconsider our consumption of violent narratives. Any simple synopsis, like that above, which does not account for the direct address would belie the rhetorical function of the events. It is primarily in the manner of the filming, conjoined with Paul's straight-to-camera address, that the film's message presents itself.

In total, there are four instances where Paul addresses the camera. The first (a frame of which features on the cover of this book) sees Paul briefly turn his head and wink at us. It comes just as the mother is about to discover the body of the family dog and seeks to make us complicit in the first of the villain's 'funny games'. This acknowledgement of the audience, in fact, merely makes explicit what the narration's rhetoric makes implicit through other means – the careful build-up to this moment has left us, in contrast to the as-yet oblivious family, in little doubt that Paul has killed the dog. In the next two instances of direct address, Paul makes explicit reference to our investment in the narrative progression and in the characters' fates. As Paul bets the family that in twelve hours they will all be dead, he turns his head to the side to face us and asks, 'What do you think? Do you think they have a chance of winning? You are on their side, aren't you? So, who will you bet with?' The next moment (fifty minutes later and after the murder of the son) also sees Paul's speech shift almost seamlessly from intra-diegetic to extra-diegetic. In fact, the crossing of the boundary is performed with even greater ease because, rather than turn his head through 90 degrees to look at us, as previously, Paul merely has to angle his head a few degrees. Throughout the exchange, the camera does not leave its fixed position on Paul and the surrounding dialogue is worth quoting:

> Paul: What do you think, Anna? Have you had enough? Or do you want to play some more?
> The father: Don't reply any more. Let them do what they want – please! Then it'll be over quicker.
> Paul: Huh, that's cowardly! We're not up to feature film length yet.
> Paul [turning to us]: Is that enough? But you want a real ending, with plausible plot development, don't you?
> Paul [turning back to the family]: The bet is still on. It can't be withdrawn unilaterally.

The verbal exchange illustrates the way Paul's speech has him occupying a position both inside and outside the fiction, a paradox that links him to the tradition of the counter-look as identified by Bonitzer. As a young man who has already frequently framed the situation and the family's experience in terms of pop cultural references, 'We're not up to feature film length yet' is a credible metaphor for such a character to deliver. However, especially with the next line, which is delivered as he breaks the fourth wall, Paul is clearly acting as a mouthpiece for a message Haneke wishes to deliver. Haneke seems to be asking us, through Paul, 'What are you expecting from this film? The child has already been killed so you know this can't end well. Why would you stay and consume more of what is to come?' Haneke's extra-textual discourse makes this intention clear. He has stated that he wished to 'rape the viewer into autonomy' (quoted in Wheatley 2009: 78) and the desire to walk out of the cinema is an active part of the film's engagement with its audience: 'Anyone who leaves doesn't need the film; anyone who stays does. People who are already very sensitised to violence are not the people for whom the film was made' (Haneke quoted in Romney 1998: 6). Paul's to-camera discourse is thus a fairly clear provocation to the audience to leave or, more appositely, a demand that they consider why they have not already left – as Haneke's comments above show, the film is not made for those who would readily walk out on it.

The film's ending, which includes the freeze frame on Paul's final look at the camera, brings the film full circle in more than one way. As already suggested, it extends the psychotic pair's cycle of violence (near the start of the film, we also saw Peter and Paul with some neighbours and we later learn that this family – and perhaps others – have been murdered). It also superimposes the film's title over Paul's face and replays the 'thrash punk' music (Catherine Wheatley's description – 2009: 79) by 'John Zorn and the Naked City' which is heard extra-diegetically at the film's start. There, the film introduces the family as the young boy Georgi watches his parents play a game in which they must guess the composer and title of the piece of classical music their partner plays on the car stereo. Shots within the car are interspersed with shots, clearly taken from a helicopter, looking down on the car as it moves along roads towards their lakeside retreat. The parents' game fills the soundtrack until Zorn's screamed vocals, thrashy guitar and arrhythmic drums suddenly come in. The film's title then appears in large red letters over a shot of the contented family. Extra-diegetic devices (the title, the Zorn music) combine with the bird's-eye view of the car to foreshadow the victimisation of the family. The scene setting could hardly establish a more complacently bourgeois family (not only is there the classical music game but the family's Range Rover pulls their yacht as they drive through the remote-controlled gates of their holiday home) and the opening message is avowedly authored in asserting that these characters will be subjected to punishment *by the film*. Indeed, the John Zorn music links the family's intra-diegetic torture to the extra-diegetic discourse of the opening and closing images of the film – when Paul pursues Georgi through a neighbour's home, he puts the same piece of music on a stereo. In each of the three major case studies (and in many other films touched upon elsewhere), the characters' ability to address us directly is tied to their ambiguous 'awareness' of extra-diegetic music. However, in *Funny Games*, there is nothing of this rich ambiguity in the use of the music. The John Zorn score is, rather, an aggressive declaration of authorial intent.

Paul is tied to extra- or cross-diegetic controlling forces at other moments too: for example, in the film's one moment of on-screen violence. (The focus of the analysis here is liable to obscure how remarkably effective the film is in resensitising viewers to violence by *not* showing it.) While forced to repeat a prayer Paul has devised, the mother grabs a shotgun and shoots Peter. In an unrealistic fashion expected of a Hollywood action movie, Peter flies across the room in a bloody explosion. However, Paul wrestles the mother to the ground and desperately hunts for a remote control. Having found it, we see Paul's gloved hand hitting the controls. The film's image track then appears to rewind until we return to the prayer, only for Paul to prevent his partner's killing. With the music, Paul is aligned with an extra-narrative authority. Here, his control is displayed, particularly directly, in the foregrounding of film and video technology. As Richard Falcon writes: 'he [Haneke] thus foregrounds our satisfaction at the victims' relief from the helplessness while at the same time victimising us as spectators. This alienation technique is typical of a film that is nothing if not lucid in its cruelty' (1998: 11). Haneke offers the horrific satisfaction of bloodshed and cathartic violence ('the villain gets his just deserts') only to withdraw it cruelly. Paul's gloved hands are particularly appropriate symbols of Haneke's clinical approach. Their manipulation of technology (the CD version of the John Zorn music played during Georgi's pursuit and the video remote control) demonstrate an authorial desire to turn the media back on the viewer and project anxieties of control on to us. The aggressiveness of Peter and Paul is matched by the aggressiveness of the text, the former being the *authors* of the family's torture. The characters and text are especially inseparable when Paul addresses the audience directly.

In the passage cited above, Richard Falcon describes the rewinding of events as an 'alienation technique'. This immediately brings to mind Brecht and his strategies of *Verfremdung*. The use of direct address in *Funny Games* makes the comparison with Brecht almost inevitable, yet I would suggest that there is little that is truly 'Brechtian' about Haneke's recourse to the device. In a chapter entitled 'The Narrative Sequence' in his remarkable book, *The Material Ghost*, embedded alongside a discussion of Jean Renoir and André Bazin (one filmmaker and one theorist often placed crudely in opposition to the kind of practice Brecht is taken to represent), Gilberto Perez offers the following account of Brecht's techniques. Discussing a scene from Brecht's *The Caucasian Chalk Circle*, in which an actress plays the comforting of an abandoned baby in pantomime, while another actor presents a sung accompaniment, Perez explains:

> The action, what happens in the scene, is not to be identified with either way of playing it on the stage, the song or the pantomime, two different versions calling each other into question, throwing open in our minds the possibility of other ways in which the action could have been played. We are, by an 'alienation effect', distanced from the played scene, as the played scene is distanced, made distinct, from what happens in the scene being played. We are prevented, in Brecht, from taking the enactment for the action: the action is not performed, no longer there on stage, but referred to by the performance. (1998: 81–2)

This passage builds upon a distinction between 'narrative' and 'drama' that the wider chapter develops carefully and at some length. In brief, for Perez, narrative is story as an accumulation of things that happen, while drama is enactment. Pointing to the way the words for 'count' (as in numbers) and 'tell' (as in stories) are the same or very similar in various languages (in English, of course we have 're*count*' – Perez: 1998: 50), Perez defines narrative as an accumulation of elements that can be reordered – 'a' precedes 'b' in many stories but it is perfectly possible for the storyteller to give us 'b' before 'a'. Drama, on the other hand, in the form of either a painting or a performance of an actor 'being' someone on stage, is more self-sufficient; it has inherent plenitude as *enactment* – in the theatre, 'the self-sufficiency of the stage as a substitute reality' (Perez 1998: 82). This makes sense of Perez's formulation that 'the played scene [the drama] is distanced, made distinct, from what happens in the scene being played [the narrative elements the drama enacts]'. In the Brecht example Perez cites, the two ways of recounting the action prevent the audience from taking the dramatisation for the actual events being dramatised – we are thus 'distanced' from the representation. Brecht is thus a narrative artist who makes use of various and sometimes conflicting dramatic means. Haneke's use of the rewinding of the image does approach the Brechtian because it can be seen to present 'two different versions [of events] calling each other into question'. However, Haneke's is a 'negative' kind of Brechtianism because, I would suggest, the effect of rewinding and then removing the shooting of Peter is ultimately to condemn the spectator's desire for an alternative that the film's discourse presents as inappropriate – it is inappropriate because explosive and stylistically heightened film violence is morally inappropriate and narratively inappropriate because the family's defeat feels inevitable. Crucially,

Haneke's practice here differs from that of Brecht because the latter wished to make the viewer active in imagining alternatives (political and / or narrative), while Haneke seeks, rather, to victimise and condemn and use our passivity as removed spectators against us.

If the business with the remote control is partly 'Brechtian' (perhaps in technique, if not in spirit), I would suggest that the direct address is not remotely so. If Brechtian techniques seek to make spectators active, Paul's direct address is an explicit marker, rather, of our passivity. Other parts of the film demand the viewer's 'active' involvement, though, admittedly, in a highly circumscribed way. For example, the rigorous maintenance of the violence off screen, especially in the son's murder, denies us the 'voyeuristic' satisfaction of seeing violent events but forces us to imagine what is going on (we hear the shot and screams of the aftermath of the son's death but we see nothing of the event itself). When we do see the scene of violence, the son's dead body is merely a crumpled heap in the corner of the room by the bloody television set. This is the film's longest take, lasting almost twelve minutes, and it only pans slightly to reframe the characters – it is literal *temps-mort*. The duration of the shot overdetermines the camera's (and our) gaze, and is especially disconcerting when the father begins to wail uncontrollably. While our gaze is overdetermined and we search through the image for meaning, attention is called to our lack of control. First, our voyeuristic satisfaction is denied, then teasingly satisfied, but to the point where we are made to feel obtrusive observers. In Catherine Wheatley's analysis of the film and this scene, she links the long take to 'first-generation modernism' (2009: 94) in its recourse to a duration and a fixed camera position that distances the viewer from the events and makes them reflect on their manner of representation. The direct address is linked to 'second-generation modernism', which is more aggressive in its confrontation of the viewer. However, I would suggest that, in comparison with the extraordinary feelings of dread and guilt produced by the son's shooting, Paul's asides to the viewer are moments of relative relief. Perez's distinction between narrative and drama might be instructive here. The narrative techniques Haneke employs through the son's death and at other moments encourage the viewer to reflect actively on their desires for violence and redemption that have been generated from watching the kind of genre cinema *Funny Games* satirises. The direct address is, in contrast, the dramatisation of an authorial rhetoric that distances us from this kind of active involvement. This returns us to the notion of instantiation tentatively introduced earlier on. Here, however, rather than the instantiation of a character's individual subjectivity, we have an authorial position and message made vividly present to us. One might even question why Haneke used the device in the first place. I would suggest that it might have been felt necessary as a clear and explicit marker of the seriousness of the film's ethical project. Certainly, Haneke's comments (as quoted in Wheatley

2009: 110–111n38) suggest that his sense of the ability of direct address to make the audience complicit is a rather simplistic one.

Catherine Wheatley discusses the direct address of *Funny Games* relatively little. This is perhaps unsurprising because, I would suggest that its use of direct address is one of the least effective aspects of the film's project. This may seem like a surprising conclusion for a book focused on direct address to come to; or, rather, it makes it surprising that I have discussed this individual film at relative length. However, analysis of the relationship of *Funny Games'* project to Brecht's radical practice clarifies the latter's aims and aspirations. Moreover, *Funny Games* exemplifies the symbolic value of direct address for certain theoretical positions vis-à-vis the rules and conventions of mainstream cinema. It exemplifies a 'counter-cinema' use of direct address.

GODARD AND 'COUNTER–CINEMA': *DEUX OU TROIS CHOSES QUE JE SAIS D'ELLE* (1967)

The direct address employed in the films of Jean-Luc Godard, particularly those he produced into the 1970s, have generally been ascribed to a 'counter-cinema' project. In Wheatley's analysis of *Funny Games*, she suggests that Haneke's film does not possess the purism of Godard and his contemporaries as a work in this vein (2009: 87). On one level, she is correct; Godard, during this period, was fully committed to questioning mainstream cinema's traditional values and techniques. However, on another, and in terms specifically of the audience address encapsulated in its direct address, *Funny Games* has a didactic clarity that is more presumed than really present in much of Godard's practice. Before reappraising Godard's undoubtedly radical use of direct address, I wish to reflect upon another theoretical text that has been influential in associating direct address with counter-cinema and opposing it to the standard practices of classical Hollywood cinema.

Peter Wollen's essay, 'Godard and Counter Cinema: *Vent d'est*', was another important text from amongst the body of radical film theory that did most to circumscribe critical understandings of direct address. Originally published in 1972, Wollen's essay is best known for outlining in tabular form 'seven cardinal sins' associated with 'Hollywood-Mosfilm' and 'seven cardinal virtues', which are effectively the antonyms offered by Godard's counter-cinema practice:

Narrative transitivity	Narrative intransitivity
Identification	Estrangement
Transparency	Foregrounding
Single diegesis	Multiple diegesis

Closure   Aperture
Pleasure   Unpleasure
Fiction   Reality (Wollen 1985: 501)

Direct address is implicitly related to a number of the virtues: as a presenta-tional means of performance, it is clearly a form of foregrounding; in opening up the textual boundaries (in, at a minimum, drawing attention to the fact that on-screen actions are being performed for an audience), direct address is, arguably, multiple-diegetic; 'aperture' implies a more radical form of self-consciousness / reflexivity than what is offered by the mainstream (ibid.: 505) and, certainly, direct address can strike a tone that aids this kind of critical project. We shall return to direct address's association with 'reality' or, rather, 'documentary' towards the end of this chapter. Direct address is explicitly mentioned with regard to 'identification v. estrangement', where Wollen offers the following definition: 'Empathy, emotional involvement with a character v. direct address, multiple and divided characters, commentary' (ibid.: 502). It may seem churlish to pick apart formulations that are deliberately constructed in this form for the purposes of a polemical, vivid, direct and accessible pres-entation of an argument – that is, Wollen's argument is clearly painted in deliberately broad-brush strokes. However, given the highly limited analysis of direct address that has resulted, I would contend, in part from influential work such as Wollen's, that it is worth underlining some problems with where Wollen places direct address. Though Wollen is open about the cardinal virtues being 'revolutionary' and 'materialist' (ibid.: 501), it seems specious to oppose something so abstract as 'empathy' with category terms of such a completely different order. 'Direct address' and 'commentary' are really only names of techniques and their use as antonyms does not acknowledge even the *possibility* that they might be used to create empathy themselves. More gener-ally, the Hollywood cinema Godard is seen to be counter to is formulated in a way that is entirely consistent with then-prevailing conceptualisations and is, in some respects, continuous with dominant notions of film 'classicism' now:

> In Hollywood films, everything shown belongs to the same world, and
> complex articulations within that world – such as flash-backs – are
> carefully signalled . . . The basic principle [which] remains unshaken
> [is that] the world represented on the cinema must be coherent
> and integrated, though it need not observe compulsory, statutory
> constraints. (ibid.: 504)

Though Wollen's description of a 'liberalized classicism' (ibid.: 504) has suf-ficient caveats to imagine a degree of stylistic flexibility ('need not observe compulsory, statutory constraints'), it presents a fairly monolithic account of mainstream film's unified diegesis that will be challenged in quite specific ways by what is found in the films examined in the subsequent chapters. Though one must be careful not to overstate the extent to which direct address represents a challenge to these norms, we shall see how the device finds a place in many comedies because it is consistent with *underlying structures* that would need to be described in quite different terms from those Wollen offers. As we shall see, comedies (and musicals) regularly present performers who embody both fictional characters and versions of themselves; rather than being 'coherent and integrated' in the way Wollen suggests, comedies regularly blur the boundary between fiction and 'documentary' (broadly defined). Another aspect of Wollen's argument that has proved problematic is the extent to which the effect of certain counter-cinematic techniques is more presumed than concretely demonstrated. At one point, Wollen writes, 'It is hardly necessary, after the work of Brecht, to comment on the purpose of estrangement-effects of this kind' (ibid.: 502). Wollen is by no means alone in letting 'Brecht' be a shorthand for certain kinds of estrangement techniques but few film studies scholars have been precise about what exactly 'Brechtian' means (Gilberto Perez is rare for his precision; however, see also Polan 1985, who interrogates this very gap in film studies scholarship). Counter to Wollen, it *is* necessary to comment on the purpose of these estrangement techniques.

A quotation from Brecht comes near the start of *Deux ou trois choses que je sais d'elle*. Direct address in Godard could be a book in itself (no other director is so associated with the device) and the analysis here can only provide a snapshot of his practice. The device appears in a high proportion of the director's prolific output and through each stage of his long and varied career; it is found in the vividness and immediacy of his early New Wave work (including his debut feature, *À bout de souffle*, 1960) and in the increasingly politicised experiments with form up to and beyond May '68 (such as the Dziga Vertov group's *Le Vent d'est* from 1970, the locus of Wollen's analysis and a film also cited by Pascal Bonitzer); even his recent feature, *Film Socialisme* (2010), involves numerous characters – and one may still call them characters, though this is a complex issue – looking into the camera. Here, I shall focus mainly on one of the Godard films in which direct address has particularly complex and varied functions.

Deux ou trois choses que je sais d'elle (henceforth '*Deux ou trois . . .*') begins by setting out the various 'she' to which the *elle* of the title refers. First, a title in the red, white and blue of the French Tricolour indicates that the first *elle* is *la Région parisienne*. Godard's whispered voiceover then tells us some facts about recent changes to the region's governance, while the image track presents views of what might be described as 'alienated' urban landscapes. The film's structured use of direct address begins as we are then given images of a woman standing in front of a similar landscape, with a large tower block dominating frame-left (we might extrapolate that she is standing on the balcony of one herself, as we are high up). She looks around herself and at the camera, adjusting her hair somewhat idly. Her comportment has the appearance of a person who a director has pointed a camera at with no instructions as to what to do. She appears a little self-conscious but not too abashed by the camera's attention; these sequences feel something like a screen test. The voiceover begins again: 'She: It's Marina Vlady. She's an actress. She is wearing a midnight blue sweater with two yellow stripes. She is of Russian origin. Her hair is dark auburn or light brown, I'm not sure.' It turns out that the actress is in place, prepared to assume a role, because she begins to speak, in slightly halting language, as if feeling the effort of remembering lines. The lines themselves are precisely concerned with the manner of speaking lines: 'Yes. "Speak as though quoting the truth." It was father Brecht who said that. . . . that actors should *quote*' [emphasis in original speech]. The woman – for the question of what to call her is and will become more difficult – turns her head to her left and looks off into the distance. We see her features more clearly as, before, in what might be described as an 'amateurish' lighting set-up, her face was partially obscured because framed against a lighter background. The voiceover speaks again: 'Now she turns her head to the right, but that has no importance.'

We cut to a shot, similar in key respects. As before, the cut is on the same woman, centrally framed, looking directly into the lens and then 'idly' caressing her hair and looking around her. She remains almost silhouetted against the background. The background itself seems to be the same but viewed from a different angle or a position somewhere to the right of the previous one. Landmarks show that this is the same locale reframed – for example, we can draw a line between a building and a gas tower (perhaps, it is blurred) receding to the horizon (this had been frame-right in the previous shot but now it is frame-left). The effect of the juxtaposition of shots is one of mirroring, felt most strongly in the presence of a very similar tower block, which is now on the right of the screen. The voiceover begins again: 'She: It is Juliette Jeanson. She lives here. She is wearing a midnight blue sweater with two yellow stripes. Her hair is dark auburn or light brown, I'm not sure. She is of Russian origin.' The voiceover has moved now to indicate the fictional character who is continuous with the actress who will play her in some ways but not in others; both are of Russian origin and both wear the same clothes but only the character 'lives here'. The character now speaks but the dialogue, her manner of speaking it, and of course the fact that she still speaks directly to the camera, mean that we have crossed no definite boundary from the previous shot: 'Two years ago in Martinique . . . exactly like in a Simenon novel. No [she quickly shakes her head], I don't know which. Oh yes, *Banana Tourist*, that's it.' She breaks off, looks away and then looks back to the camera. 'I've got to manage somehow. Robert I think earns about 1000 Francs a month.' The voiceover again then describes her actions from the camera's perspective: 'Now she has turned her head to the left, but that has no importance.'

Even describing these two shots is a challenge because language is explicitly problematised – the opening is successful in 'estranging' what we would normally take for granted. For example, the voiceover's hesitancy as regards the colour of the woman's hair anticipates moments from later in the film, such as Juliette Jeanson / Marina Vlady wondering, 'what if blue had been called green by mistake?' (This worrying over language is a constant in Godard's films.) The objectivity of language is also called into question by the voiceover's description of her head turning: 'She turns her head to the left' is correct in describing the movement on screen. However, it is arguably significant that the voiceover chooses not to say 'She turns her head to the [that is, her] right,' which could equally describe the same action. Moreover, fundamental ontological categories such as 'person', 'character' and 'actor' are questioned. With the second shot, we shift to the fictional but the shift is as halting as the speech. The recourse by the character 'Juliette Jeanson' – if we can say certainly that it is she – to the analogy with the Simenon novel is incomplete and makes little sense in itself. Moreover, these lines are performed as if she were answering an unheard question. Crucially, they are delivered in a halting fashion that does not allow us to imagine that they are emanations from the character's interiority, at least not interiority in any naturalistic or unified sense. In line with the explicit allusion to the German playwright and theorist, the performance is truly Brechtian in its manner of its estrangement, its distancing:

> This sense of incompleteness . . . Brecht sought to induce in the theater: a sense of the play not as a presented whole but as a series of fragments, a narrative sequence, someone's choice of what to play to give an account of the action . . . The alienation effect is not a style of performance but the negation of the performance by making the spectator aware of what it is not. (Perez 1998: 82–3)

As with the techniques Perez describes, the fragmentary nature of the speech and the repetitions of the voiceover make us aware not of action / story in and of itself but of 'someone's choice of what to play to give an account of the action'. The narrative premise, or at least the premise on which the film's promotion is most often hooked (Jeanson prostitutes herself in order to make ends meet), is anticipated when she says, 'I've got to manage somehow. Robert I think earns about 1000 Francs a month.' However, the sense that both the character and the actor incarnating her are quoting lines which are not her own frames the story in a very particular way.

The above sequence takes us to the heart of some quite complex questions concerning character agency and interiority. It will be instructive to return to Pascal Bonitzer's notion of the counter-look or, rather Marc Vernet's extrapolation of Bonitzer's argument. Vernet returns to the notion of the counter-look as 'abject' but is more forceful in ascribing this effect to Godard when he says that in Godard's use of the counter-look, 'the actor is brutally stripped of his character' (1983: 35; my translation). However, rather than illustrating Bonitzer's schema, the opening of *Deux ou trois . . .* complicates it. First, it is ambiguous whether Vlady / Jeanson's looks to camera would be best described as 'the hidden look' or 'the counter-look'; in line with the former, we feel clearly at times that she is looking to Godard (it is Godard's voice we hear in whispered voiceover, after all) and her performance is more tentative, almost submissive, than provocative; however, in the role it plays in a clearly 'Brechtian' strategy of estrangement, the looks towards us are clearly 'counter'. Deciding rests partly in the force, the agency, one ascribes to the woman looking at us.

Crucially, however, the problem in deciding results partly in the very existence of such binaries and the assumption, at least as present in much film theory of the 1970s, that Brecht stands for radical opposition to the very concept of fictional characterisation / embodiment. In reality, Brecht's practice did not destroy characters or 'brutally strip them' out of the text. Rather, Brecht suggests that characters, like all real people, are contradictory and the 'reality' of their situations is ultimately not fully knowable – the techniques of estrangement draw attention to this fact rather than to the *absence* of character. With his typical acuity, Robin Wood links Brecht's practice to another Godard film in which direct address plays a very prominent role, *Tout va bien*. Here, in contrast with the way much classic film theory alluded to Brecht, Wood underlines how Brechtian techniques are not incompatible with our engagement with characters as such:

> The characterization in *Tout va bien* may be tenuous, and our awareness of [Yves] Montand and [Jane] Fonda as themselves constant, but the film none the less refers us to the imagined predicaments of a fictitious couple – predicaments with which we are clearly meant to become involved, to which we are invited to relate on a personal level. (2006: 99)

Clearly, in the opening of *Deux ou trois . . .* , Godard employs Vlady to construct a character, 'Juliette Jeanson'. And rather than an 'abject' absence of character (we should remember that Julia Kristeva tells us the abject is where meaning collapses – 1982), the spectator's reading of character interiority is, instead, problematised. This is how I read the moment in the first shot in which the voiceover says, 'she turns her head right but that has no importance.' The voiceover estranges us from what I believe we would *wish*, by our familiarity with filmed fictions, to read in the image. The effect of Vlady's turning her

Figure 2.1 *Deux ou trois choses que je sais d'elle* (Argos Films et al., 1967): Marina Vlady / Juliette Jeanson looks 'thoughtfully' into the distance.

head into the light (see Figure 2.1) and her movement to gaze – I find myself wanting to say 'thoughtfully' – into the distance is as if to bring her personality to light.[4] That Godard seeks this effect upon us is suggested by his choosing previously to have her almost silhouetted against the sky in the background.

Peter Wollen cites *Deux ou trois . . .* as a step in Godard's 'retreat from (and eventual attack on) fiction':

> Especially since May 1968, the attack on fiction has been given a political rationale (fiction = mystification = bourgeois ideology) but, at the beginning, it is much more closely connected with Godard's fascination (Cartesian, rather than Marxist) with the misleading and dissembling nature of appearances, the impossibility of reading an essence from a phenomenal surface, of seeing a soul through and within a body or telling a lie from a truth. At times, Godard seems almost to adopt a kind of radical Romanticism, which sees silence (lovers' silence, killers' silence) as the only true communication, when reality and representation, essence and appearance, irreducibly coincide: the moment of truth. (Wollen 1985: 507–8)

Here, Wollen makes use of his binaries (in this case, 'fiction v reality') brilliantly because he treats them as a spectrum, with Godard's practice moving forwards and backwards along this scale. As Wollen suggests, there is romanticism in Godard and in *Deux ou trois . . .* , a 'radical romanticism'. Not only does the whispering voiceover (approaching and surrounded by moments of silence) suggest a tentativeness, perhaps a self-deprecation that might be one of Godard's most sincere expressions of truth, but also this voiceover is used to brilliant effect over an image I take to be the film's most sincerely romantic image, an image a colleague described to me as 'the coffee cup of the cosmos'.

In a scene in a café where Juliette seems about to pick up another client, the film presents a series of relatively disembodied shots of the surface of a cup of coffee, on which bubbles form and dissipate. The philosophical content of the voiceover that accompanies these images cannot be dealt with succinctly here except to note that they see the juxtaposition of ideas of real vastness (life, the universe and everything, more or less) with imagery that focuses on the banal (a cup of coffee) in microscopic detail. The combination is ironic but I take the romanticism of the images to be, ultimately, sincere because of the beauty of the coffee's bubbles and the perfect fusion of voiceover and accompanying image when the voiceover speaks the words, 'but if, by chance, things again become clear [*nettes*]' – here, the images come into sharp focus. The combination of vast philosophical ruminations with the close-up on the banal could be said to dramatise contingency. So too does the film's passages of direct address but, of course, with the added contingency presented by 'real' filmed human figures.

The film is interspersed with the straight-to-camera testimony of a range of what seem to be 'real women'. One such woman, 'Paulette Cadjaris', speaks to the camera from the hair salon where she apparently works. There are halts in her speech like Vlady / Juliette's earlier, which seem to suggest she is answering some unheard questions. However, her performance and testimony are genuinely moving, as she offers an insight into her life and her prospects for the future that only include 'a load of everyday things [*un tas des choses banales*]'. Whether Paulette is a 'real', documented subject or not is difficult to ascertain but, either way, her testimony makes the viewer reflect on the limitations of our capacity and the capacity of film to offer insight into the interior lives of people and characters. Direct address is one of the most expressive devices for the exploration of such questions because, I would suggest, something of the 'real' human subject always presents itself (the actor and / or the character built from the material that actor presents), even if that 'real person' is contingent and contradictory. Though critical of the notion of a soul and radically different in attitude to the 'romantic' films examined in the case studies chapters, Godard's use of direct address has nothing to do with 'abjection' but everything to do with the contradictory nature of film performance. Crucially, the above analysis has sought to stress the ambiguity and multivalence of Godard's direct address – the necessarily brief analysis could only scratch the surface of this. It contrasts with the didactic clarity, the 'director's address', offered by *Funny Games* to-camera discourse. To cite Robin Wood again:

Except when Vladimir and Rosa supervene [Wood refers to a film made by the Dziga Vertov group, in which Godard appeared as Lenin and Jean-Pierre Gorin as Karl Rosa], it is difficult to think of a single statement in a Godard film that can be unequivocally construed as 'Author's Message': the statements are set side by side as so many pieces of evidence for our serious consideration, Godard's point of view being defined only in terms of the areas of interest implied by the selection. (2006: 80)

Seeing the 'fiction'–'reality' distinction as being on a continuum rather than as a binary, we shall see links with the films examined later, such as the moment, in *La Ronde*, in which the camera shifts to show us filmmaking technology in the background – this shot might be compared with the reframed shots of 'Marina Vlady' and then 'Juliette Jeanson', though the contingency of Max Ophuls's[5] filmed world is very different to that of Godard's. We shall see other films that share 'Brechtian' characteristics with Godard but are more invested in creating unified characterisations, though, as we shall see, direct address complicates this unity considerably.

As a conclusion to this chapter and in anticipation of the next, I wish to introduce the notion of 'documentary' that will inform the discussion of comedies and musicals. Emerging out of Gilberto Perez's work in *The Material Ghost*, this concept clearly links Godard's practice with wider film form. Indeed, Perez draws on one of Godard's own sayings:

> Jean-Luc Godard said that every film is a documentary of its actors . . . In his own films Godard purposely brings forward the documentary of the actor as distinct from the character being played. If an actor's performance is an icon of the character, the documentary of the actor is an index of the person giving the performance. (1998: 37)

Working with the semiotic terminology of 'index' and 'icon', Perez elegantly suggests that Godard's difference from wider practices is a matter more of degree than of kind. Perez compares Godard to the neorealist, Vittorio De Sica, who was famed for using non-professionals, but, further on, Perez also underlines the documentary aspect of star performances familiar from 'classical' Hollywood:

> The faces of the great movie stars, their ways of being on the screen, all have the distinctive particularity of the documentary image. But out of the documentary image the screen makes a fiction, a world of the movie – of many movies in the case of a star – and the documentary particulars become part of that fiction. (ibid.: 38)

Perez's analysis is not born of some naive belief in the innate 'realism' of the cinema. He is measured in his reappraisal of the theoretical heritage of André Bazin (whose naivety has been greatly overstated by his critics): 'Every film may be a documentary of its actors, but most films are documentaries of little else; they may be shot on location yet they take place nowhere near the real world' (Perez 1998: 39). In the previous quotation, Perez's final point about the documentary particulars making up the fiction is crucial. To give the example of a performer whom Perez discusses and who will be touched upon in the next chapter, the documentary of Charlie Chaplin looking at the camera (documentary because it is a material fact of the filming) becomes part of the on-going fiction (on-going across many Chaplin films) of the Tramp's search for communion with 'us'. I will suggest that the comedic mode is, in fact, especially 'documentary'. However, in line with Perez's warning that all films may be documentaries of little else than their actors, I would suggest that comedies are generally only documentaries of their own making – this is documentary of a clearly quite solipsistic kind.

NOTES

1. Wheeler Winston Dixon's book *It Looks at You: The Returned Gaze of the Cinema* (1995), by dint of its length, would seem a more likely candidate for this title. However, Dixon subsumes direct address into a broader account of the 'look back' – he suggests that some films actually 'surveille' the audience. Dixon's focus is too diffuse, too casual (production photos are regularly taken for film stills), and, I would contend, too obfuscatory to be useful here.
2. If Godard exemplifies the 'counter-look', Bonitzer formulates the other principally with reference to largely non-narrative films by Stephen Dwoskin that are also the focus of an earlier-cited essay by Paul Willemen (1976). Bonitzer does make reference to Ingmar Bergman and brief mention of Fellini (Bonitzer 1977: 46). However, I find his auteurist account of both kinds of looks rather limiting.
3. As in most accounts of the film, I shall designate the two young torturers 'Paul' and 'Peter'. These are the names they use most often but are clearly assumed as a part of their 'funny games'. They alternately call each other Tom and Jerry, even Beavis and Butthead – hinting at Haneke's disdain for television and particularly youth culture. The jokes with their names suggest their primarily rhetorical function and also evince Haneke's desire to problematise 'identification'. The family are given proper names (Anna, Georg and Georgie – in the US version, the names are Anglicised but not changed), probably with the aim of humanising them and making their

torture, for us, more painful. However, I shall generally refer to them as 'mother', 'father' and 'son' because they seem too to have a primarily rhetorical function.

4. This tendency to read interiority on to filmed subjects might be described as the anthropomorphism of film. I take this theme to be key to the inclusion and particular use of child 'performers' within *Deux ou trois* . . . For example, the vexed question of interiority is treated quasi-comically in a scene between Vlady / Jeanson and the boy playing her fictional son (Christophe Bourseiller). After he asks, 'Mummy, do you dream?', he tells her a story of *his* dream, which is a ludicrous (for a small boy) allegory of the Vietnam war. Attention is drawn to the peculiar ontology and, one might say, anthropomorphism of child performances for brief comical effect here, but elsewhere, probably the most authentic performance in the whole film is offered by the small girl (Marie Bourseiller) who plays Jeanson's other child. She screams uncontrollably for her mother and, though the performance is visibly and viscerally authentic, it is evident that its framing is not; neither Jeanson (obviously) nor Vlady is her real mother, though her real brother plays her fictional brother! (See Robin Wood 2006: 208–12 for a discussion of children in Godard.) Some of Godard's choices in his worrying over interiority and inter-subjectivity are highly problematic, however. At a recent research group in my university department, a number of colleagues felt that, though the film gives voice to female figures in a way not often seen, women often seem here to provide 'a convenient metaphor' for the emptiness of modern personality formation and the consumer culture that produces it.

5. I have chosen to use the more anglicised version, 'Ophuls', over 'Ophüls', as it is also often written. Susan White discusses some of the issues behind the different permutations of the director's name, also opting for 'Ophuls' for her own purposes (1995: 11).

CHAPTER 3

Looks of invitation: comedic and musical direct address

Comedy is the most common, the most 'natural' home for direct address within mainstream cinema. Following, principally, the work of Deborah Thomas (2000) and Alex Clayton (2010),[1] I will discuss comedy as a 'mode' rather than as a genre *per se*. Thomas sees comedy and melodrama as the two dominant modes of Hollywood cinema (with 'romance' a significant inflection of each) and Clayton has offered a new definition of the comedic mode ('since comedy is merely a genre in which the mode is dominant' – 2010: 62). In line with the above schema, musicals are treated as a sub-strand of film comedy ('musical-*comedy*' is dominant in the 'classical' American cinema I favour here). However, I will attend briefly to the specific relationship of direct address to the performance of song and dance.

I wish first to return to the documentary aspect of film as introduced above. Remembering Godard's comment that every film is a documentary of its actors, we can see clear links with stylistic traits found regularly in comedies. In most traditions of comedy (those involving elements of slapstick, for example), the actor's 'business' is central and what is funny often emerges from the camera's close observation of someone '*being* funny'. Moreover, it seems especially true of comic performers such as Will Ferrell to say that he is always, to some extent, playing the same role: 'Will Ferrell'. Stan Laurel and Oliver Hardy (two performers examined below) always play characters called 'Stan' and 'Ollie'. Unlike in Godard, the documentary aspect of the filmed material is not here brought out in order to deconstruct the fictional elements; 'deconstruct' implies something too analytical, not to mention too serious. However, mainstream comedies are often at least as reflexive as the films examined in the previous chapter. James Naremore writes that, 'By its very nature, comedy undermines our involvement with the characters, barely maintaining a dramatic illusion . . . [and] invites us to observe plot machinery *as* machinery' (1988: 115). The latter description is of something documentary in spirit.

One could go as far as to suggest that comedy is the filmmaking mode closest to documentary. If this appears counter-intuitive, it is because, tonally, 'documentary' feels far removed from comedy's concerns. However, a range of examples suggest a long-standing affinity. For example, Chaplin's first appearance as the Tramp in *Kid Auto Races at Venice* (1914) was a prototypical 'mockumentary' performance, the conceit being the Tramp's unwanted interruption of the shooting of a soapbox race.[2] The event, its participants and spectators were real, the Tramp and the diegetic film crew, fictional. James Naremore uses the film to open his investigation into both film acting and social life as performance, imagining it to be a film made by 'some Los Angeles-based Dziga Vertov' (1988: 9). An example less obviously documentary-like is *Road to Morocco* (1942), one of the long-running *Road to . . .* series in which Bing Crosby and Bob Hope starred. Very near its start, the two leads (ostensibly playing characters called 'Jeff' and 'Orville') sing a song, 'We're on the road to Morocco'. This most self-conscious example of this most self-conscious of genres (comedy / musical) has them sing lines that include, 'I'll lay you eight to five we meet Dorothy Lamour' and 'Paramount will protect us 'cos we're signed for five more years.' Of course, Lamour does show up (she was a regular co-star in the series) and references to the producing studio and other in–jokes abound. Indeed, the extremely formulaic aspect to the narratives of the *Road* series is commented upon in the final scene. Lamour says, 'I get the strangest feeling that we've been through all of this before' – *Road to Morocco* was the third in the series. Jumping sixty-three years, *A Cock and Bull Story* (2005) takes the comedy–documentary relationship to its (post)modern conclusion. The film intersperses an adaptation of the novel *Tristram Shandy*, in which Steve Coogan plays the title character and Rob Brydon his uncle Toby, with a fictional documentary frame about the filming of this 'Tristram Shandy', in which Coogan and Brydon play versions of themselves but in which many other actors (some well known) incarnate fictional versions of directors, costume designers and so on.[3] The ontological complexities of the various performances within performances in *A Cock and Bull Story* make it impossible to describe succinctly. What it has in common with the other two examples I have chosen, however, is that direct address is embedded throughout. In this case, it is embedded in the fiction within the fiction ('Tristram Shandy'), not the (fake) documentary frame. I would suggest that, ultimately, direct address helps convey the sense that, paradoxically, the meta-film, 'Tristram Shandy', is 'truer', more 'real' (a truer documentary?) than the 'behind-the-scenes' footage.

In these and other ways, comedies, even when they do not include allusions to documentary as genre, are frequently 'documentaries of their own making'. Comedies often become quite literally documentaries of their own making for the duration of a 'blooper reel', which may appear over the closing credits (even if it appears nowhere else in that comedy, addressing the camera is likely to crop up here). And the documentary spirit of screen comedy is often tacitly acknowledged by film spectators when they positively evaluate films (or mitigate their negative reactions) by saying that 'They [the actors] clearly had a great time making it [the film].' This is a common response by film spectators and / or critics, even in the absence of a blooper reel, whose principal function seems to be to testify to the fun had on set.

Before further analysing these and other issues, an example from *Wayne's World* (1992) can provide a more extended example of comedy-as-documentary, as well as set up a number of issues pursued in the subsequent analysis. In the first minutes, we are taken into the basement where Wayne (Mike Myers) and Garth (Dana Carvey) film their titular cable TV show. We see the pair look into diegetic television cameras but the film initially avoids having their gaze meet ours directly – we only see the diegetically located direct address of Wayne and Garth on story world televisions and studio monitors. Through contrast, this lends added intimacy to Wayne's testimony direct to *us* in the subsequent scene, where, as external spectators, we are granted a position more privileged than the television viewers within the film's diegesis. Wayne leaves his studio and enters the upstairs house to tell us, 'Let me bring you up to speed.' He then provides a quick recap of his life so far and information about, for example, the setting for the action (Aurora, Illinois). Myers / Wayne seeks to win us over with his self-deprecating outlook: 'What I'd really like to do is make Wayne's World for a living. It might happen! Yeah, and monkeys might fly out of my butt.'

The film here evokes one of the claims I earlier mentioned as common to cinematic direct address: its evocation of a character's superior epistemic relationship to the fiction. In this case, it is done through irony, as Wayne is ostensibly unaware of what is to come. Most viewers will, however, be pretty confident, contrary to Wayne's sarcastic take on the likelihood of his success, that he *will* begin to make a living from Wayne's World – we have already seen the television executive, Benjamin Kane (Rob Lowe), take note of the show and, it should be remembered, spectators often know the rudiments of a film's story arc before sitting down to watch a film.[4] Also, Wayne's dismissal of this possibility is *so asserted* and, indeed, the fact that it is articulated at all (out loud to the camera no less!) suggests that, ironically, Wayne / Myer's (the distinction quickly blurs) is being 'knowing' about what is to come. (Irony is a complex issue we will return to at numerous points over the coming chapters.)

Within screen comedy, *Wayne's World* is unusual for the extent, though not necessarily the manner, of its reflexivity. After Wayne is picked up by Garth in their 'mirthmobile', a scene in a diner sees the manager Glen (Ed O'Neill, from long-running US TV series *Married with Children*) beckon the camera towards him. His crazed ramblings are interrupted by Wayne: 'What are you doing? Only me and Garth get to talk to the camera!' (In having more than one character address us directly, the film *is* actually unusual.) The camera switches to follow Wayne and then, finding Garth, the latter flees from it. The camera here is a physically active presence in helping convey their distinct characterisations: Garth is a much shyer character. In their later to-camera discourse, Wayne is often ironic or warmly sarcastic, while Garth is ingenuous. Yet the direct address of both is a marker of their shared 'authenticity', in contrast to the 'phoniness' of the business world and, especially, its representative, Benjamin.[5] Also, Garth's direct address, like Wayne's, suggests his awareness of the narrative trajectory in which they find themselves. When Benjamin presents the pair with a contract for producing *Wayne's World* commercially, Garth deliberately (and rather artlessly) drops his pen on the floor and beckons the camera to follow him as he goes to pick it up:

> Does this seem weird? Why does this guy have contracts? Did you ever see the *Twilight Zone* where the guy signed a contract and they cut out his tongue and they put it in a jar and it wouldn't die and it just grew and grew and pulsated and gave birth to baby tongues . . . Pretty cool, huh?! I gotta go.

Here, as elsewhere, the infantile (more infantile) Garth is actually more nearly perceptive than Wayne. Both characters inhabit a fiction made up of clichéd tropes (Rob Lowe's slick exec is comedic in the obviousness of his mendacity) and, at various moments, the on-screen figures appear aware that they are in a film without ceasing to be characters in it. Garth's babbling about tongues in jars alludes to a ridiculous narrative from television, suggesting the narrative of *Wayne's World* is similarly – gleefully – ludicrous. However, it *is* prescient for the Faustian narrative situation in which he finds himself and, as a metaphor that becomes steadily more incoherent, it is also symptomatic of a naivety (more generously, we should call it 'innocence') that will continue to make him and Wayne hapless fall-guys in Benjamin's devious plans.

Wayne's World's 'intertextuality', its genesis as a television sketch on *Saturday Night Live*, and its use of the world of television as a fictional setting partly explain its playful form and its mockery of the convention of the 'fourth wall'. However, we are not far from the *Road to Morocco* here. The ending of *Wayne's World* (in which we are given multiple alternate endings, including a 'mega happy ending' and 'a Scooby Doo ending') is clearly in line with the tone and tenor of Hope and Crosby's exchanges:

> Orville / Hope: 'First you sell me for 200 bucks, then I'm gonna marry the princess, and then you cut in on me. Then we're carried off by a desert sheikh and now we're gonna have our heads chopped off.'

Jeff / Crosby: 'I know all that!'
Orville / Hope: 'But the people who came in in the middle of the
    picture don't.'
Jeff / Crosby: 'You mean they missed my song?!'

Wayne's World's multiple endings follow through its mockery of the contrivances of conventional film storylines and the arbitrary resolutions of narrative problems. This does not make *Wayne's World* 'radical'; this is the common currency of 'spoof' films.[6] In comedies such as *Wayne's World*, the supposed 'goal-oriented' unfolding of narrative is almost irrelevant next to the more important drive to engage and play with the audience's emotions and awareness of generic conventions quite directly[7] – self-referentiality is one way to achieve this. The film can, however, be considered, on certain levels, a documentary about film narrative and its direct address is intimately linked to this. In order to talk more precisely about the conventions in which *Wayne's World* and other direct-address films participate, let us consider some other overriding performative traits of the comedic mode.

ACTING UP AND ACTING OUT: DIRECT ADDRESS AND COMEDIC PERFORMANCE

It should be stressed that I do not treat the documentary aspect of comedy as its *defining* characteristic – the notion of 'documentary' I am following is found in all fiction film, to some extent.[8] In order to understand the specificity of comedy further, in this next section I shall draw heavily upon the work of one writer[9] who has offered a new definition of film comedy that enables a more developed understanding of the complex role direct address might play in it.

Alex Clayton's essay, 'Play-acting: A Theory of Comedic Performance', seeks to shift the terrain of debate about what constitutes screen comedy from an emphasis on effect and affect (primarily laughter) to one of intention: he argues that 'a performance is comedic in as much as we recognize that it seeks to amuse' (2010: 62). The most simple justification for Clayton's questioning of the bias of previous comedy theory is because a comedy that fails to make us laugh is still a comedy, though it might be considered a failed one: 'the joke that goes down like a lead balloon is a joke regardless, the defining feature being ambition rather than accomplishment' (ibid.: 63).[10]

Clayton's analysis of the displayed intention to amuse as central to screen comedy encompasses many different aspects of performance and its framing. These include direct address. Talking of a moment from Chaplin's *The Circus* (1928), Clayton writes:

Such moments awaken a dynamic, always latent in performed
fiction, between actor and character – polarizing them . . . Comedic
performance crucially exploits the duality of actor–character
co-existence in a single embodied figure. This complex dynamic is
brought boldly and comically to the surface in the banana moment
when Chaplin looks at the camera *in character* (a wholly conventional
paradox). (ibid.: 67)

The 'polarising' of the dynamic between actor and character relates to our
previous linking of comedy to documentary. Indeed, if, as we have suggested,
all filmmaking has a documentary edge – Godard's comment about every
film being 'a documentary of its actors' is similar in content, if not tone, to
Clayton's acknowledgement of the dynamic between character and actor being
'always latent in performed fiction' – we can see how comedy is especially close
to this heritage. Clayton underlines the consistency of a comedian's characterisations across their film vehicles (ibid.: 77) and we might say that, because
the persona of the little Tramp is so recurrent, many of Chaplin's comedies
can be considered documentaries of 'Chaplin being the Tramp'. However, the
performativity of the Tramp is also crucial to his *character*:

One reason [Chaplin's Tramp] is a comic hero is that there is usually a
disparity between his grand actions and his humble 'essence'. In every
way he is what Leo Braudy describes as a 'theatrical character' – a
figure who *acts* and who lets us see the artificiality of his performance.
(Naremore 1988: 122–4)

According to Clayton, Chaplin's camera-look is *in character*, making the
moment Clayton cites from *The Circus* a core example of what I have been
calling direct address. He also makes the rarely acknowledged point that this
paradoxical look (paradoxical because, following V. F. Perkins's formulation,
there is no camera in the character's world) is 'wholly conventional': that is,
conventional to the comedic mode. He goes on to suggest that 'looking at the
camera is only one (albeit perhaps the most overt) form of comedic address'
(Clayton 2010: 67) and moves on to consider other aspects of performance.[11]
However, these other performative postures remain relevant to our more
specific focus on direct address:

How is it we recognize, even without extratextual knowledge of the
performer, a stance, gesture or look as comedic? We find ourselves
wanting to point at something in the body itself – the way the limbs
are held, the way the gaze is fixed – a feature I want to call the *comic
twinkle*. Difficult to pinpoint but impossible to ignore, the 'twinkle' is

that oblique bodily disclosure of comic intent – call it irony, cheekiness, a certain sense of 'I-know-you-know-I-know' – which appeals to our sense of humor. As with direct-to-camera address, it visibly acknowledges the discrepancy between actor and character, even as that role continues to be played. (ibid.: 67)

Crucially, the 'comic twinkle' as a disclosure of the individual performer's intention to amuse is not the only way in which film comedies define themselves as such: 'bodily *placement* may alone yield a disclosure of comic intent' (ibid.: 67). Clayton cites various examples, such as the 'deliberate accident', where the *film* could be said to perform the setting-up of a gag to which the oblivious character will fall victim: an oblivious character performed by a 'knowing' actor. This is important because, shifting for a moment from the emphasis on intention to effect, it strikes me that what is most often *funny* is the obliviousness of characters to the pratfall and / or moment of acute embarrassment that is awaiting them. Following Clayton, we can see how the placement of a figure on screen is often central to that common experience we have as spectators of cringing in anticipation of something of which the comedy character is unaware. However, this begs the question, where does this leave direct address? In the Introduction, I suggested that direct address is often a marker of a character's realisation, their coming to consciousness, thus their awakening *from* obliviousness. In order to understand its place within the conventions of comedic performance, as well as why direct address might be funny (not the same things, as Clayton reminds us), some concrete examples are needed.

First, an extended quotation from Andrew Klevan, part of a passage cited earlier, in the Introduction. Here, Klevan attends with extraordinary care to a moment in which Oliver Hardy performs direct address in *Sons of the Desert* (1933). The sequence involves Stan and Ollie's floundering attempts to lie to their wives, who are interrogating them about their whereabouts over the previous days – they are trying to conceal that, against the wives' express wishes, they have attended a convention for the 'Sons of the Desert' club. What follows takes up the scene from a moment where Laurel and Hardy, who previously shared the frame, are now separated by an edit:

With this distance [now] between them, Stan naturally confesses, and cries hysterically. The film cuts back to a (waist up) shot of Ollie who is now sitting at the table, with his head leaning on his arm; he looks in the direction of the camera. There is no attempt to shut Stan up, no attempt to excuse Stan's confession, no attempt to prolong the cover-up, no equal show of panic and after all their combined efforts at gesturing, Ollie now sits still, and separate. There is humour in the suddenness of his restraint. He looks towards us, now that he can no longer look to Stan, with the hope that we, at least (all of us, some of us, one of us), might recognise that his partner has let him down. His look is made more potent by the fact that he stares, not merely elsewhere, but as if into another world, out of his own (fictional) world, the one that includes Stan. (2005: 31–2)

The resignation of Ollie's direct address seeks communion with the spectator and our recognition of his predicament. It is, in narrative terms, a pretty passive gesture as, defeated by the wives' insistent questioning and Stan's sudden capitulation, it marks his resignation to his fate – Ollie's famous catchphrase ('That's another nice mess you've gotten me into') is passive-aggressive; in reality, Ollie is often equally active in the pair's messing things up. As Klevan underlines, the gesture itself is humorous and this derives from its strong contrast with what has gone before (we have 'the suddenness of his restraint') and its contrast with Stan's hysteria. This seems to me paradigmatic of the way direct address is often comic (that is, funny) in screen comedies: our cringing anticipation leads to the sudden release of the pratfall (in this case, capitula-tion to the wives), which can then be followed by a moment of recognition / realisation 'shared' between spectator and character / performer. Direct address is here, something like a pause, a sigh perhaps. As suggested in the Introduction, a sensation of 'stillness' seems often a quality of direct address and this stillness can help shape the contours of a scene's humour. (Though, following Clayton, debating the presumed effect on audience members is more problematic than seeking to identify the apparent intention of a given performative gesture or posture.)

Klevan is cautious in avoiding describing Ollie as looking 'at' the camera or 'at' us; I would suggest, overly cautious. However, it is true that throughout this and so many other Laurel and Hardy films, Ollie often looks so close along the line with the camera that it can be difficult to tell where, physically, the gaze is fixed. Interestingly, Ollie also looks at the camera in partial axial shot-reverse-shots. Just after the sequence Klevan analyses, Ollie has an exchange in shot-reverse-shot with his wife and then with Stan. In both cases, Oliver Hardy is looking straight into the camera (or very nearly) and the other fig-ure's gaze is more clearly off; camera looks *and* direct address are generally the province of Hardy in these films. They are consequently marked moments of his aloneness. Klevan (2005: 25–32) and Clayton (2007: 105–22) have done brilliant work in exploring the togetherness of Laurel and Hardy on screen. However, the comic effect of Ollie's direct address generally resides in the way it separates him from Stan, much in line with the moment analysed by Klevan above. Stan does on occasion look at the camera, perhaps in a moment of clarity.[12] However, generally, Stan's performance style is defined by his gaze *not* connecting with ours; the comedy of Stan's performances lies largely in his near-perfect obliviousness. Ollie is the one who repeatedly and insistently looks 'at' us. Klevan on the camera-look in *Sons of the Desert* again: 'We might sympathise with the collapse into resignation and exhaustion, but we cannot confirm Ollie in his superiority, and not simply because, as is often claimed, he is in no position to condescend' (2005: 32). Klevan goes on to make a further point about their togetherness but the point that Ollie's direct address is ironic because he is in 'no position to condescend' still holds (even if it is 'not simply' this). The comic effect of direct address as a marker of realisation / consciousness is again complex. In this case, the often-perfect obliviousness of Stan contrasts with the false dawn(ing) of Ollie's to-camera realisations. The failed superiority reached for by Ollie's direct address makes him, in these moments, all the more alone and makes us, perhaps, all the more sympathetic towards him.

In very similar terms, Gilberto Perez describes arguably cinema history's most famous performer of direct address:

> Even when the Tramp finds himself all alone, rejected by everyone in the film, he still has us, the main recipients of his personal appeal. His directing that appeal to us of course stresses his alienation from his milieu, but it also indicates Chaplin's confidence that the appeal will be heeded, and thus his hope that the established order will be changed. (1998: 117)[13]

With the latter part of the quotation, Perez shifts from character to actor and makes a point about the latter's socio-political hopes and wishes. However, the point about the character's 'alienation from his milieu' is very close to Ollie's isolation in his appeals to the spectator. An example from Chaplin's *The Circus* not examined by Alex Clayton can further develop our impressions of how direct address might be funny and the multiplicity of things it might be said to mean in the context of comedy.

Midway through the film, the Tramp is chased by a donkey that has taken a dislike to him. He runs up some steps and through a door, only to discover he is in the pen of one of the circus's lions. Realising his error, he tiptoes away from the beast, which, for the moment, is fast asleep. A reverse cut shows us his hand as it reaches through the bars and round the side of the pen as he tries to move the catch on the door. He only succeeds in causing the catch to fall firmly in place, locking him in with the lion. The shot of the Tramp's hand inadvertently locking himself inside is a simple example of the 'superiority principle' (Clayton 2010: 63) as it pertains to film comedy (its impact derives from our momentary appreciation of our superior view of the catch falling and the sight of the Tramp's hands fumbling uselessly for a few beats more). Believing he has discovered another way out, we have slightly longer to appreciate the Tramp's inferior awareness as he peers through a hatch into the adjoining pen: while he looks screen-left, a fearsome tiger approaches on the right.

We could point to the 'comic twinkle' in Chaplin's posture, in his expressions and in the Tramp's bearing, but, following Clayton, we can see how bodily placement is at least as crucial in disclosing comedic intent. As he withdraws from the tiger's pen, a reverse angle cut shows him back in with the lion. He stands up slowly with two shelves perilously close on either side of him. The spectator can observe large metal trays on the ends of each of these shelves, one being particularly precariously poised on the edge of the right-hand shelf, which, moreover, hangs unevenly off the wall. Sure enough, in a beautifully choreographed set of movements, an especially violent flick of the sleeping lion's tail causes the Tramp to spin round, almost hit the shelf on screen-left and then, backing up quickly, actually knock over the more precarious tray on screen-right. In the nick of time, he catches the tray, its movement through space and in his hands allowing us to appreciate its considerable heft. A further series of incidents conspires to deepen the Tramp's predicament: a dog starts yapping at him through the bars; the dog's yelps alert the Tramp's love interest (Merna Kennedy) but she only faints when she sees the mess he is in; he tries to use water left in the tray to splash her awake through the bars but to no avail. The Lion wakes up.

The Tramp flees to the far end of the pen and tries the door again. The Lion moves over to the Tramp, but then turns round and moves back to sit down where it had been sleeping. We cut closer in on Chaplin as he looks at the camera for the first time in the scene, the Tramp's eyes wide in continued fear (Figure 3.1). He feels his body in a pantomimic checking that he is intact (his bottom gives him pause to turn round and check it is still there – perhaps his famously baggy trousers cause him doubt). He takes a huge intake of breath, closes his eyes and exhales an enormous sense of relief. He looks over to the lion, which now rolls around on its back like a kitten. He looks back to the camera, raises his eyebrows and begins to swagger as he moves forward to the bars. His gaze moves between directing looks at us and looking somewhere in the middle distance. The latter glances seem to be looking around the diegesis for someone but, suddenly, there is no urgency in this search; something in his expressions suggests he perhaps is looking for a chance to show off rather than a chance at rescue. The looks at us and around him seem to say, 'So, I'm in with a lion . . . Oh well.' In a short passage, his direct address has moved from conveying frozen panic (Figure 3.1 again) to a highly mobile (over)confidence (Figure 3.2). Sure enough, when the girl awakens and opens the door for him, he is in no hurry to leave. Chaplin performs the Tramp's sense of invulnerability as a parody of 'masculine' certainty and bearing. He goes over to pet the lion. However, rather than continue its supplication, it

Figure 3.1 *The Circus* (Charles Chaplin Productions, 1928): Chaplin's terrified Tramp looks to us.

roars at him. The Tramp flees out of the now-open cage, up a pole, where he responds to the girl's beckoning to him with unabashed 'girlishness'.

The meanings of the moments of direct address in this scene are shifting and mobile. However, they have things in common. They are humorous through their contrast with what surrounds them: a sudden freezing as if, literally, petrified and then as a commanding swagger utterly inappropriate to the situation. They both have something to do with realisation. The first is realisation as startlement or shock (though this leads to doubt, rather than certainty: 'Am I still intact?'); the second is classically an instance of marking a character's superior position within their fictional world (the Tramp, alone, can 'see' the spectator and his gaze also seems to say, fantastically, 'I'm safe from lions'). However, the film makes this ironic because the character's superiority is misplaced – in this, the second moment of direct address is very close to that of Ollie. I take these examples to be paradigmatic of comedic direct address because they inflect comically the 'honesty' I have suggested direct address often vivifies. The playfulness with the distinction between the actor and the character they incarnate is complexly played: 'Comedy depends on and exercises our skills of recognizing strategies of self-presentation, of discerning and weighing intentionality, and of acknowledging varieties of pretence' (Clayton

Figure 3.2 He looks again, now too sure of himself.

2010: 79). The special claims direct address makes and the particular effect of this illusion of 'eye contact' tests these skills. However, only the case studies chapters will provide sufficient space to explore the 'varieties of pretence' and their unmasking (via direct address) that are uniquely configured in individual films.

MODE AND MOOD: DIRECT ADDRESS AND COMEDIC LIGHTNESS

Above, we discussed the documentary aspect of film comedy as well as outlining some of the recurrent meanings and effects of direct address within this filmmaking mode. This is only part of the picture, and other crucial aspects of film comedy, particularly in relation to its tone and mood, can help explain its special affinity with direct address. To examine this, I will draw upon Deborah Thomas's work in *Beyond Genre*. Thomas proposes the move signalled by her title because, despite the apparent ease of identifying some films as falling within specific genres (such as westerns, musicals and so on), particular problems ensue when trying to identify the boundaries of the categories of comedy and melodrama:

As well as being aware of the difficulties posed by such terms both for students and for many critics and theorists, I have a powerful sense as an ordinary movie spectator (a sense which I believe is widely shared) that different kinds of viewing experience are available from different kinds of films in ways that go beyond genre. Thus, when I approach films (from a variety of genres) in which it is clear that the main characters will be dogged by an unforgiving fate and that they will almost certainly be caught and punished in some way, I often have to steel myself to watch them. In contrast, my body relaxes when I'm about to look at other films whose tone is very different . . . on one hand, there are narrative worlds that feel repressive and full of danger and, on the other, those that feel more benevolent and safe. Settling down to watch a film is, crucially, a case of getting in the mood for the sort of film one is about to watch. (2000: 9)

In the above passage, Thomas describes the mood and feeling of fictional worlds in a way that crosses the narrower categorisations of individual genres. Comedy involves fictional worlds that 'feel more benevolent and safe' while melodramatic worlds 'feel repressive and full of danger'.[14] Thus, even some 'war films' may feel quite 'safe' (a comedy war film, such as the 1966 *La Grande Vadrouille*, for example), whereas most others in the more narrowly defined genre, obviously, do not. This emphasis on 'feeling' is both a description of the general tone and mood of the film's world and the evocation of something physically felt – the experience for a spectator of one fictional world is (broadly put) tense and, of the other, is relaxed. From Thomas's wide-ranging argument, some elements are worth highlighting as they will prove instructive to the analysis of how direct address may 'fit' in some fictional worlds but can feel incompatible with others: the lightness of comedy versus the repressive, 'heavy' nature of the melodramatic; also, how this relates to the self-consciousness of characters and their awareness (or not) of their situation. The latter, especially, returns us to notions of the documentary aspect of comedy earlier noted.

The 'safety' of film comedy needs qualifying, as the narrative situations of comedies are clearly not without peril. Indeed, as was earlier hinted, the threat of physical or social mishap is often central to what is 'comic'. *The Circus* lion scene, for example, provides a clear instance of the importance of quasi-danger to comedy. However, crucially, we, as spectators, know that comedic characters are safe. One of Thomas's key examples of the essential safety of comedic film worlds is the scene from Howard Hawks's *Monkey Business* (1952), where Dr Barnaby Fulton (Cary Grant) drives a car as his eyesight begins to fail (Grant's chemist has created a youth elixir, the effects of which are beginning to wear off). Just as his car seems about to crash into another vehicle, we see that the latter's chassis is elevated fantastically high above Barnaby's car bonnet: 'the oddity of this vehicle, whose only purpose is to guarantee Barnaby's well-being, provides a strange but apt symbol of the generosity of this film's world' (Thomas 2000: 67). We find here an interesting play between the character's blindness to both his imminent danger *and* his ultimate safety and our awareness as audience members of the essentially benevolent fictional world the character inhabits:

> the world of comedy appears to be safe partly because we perceive it as a fictional world with a benevolent director pulling the strings. In contrast, the oppressiveness of the melodramatic world seems to be inherent in its social fabric and conditions rather than originating in a melodramatic figure outside. For characters in comedic films to know that they are safe, they would need to be aware that they are characters in a comedic film, whereas melodramatic characters can feel the weight of their oppression without the same degree of self-consciousness. (ibid.: 12–13)

Thomas's speculations about the self-consciousness of comedy characters raise some complex issues. As we have already seen, it *is* a possibility of the comedic film that its on-screen figures may know (or at least have flashes of awareness) that they are in a comedic film and, by extension, that they are safe. To cite *Wayne's World* again, Wayne and Garth interrupt a dénouement to the narrative in which a series of disastrous events and outcomes have been visualised: 'As if we'd end the movie like that! . . . Let's do the Scooby Doo ending.' Moreover, in terms specifically related to Hope and Crosby's safety, we can cite the opening of *Road to Morocco* once more: 'For any villains we meet, we haven't any fear. Paramount will protect us 'cos we're signed for five more years.' The latter example may be objected to because the *actors* might be described as stepping out of their roles and commenting on the film as a film, whereas, at other moments, their *characters*, 'Orville' and 'Jeff', are afraid of the film's various villains. The point, however, is that such a separation of character and actor is inappropriate to comedy, which regularly 'acknowledges the discrepancy between actor and character, *even as that role continues to be played*' (Clayton 2010: 67; emphasis added). Deborah Thomas takes the example of *Monkey Business*, which opens with Howard Hawks's own voice being heard telling his lead actor, 'Not yet Cary,' as the actor is (fictionally) premature in reaching his mark. Thus the safeness of the comedic fictional world is in this instance related to the documentary aspect of screen comedy and, in Thomas's words, *Monkey Business*'s 'space [being] simultaneously the space of the film's narrative world and that of the film set on which it was made' (2000: 62). Of course, some traditions within the documentary genre are known for their featuring of the documentary's own filmmaking technology and personnel (see Nick Broomfield's films, for example).

If it has not been stated already, it is worth underlining the obvious point that 'comedy as documentary' is not to be confused with any aspiration towards 'realism'. As Thomas suggests, it is 'melodrama [which] shows us a version of the world in some sense as it is, rather than [as in comedy] as it might be' (ibid.: 72). In the more extended quotation from Thomas above, she draws a distinction between our understanding of the fictional worlds of comedies *as* fictional worlds, and the 'oppressiveness of the melodramatic world [which] seems to be inherent in its *social* fabric and conditions'. In this way, our (intensely emotional) experience of melodrama as viewers and the (often intensely emotional) experience of the characters are closer in melodrama. Why, then, is the gesture towards communion between viewer and character / actor represented by direct address not more at home in melodrama, rather than less, as I am arguing? For one thing, Alex Clayton has shown that the separation of our experience / knowledge / awareness as viewers from that of the character (often by means of our 'superiority') is only one half of an (at least) dual play with the audience common in comedy. The 'comic twinkle' displays the intentions of the *performer* and, to connect Clayton with Thomas's analysis, can be said to say, 'I know you know I know . . . that no harm will ultimately befall me.' The thrill of danger (danger of, at the least, embarrassment) combined with the ultimate guarantee of safety is one of comedy's chief pleasures and, as we have begun to see, direct address plays a role in these films' playfulness with their audiences. This special duality of actor and performer must be kept in mind throughout our discussions of comedies as well as musicals.

Approaching the issue from another tack, direct address's common function as a marker of coming-to-consciousness would be out of place in many classic melodramas:

> Of course, melodramatic characters may mistakenly believe themselves
> to be free from oppressive determinants, unaware of the malign
> fate closing in on them as well as of its institutional and ideological
> underpinnings. Indeed, such blindness has sometimes been taken
> to be a central characteristic of the melodramatic protagonist . . .
> Nevertheless, melodramatic characters are far more likely than comedic
> characters to experience the mood or 'feel' of their narrative world in
> ways that match the viewers' experiences of it. (Thomas 2000: 13)

Notwithstanding Thomas's final stress on the ways melodramatic characters exist in concert with the tone of their film worlds, I would argue that direct address is ill suited to the oft-cited 'blindness' of melodramatic characters. A scene from one of the classic melodramas examined by Deborah Thomas (2000: 32–42), *Bigger than Life* (1956), can serve as an example. In the grip of the

Figure 3.3 *Bigger than Life* (Twentieth Century Fox Film Corporation, 1956): Ed Avery (James Mason) blithely looms too large in the CinemaScope frame.

delusions of grandeur engendered by the steroid cortisone prescribed for a condition that otherwise would be terminal, primary schoolteacher Ed Avery (James Mason) stands addressing the audience at a meeting of the Parent–Teacher Association (PTA). Ed's speech builds to a crescendo in which he implies that the Republic's very future is being endangered by an education system that is 'breeding a race of moral midgets'. One parent, clearly a reactionary thrilled by the authoritarian message of Ed's oration, turns to the actual principal of the school (Rusty Lane) and says, 'Mister, that young man ought to be the principal of this school.' We cut to a close-up, one of the closest in this CinemaScope film, of Avery raising his eyebrows, eyes fixed somewhere to his left and puffing out a great plume of smoke (his smoking in the classroom and casual discarding of his match have already scandalised his audience; see Figure 3.3).

Let us imagine for a moment that Ray had asked James Mason to look into the camera at the end of the shot and that this has made it into the final edit. I have no reason to suppose this happened – I have, rather, many reasons to imagine it would not 'fit' – but an imagination of alternatives can be highly instructive (see Gibbs 2006: 8). What would the effect have been? The existing shot already feels deliberate in its overdetermination (Mason's face looms 'too large' in the CinemaScope frame) and I would imagine a look at the camera here to be a step, stylistically, far too far. Also, crucially, what is at stake in Ed's position in the frame (he is shot from a slightly low angle; he is generally seen from low angles in the scene, looming over his audience of parents) and in his blithely self-satisfied gaze outwards is the utter inappropriateness of his extreme authoritarian stance vis-à-vis the education of young children. In the next scene, Wally (Walter Matthau), who witnessed Ed's performance, tells Ed's wife (Barbara Rush), 'He isn't the same guy . . . You know . . . big shot. He even looks bigger.' If Ed had looked at the camera, the film might have been experienced as, in some ways, validating the 'bigness' that it is, rather, concerned with criticising. Yes, the 'epistemic authority' might here have been used ironically (as I have shown it to have been in a number of actually exist-ent examples) but, still, Ed's look at the camera could never be *at us*. This is a man deluded – his delusion is a key condition of the film's world as a melodra-matic one – and he is so tragically and so pathologically locked in a distorted worldview that it would be patently inappropriate for the film to conjure such a 'direct' connection with us, even if the connection were ironically inflected.

Thomas provides a table that can further underline the seeming 'inappro-priateness' of direct address to melodrama and the characteristics of comedic film worlds that make direct address more freely assimilable therein:

MELODRAMATIC FILMS *are characterised by*	COMEDIC FILMS *are characterised by*
Danger	Safety
Repression, displacement	Expression, satisfaction
Hierarchical power	Mutuality, community
Rigidity	Improvisation, spontaneity
Malign fate	Benevolent magic (Thomas 2000: 92)

There is a 'lightness' and a transformative quality to comedic film worlds that make them both, tonally, less continuous with our own 'real world' than those of melodramatic narratives, and more susceptible to direct address as a gesture towards communion. This transformative quality is also manifest in the importance of performativity to comedy and the recurrence of actors performing characters performing. This is suggested in Thomas's contrasting of melodramatic rigidity with comedic improvisation and spontaneity. The diaphanous or shifting relationship between actor and character in comedy is consistent with the cross-diegetic nature of direct address. In contrast, melo-dramatic characters are 'inhabited' by their actors and are 'rounded' in a way comedy characters are often not (a reason why actors in comedies are notori-ously under-rewarded in the Academy Awards and by other such prizes). In the example (partly imagined) from *Bigger than Life*, Ed Avery remains too much 'Ed Avery' to look at us.[15]

PRIVATE CONVERSATIONS IN PUBLIC: *MAKE WAY FOR TOMORROW* (1937)

The above has indulged in the, I hope, productive essentialising of broad modes of filmmaking and suggested the suitability of direct address to certain traditions and its apparent incompatibility with others. Before moving on to saying something more specific of musicals (a genre that is part of the larger comedic mode but whose use of direct address has its own particular qualities), I wish to complicate these neat divisions. Indeed, it would not be in line with the analysis undertaken in *Beyond Genre* to employ the melodrama–comedy distinction in a bald either / or way. Thomas's schema is highly flexible, with many films moving backwards and forwards between the extremes of melodramatic and comedic poles. Thomas's points about romance give a flavour of this flexibility:

> I observed earlier that romance is rarely free-standing and that to classify a film in this way – simply as a romance – provides only part of the picture. Romantic melodrama or romantic comedy? Is desire the ingredient that locks the romantic couple into a tight and repressive world, or can it in some way liberate them? . . . As we shall see . . . it is not always easy to determine whether romantic films are essentially melodramatic or comedic, since to some extent many of them have aspects of both. (ibid.: 99)

Leo McCarey's *Make Way for Tomorrow* (1937) is a prime example of the problems of generic pigeonholing (is it a 'social problem picture', a 'family melodrama'?; or is it just a 'drama' or a 'romance', as imdb.com classifies it?) but also of the potential rewards of attending to the underlying structures *beyond genre*. The film might be best described as a romantic melodrama, but one punctured frequently by the comic. It concerns the plight of an elderly couple, Lucy (Beulah Bondi) and Bark (Victor Moore),[16] whose house is being repossessed. None of their five children is able (or, really, willing) to take both parents in, so the decision is made that the father will live with one of the daughters (Elisabeth Risdon) and the mother with one of the sons (Thomas Mitchell). Unable to live together, each parent becomes increasingly unwelcome in the homes of this child's family. Events come to a head and the father is to be moved on to California and the mother to a retirement home in New York. It appears highly unlikely that they will ever see each other again.

Not just sad, the world of the film is melodramatic because its oppressiveness is 'inherent in its social fabric and conditions' (Thomas 2000: 12) – that is, the weak fabric of modern (1937) family bonds and the absence (though unmentioned) of a social security safety net.[17] The comic qualities of the film emerge often from the good humour with which the old couple meet this unforgiving trajectory and, always, through the space, both literal and metaphoric, given to all the film's actors – McCarey is a director famed for his ability to encourage 'spontaneity' in his performers (often in comedic films) through techniques of improvisation. Also following Deborah Thomas's model, we can see how the scenes in the hotel just prior to Bark's departure for California can be understood as the couple's temporary liberation through their mutual romantic desire. However, because this film's world is ultimately melodramatic, we always know that this space is a respite from wider socio-economic and narrative strictures, not an escape. The couple are returning to the hotel in which they honeymooned fifty years previously, and the scene's poignancy rests with our knowledge that soon Bark must catch his train.

Having decided that they are enjoying each other's company far too much to keep an engagement with their mostly unsympathetic children, Bark takes the decision to call their daughter, Nellie (Minna Gombell). Lucy is clearly the more anxious about the children's feelings but Bark promises he will 'fix it up . . . in a nice way' (a suppressed edge in his voice suggests he is really more concerned with Lucy's feelings about the children's feelings than with those feelings themselves). On the phone to his daughter, he tells her fairly bluntly that they are not coming. Unseen and unheard on the other end of the line, Nellie is evidently protesting. Then, Lucy comes over and tugs at Bark's coat and begins to say, 'Bark . . . maybe we should . . .'. 'Excuse me, young lady, this is private,' Bark gently shoos her out of the phone cabin and closes the door on her. He now moves right up to the receiver, cupping his hand over it. We, like Lucy, are no longer permitted to hear what he says. A cut to Nellie conveys her mute shock at what we surmise are even blunter words. Bark leaves the cabin, assuring Lucy, 'She took it very nice.' Loosely diegetic music (they will approach the ballroom shortly, so it may emanate from there) builds to consummate our enjoyment as spectators of this small triumph of Bark's. The parents have been undermined by the children throughout and, though the film's (and Bark's) gentle tone mean an explicit telling-off of the children would be out of place, we appreciate Bark's success in privately admonishing Nellie.

The mostly one-sided filming of the phone conversation echoes other private conversations conducted in public earlier in the film, where the intimacy of the exchange is made more poignant by the pressures of an audience: first, there is Lucy's phone call from Bark, which she takes in the middle of her daughter-in-law's (Fay Bainter) bridge night – the guests, previously irritated by the mother's intrusions, are clearly touched by what they hear; second, the letter from Lucy that Bark's friend Max (Maurice Moscovitch) reads to Bark until he becomes too choked – 'maybe you'd better wait until you have your glasses fixed,' Max concludes. The loss of their privacy (Bark has been sleeping on a couch, Lucy sharing a room with a teenage granddaughter) has been at issue throughout the film and, thanks to the phone call, Bark has temporarily won for them a space in which they can be lovers again, not merely parents. Shortly, direct address will play a role in developing this private–public dynamic in a most striking way.

Bark and Lucy decide to stay at the hotel for dinner. The more than hospitable hotel manager (Paul Stanton), having heard about the couple's return fifty years after their honeymoon there, joins them for a drink. After he has left, the film cuts to a position behind them (incidentally breaking the 180–degree rule). The couple are framed symmetrically against the dance floor and stage, halfway between facing forwards towards the dance floor and facing each other. Their facial expressions are only available in profile when they turn their heads to look at one another. Dialogue, tone of voice and gestures are enormously expressive, however, and combine to create a touching moment when Bark speaks more affectionately to Lucy than at any other point of the film – the eloquence of performance is evident, for example, when Lucy self-consciously tugs at her high collar (a garment she presumably wears for its modesty) when Bark says to her, 'You've held your looks better than anyone I know.' Lucy is touched and moves to look at Bark more insistently than before. The couple lean in to each other very steadily. Just as their lips are about to meet for what would be their first on-screen kiss, Lucy suddenly stops with a start, recoils slightly from Bart, then looks towards the camera, realising they are being watched. Her eyes, first wide in startlement, narrow as if in rebuke of those watching, before she looks down and away, her face breaking into a bashful smile – all this occurs at a pace and with a fluidity a prose description could never match (see Figure 3.4).

Her sense of being watched is partly diegetic; there are people placed on tables behind and above the couple in the direction of and beyond the camera, and Lucy's gaze may take in these off-screen figures (precise eye-line *is* difficult to discern at this range – certainly in pre-HD filmmaking – and moving frame by frame through the sequence distorts rather than clarifies the gesture). However, this *is* a moment of direct address. Not only does Beulah Bondi make eye contact with the camera, but also the whole set-up of the shot (an approximately 135–degree cut across the axis of action so that we peer over shoulders rather than being faced by these figures head-on) makes us aware of our own position as watchers. Lucy's look is then experienced as one at us. It is an arresting gesture by the film; it arrests us from the normal comfort of watching these characters – any characters in the film – being together. Its force is derived partly from the duration of the shot and the duration of the shots around it. McCarey's generally unobtrusive visual style is marked by the length of his takes, often 'invisible editing' and spare use of close-ups; long- and two-shots predominate and give primacy to the interaction of his characters. Though the take containing Lucy's direct address is by no means the longest in the sequence (a number of preceding shots last well over a minute), because its content is, in various ways, 'private', its fifty seconds start to feel like an intrusion. It is imbued with a weight one might describe as 'to-be-watched-ness' (this is a part-neologism I shall discuss below). The

Figure 3.4 *Make Way for Tomorrow* (Paramount Pictures, 1937): Lucy (Beulah Bondi) senses our prying eyes.

length of the take is absolutely crucial to the effect McCarey derives from the performances he elicits. Yet, before this shot, Lucy and Bark have been comfortable in our company and the long-takes brought their emotions close to us as film spectators. However, in having them turned away from us and then, finally and most boldly, in having them actually notice us, the film brings to fruition a whole trajectory whereby this scene in this hotel is the one where, finally and temporarily, the couple have won out a private space away from the interference of their children and away from prying eyes . . . even, at least metaphorically, ours. This is extraordinarily skilled filmmaking but extraordinary in a way entirely consistent with stylistic systems of the 'ordinary' studio filmmaking often called 'classical'. It is a bold rupture of the film's established style of playing but utterly consistent with its dramatic preoccupations. This paradoxical position – a wholly consistent stylistic rupture – might well be paradigmatic of the practice of direct address valued most highly in this book.

As a final note, we should acknowledge that it is well established that film narration can limit our access to the actions and / or speech of characters through choices in editing and / or sound design – the decision to shut us out of the phone booth when Bark gives Nellie a piece of his mind is an example.

Such devices are regularly acknowledged by film critics or theorists and one might call the choice to make Bark's final words to Nellie inaudible an 'editorial' move. Also, the language available from work on cinematic point of view can help us consider how, in Bark's shutting the door on Lucy and in the film's suppression of what Bark says, we are made, for the moment, to share key aspects of Lucy's experience. Moreover, Bark's loving 'Excuse me, young lady, this is private' is lent force by the film narration, and one can talk easily of a synthesis between the editorial moves of the narration and the meanings of the drama. Much more could be said of that moment, of course, but my point is simply to underline that, as viewers and scholars of film, we can easily and regularly do acknowledge how film narration might dramatise the 'privacy' of a moment, action or exchange through various moves. However, to my knowledge, films scholars have never acknowledged the possibility that such narrational rhetoric might also include direct address. In the example analysed above, our 'presence' as spectators and the camera's attention on the characters (normally a given) suddenly become active in the dramatisation of the narrative, and a part of our conscious experience of the film. *Burlesque Suicide* from 1902 (discussed briefly in the Introduction) might be crude in comparison but it shows that such possibilities were alive from cinema's beginnings. They persist still.

MUSICAL DIRECT ADDRESS

The analysis of musicals will be more condensed than the analysis of comedic films because, first, following Deborah Thomas's schema, the classic musical tradition of Hollywood can be identified as a sub-division of the comedic mode (some other national cinemas have had a greater emphasis on musical melodrama but that is beyond the purview here); second, I would suggest that much of what can be said of the 'documentary' aspect of comedies can also be applied to musicals; and, third, I have found actual direct address to be less frequent in musicals than I had assumed before undertaking this research. The latter discovery was surprising chiefly because direct address has been *relatively* more readily acknowledged in scholarship on musicals than in work on other genres. For example, Jim Collins touches upon direct address in his essay on the textual mechanisms of musicals (1981: 134–46); Jane Feuer devotes a short section to direct address in her canonical *The Hollywood Musical* (1993: 35–42); and, though these are only asides, the musical is the genre that Tom Gunning has most often cited as continuing the 'direct' impulses of the cinema of attractions (Gunning 1990: 57; 1999: 826). I shall begin by discussing the scholarship before moving to suggest the ways in which direct address in musicals does play some specific roles.

Both Feuer and Collins make a point of contrasting the musical with what had been privileged by the orthodox film theory of that time (the first edition of Feuer's book appeared in 1982): Feuer by contrasting the musical's use of direct address with assumptions of the device's 'Brechtian' effect (1993: 35–6), Collins with reference to the work of Christian Metz. Here, Collins discusses the importance of 'putting on a show' for creating 'the illusion that the work is a *discours* in the process of creation':

> This illusion of 'creation' involves another central element in the rapport between text and spectator. For Metz an essential aspect of the *histoire* quality of traditional fiction film is that 'the film is not exhibitionist. I watch it, but it does not watch me watching it. However, it knows that I am watching it. But it doesn't want to know it.' . . . this may be true of other genre films, but certainly is not true for the musical, where the presence of the spectator is continually recognized and exploited. This recognition of the viewer is stressed in both the *regard* (the look or glance of the character) during the songs, and the use of pronouns in the lyrics. (1981: 138)

This notion 'that film is not exhibitionist' is countered by a wide range of films touched upon in this book. However, Collins is right to assert that Metz's formulation is at least more broadly inappropriate for the musical – not only for the reasons Collins cites (the use of the 'I', 'you' pronouns in the songs forms a large part of his analysis) but also because of the 'aggregative' nature of the structure that brings song, dance and narrative together.[18]

The main example Collins gives for an on-screen performer addressing the film spectator directly is the final number of *Shall We Dance* (1937), one film amongst the many that Fred Astaire and Ginger Rogers made at RKO over the decade. In the 'Shall We Dance' number, Astaire does look at the camera at various points, but actually nowhere near as much as Collins's descriptions suggest. It would be more accurate to say he occasionally glances at it while projecting his performance more generally outwards – that is, until their romantic union consummated in this final dance, 'Petrov' / Astaire and 'Linda' / Rogers sing more insistently into the camera in the film's final shot. Generally, I would suggest that Astaire does not sing to the camera in his films all that often. More frequently, Astaire's characters address their songs to someone in the story world, be it a whole audience if it is a 'show number' or to another character, often Ginger's, if the number is more 'integrated'. (Maurice Chevalier, perhaps partly because he is not a dancer and therefore not so mobile, would be an example of a musical performer who addresses the camera much more insistently in musicals of this period.) Crucially, in the final number of *Shall We Dance*, the looks at the camera are grounded by the performance being situated on a theatre stage. Does the presence of a diegetic audience disqualify this (and many other musical numbers like it) from my corpus? Perhaps. However, one should be cautious of black-and-white distinctions particularly given the particular complexities and hybrid 'theatricality' of musicals. As many writers acknowledge, the presence of diegetic audiences is really an alibi for the musical to perform to *us* (though the necessity of such an alibi remains significant). Also, in the case of 'Shall We Dance', though the characters are clearly addressing themselves to people within their fictional world, the final shot involves a crane movement that sweeps forwards and offers a view that is clearly independent of any human perspective available within the diegetic auditorium – the performers still end the film gazing into the camera. This is by no means exceptional for musicals of this period. For example, the famous numbers choreographed by Busby Berkeley in the 1930s might ground their spectacle in a theatrical setting but, in the arrangement of lines of chorus girls for a camera filming from a bird's-eye view, and by the numerous individual performers who look directly out at us, their visuals assert the autonomy of the camera.

Collins moves from describing looks that seem to be 'at us' to note the more general inscription of the viewer into the film through the use of diegetic audiences (1981: 138–9). I believe this confuses the issue somewhat because Collins relies on terms such as 'subjective shot' that are both conceptually and technically imprecise – the actual shots that are filmed *roughly* from the position of the diegetic audience are not optical point-of-view shots and, even if they were, it is highly questionable whether they could ever suggest a 'subjectivity' (see Pye 2000 and Wilson 2006). Though it risks pedantry, the above corrections to Collins's description of what is, in many respects, a fairly typical musical number are necessary in order to define the scope of the analysis better here. However, Collins's essential point about the sense created of our inclusion in the musical spectacle and the encouragement to participate, at least emotionally, is valuable.

Jane Feuer offers a more extended discussion of direct address and a more refined account of the relationship between the often-present diegetic audience in film musicals and us as external spectators. Concluding a comparison with distanciation as practised by Godard:

> The goals of musicals and those of Godard must surely be opposed.
> But – as in the case of direct address – their methods are identical.
> How can this be? I believe the difference lies in what is being conveyed
> by the direct address and the traditions behind those messages. The
> narratives of musicals place themselves firmly within a long tradition
> of popular entertainment; we have seen that the musical views itself in
> direct line of descent from folk art. Godard, on the other hand, places

himself in dialectical relationship to Hollywood; he is the antithesis to which the narratives of musicals are the thesis. When performers in musicals turn to face us directly, we do enter another register, but as we have seen, the potentially disorienting effects of the break in narrative are minimized – by the presence of the audiences in the film and by mechanisms of identification. Even when the break in register does throw us out of the narrative it's for the purpose of praising show business, not burying it. (1993: 36)

Key to Feuer's thesis about the Hollywood musical is its disingenuous alliance of itself with folk art traditions: its strategies of bringing the spectator into the fiction disavow the break from the audience that the shift from a folk to a mass culture represented (a shift of which the Hollywood musical is a clear part). Similarly, her lucid accounts of moments in *The Pirate* (1948) and *Dames* (1934), moments that in other contexts might be read as 'modernist', show how a direct appeal to the spectator is recuperated for entertainment by reference to its own traditions and the specific pleasures only it can offer:

> We are called away from our immersion in the fiction, distanced in that we are asked to reflect upon the spectacle itself. But what we are asked to reflect upon is the tradition to which *The Pirate* belongs – that of the magic show, hocus-pocus, illusionism. (ibid.: 41)

The above quotation and the final point of the previous one underline how musical entertainment often refers to its own values and strategies (Feuer goes on to discuss the frequency of 'Ode to Entertainment' numbers in the genre – ibid.: 36–7). In content, then, musicals are even more vividly 'documentaries of their own making' than the comedies examined earlier. Clearly, the narratives of many musicals are about putting on song-and-dance shows (some, such as the 1952 *Singin' in the Rain*, are even about filming musicals) but musicals are also strongly 'documentary' in the kinds of performances that populate them. The skill sets required of performers in Hollywood musicals are highly specialised and musical performance can be seen as more vividly the performance of self than even the slapstick acts examined above. Steven Cohan describes something similar in the performances of Fred Astaire: 'His musical numbers exert a non-narrative, extra-diegetic pressure – *contemplation of the star performing* – that remains in excess of the conservative narrative activity of the film's plot' (Cohan 2002: 89; emphasis added). Though one might be cautious of the description of narrative immersion as inherently 'conservative', Cohan suggests that musical numbers, like direct address, create an 'extra-diegetic pressure' that creates a form of distanciation. As Feuer underlines, there is nothing innately progressive in this kind of estrangement from narrative because, if musicals are strongly 'documentary' in their content, they are often highly solipsistic in their nature: 'In its endless reflexivity the musical can only offer itself, only entertainment as its picture of Utopia' (1993: 84). The utopian aspect of musicals is something I shall return to below. However, it is worth first noting that the transformative nature that Richard Dyer's (1992) account of musical utopia describes (and many other discussions of musicals also stress) relates to the sense that, in contrast with when they 'act', musical performers often become more apparently 'themselves', more authentic, when they sing and dance.

What the above underlines, and what Collins also makes clear in his focus on the frequency of 'I' and 'you' pronouns in the lyrics of songs, is that we are addressed as audience members in manifold ways in this genre – musicals are, in their peculiar way, highly 'interactive'. It is probably fair to say that the musical is the most 'direct' of mainstream film genres. Why, then, if my earlier assertion is correct, would actual direct address not be so widespread as might be imagined? It should be stressed that by no means do I suggest the device does not recur throughout the genre's history; from the opening image of *Gold Diggers of 1933* (1933) to the conclusion of the 'New York, New York' number in *On the Town* (1949) and 'You Can't Get a Man with a Gun' from *Annie Get Your Gun* (1950), there are numerous examples of characters addressing the film audience. However, it is more *felt* than actually present in many films. For instance, in one of the main examples Jane Feuer uses to discuss direct address, the 'That's Entertainment' number from *The Band Wagon* (1953), the performers barely look at the camera at all. The four characters, played by Fred Astaire, Oscar Levant, Nanette Fabray and Jack Buchanan, look forwards, very much in the general direction of the camera, but they generally avoid making eye contact with it (Nanette Fabray looks into the lens a couple of times). Arranged in a line, each looks out into the auditorium in front of them. Feuer is right to note that 'the theater is empty' and surmises that therefore 'we the spectators are happy to fill the void' (1993: 37). However, I would call this 'nearly-direct address', and I would argue that *this* is the default mode of address for Hollywood musical show numbers. Drawing upon theatrical conventions, the performers' projecting forwards is grounded either in a diegetic theatrical setting – be that literally a theatre or a less informal space arranged for putting on a show – or in the film's creation of a quasi-proscenium space from the material of the fictional world (see Feuer 1993: 23–6). Does the distinction between direct address and 'nearly-direct address' really matter? Yes and no. No, because, as already suggested, we feel as if we are addressed by the film even if eye-line does not consummate this connection. Yes, because understanding 'nearly-direct address' as predominant helps us to understand the specific inflections looking at the camera can be given in the Hollywood musical and also to suggest, much more tentatively, what this tells us about the genre's development.

Judy Garland is one of the genre's most celebrated female performers and *Easter Parade* (1948) is interesting for the way it uses direct address to contrast her character's authenticity with its lack in another. After the successful musical collaboration of Don Hewes (Fred Astaire) and Nadine Hale (Ann Miller) ends because the latter's self-serving ambition outgrows the partnership, Astaire recruits the more modest Hannah Brown (Garland). A rough diamond, Brown needs polishing but eventually 'Hannah and Hewes' form a successful on-stage duo. Miller's Nadine Hale, though enjoying a flourishing career herself, becomes jealous and various narrative conflicts ensue. In Hannah and Nadine, the film contrasts two different versions of femininity. Nadine's femininity is highly constructed and polished, based on high fashion and her overly 'theatrical' (and sexual) bearing, designed precisely to attract as much (especially male) attention as possible; Hannah is more modest and, though her ambition is ultimately to be the subject of admiration on the Easter parade (Nadine earlier sashayed down the street while men gawped), she achieves this, in a paradoxical manner typical of the genre, by 'being true to herself'. Nadine / Miller and Hannah / Garland are both immensely impressive performers and are framed as such by the film. However, there is little doubt whose values the film prefers; Nadine presents a shallow version of musical celebrity while Hannah's greater authenticity and modesty connect her with a more 'folk' tradition of entertainment (we see her starting out performing in a lively community restaurant).

The musical number, 'The Girl I Love is on a Magazine Cover', marks the high point of Nadine's success while she dances with the Ziegfeld Follies. The production's design is based around a series of views of glamorous women, posed as if they are on the cover of high-class fashion magazines. Nadine is the final woman, who emerges as if out of a cover for *Harper's Bazaar*. Her look outwards and at the camera is thus grounded by the aesthetics of the fashion industry and of portraiture and photography more broadly.[19] Throughout the number, though there is a diegetic audience present, Nadine / Miller looks repeatedly at the camera, whose mobility clearly separates it from any diegetic perspective. This is even more strikingly the case with an earlier number, 'Shakin' the Blues Away'. Here, though performing to a large theatre, she looks at the camera throughout. The camera is constantly mobile as it follows Nadine, craning in and out, sometimes looking up at or down on the performer, often moving in very close on her, yet her gaze is constantly fixed on ours. Here Nadine's diegetic ambitions stretch outwards to an appeal to us. To return to comments by Gilberto Perez cited earlier, 'the documentary of the actor is an index of the person giving the performance' (1998: 37). Here, the documentary details of Ann Miller's camera looks are indexical of Nadine

Hale's absolute desire for the public's adulation. The film gives this appeal to the public (both diegetic and extra-diegetic) a negative inflection because of details of Nadine's characterisation and by force of contrast with Garland / Hannah – the latter *never* looks at the camera, not even in her musical numbers. It is ironic in a genre which is very often about the drive towards fame (this is a major narrative goal in *Easter Parade*), but I would suggest that this film inflects the direct appeal to the public and to the camera as slightly crass. That direct address is capable of carrying associations of 'giving too much of oneself to the audience' perhaps goes some way to explaining why the device does not appear suitable for all musical films. Perhaps in so 'direct' a genre as the musical, direct address risks being, stylistically and / or tonally, *de trop*?

A Star is Born (1954) is another Garland musical in which direct address is absent. Indeed, as a musical melodrama, it would not *feel* so appropriate for here. Garland's character, Esther Blodgett / Vicki Lester[20] does not look at the camera during any of her musical numbers, but comes close during the film's one 'integrated' number – the film is a 'backstage' or 'show musical'. However, this number (a complex medley / montage starting and ending with 'Swanee') is embedded in a film within the film – the narrative follows Esther as she becomes a star of Hollywood musicals. Generally, Garland's performance style during her songs in this film (and in many others) is characterised by what I would call 'the intense look off into space'. The emotionality with which Garland's 'incandescent' performances are associated (Dyer 1992: 21) is arguably more suited to this kind of gaze than a look into the lens. One of the principal arguments of this book is that direct address is a rich device for expressing the emotions of characters. However, the intensity of Garland's singing does not fit with direct address. For example, in 'The Man Who Got Away' number in *A Star is Born*, a look at the camera would seem incompatible with the imagined romantic object of the song's lyrics – the 'man who got away' is better evoked by a look into space rather than at us; he is 'away', while direct address is a gesture towards present-ness.[21] While I share Martin Rubin's distrust of histories of the Hollywood musical that have overemphasised a drive towards 'integration' (1993: 12–13), their emphasis is appropriate in the limited sense that the emotionality, the meaning *for characters* of song and dance, became increasingly important as the genre developed from its filmed theatre origins. 'Intense looks off into space', in the specific context of musical performance, suit this intra-diegetic emotionality better than direct address.

A brief return to Mulvey's argument in 'Visual Pleasure and Narrative Cinema' will help reflect on issues of agency as they relate to the above analysis. The following comes from a famous passage in which Mulvey coins the term 'to-be-looked-at-ness' to denote the passive female character as framed by the active male gaze, a structure supposedly inscribed into mainstream film form:

Woman displayed as sexual object is the leitmotif of erotic spectacle:
from pin-ups to strip-tease, from Ziegfeld to Busby Berkeley, she
holds the look, plays to and signifies male desire . . . Traditionally,
the woman displayed has functioned on two levels: as erotic object
for the characters within the screen story, and as erotic object for the
spectator within the auditorium, with a shifting tension between the
looks on either side of the screen. For instance, the device of the show-
girl allows the two looks to be unified technically without any apparent
break in the diegesis. A woman performs within the narrative, the gaze
of the spectator and that of the male characters in the film are neatly
combined without breaking narrative verisimilitude. (1992: 28)

We can see how a limited range of intra-diegetic looks is seen as suturing in
the distinction between active male gaze and passive female 'to-be-looked-at-
ness'. Direct address clearly disturbs the neatness of this model of repression.
What happens in the case of a show-girl whose gaze literally meets our own?

I would suggest 'to-be-watched-ness' as, if not an alternative, then at least
a formulation additional to Mulvey's, because 'watched' somehow connotes
a more active awareness of the presence of spectators than does 'looked-at'.
'To-be-watched-ness' denotes the way that some fictional characters appear
aware of the 'presence' of extra-diegetic spectators. Direct address is the
clearest indication of this awareness, though it is not its only example. For
example, in both *Le Notti di Cabiria* and *High Fidelity*, examined in the next
chapters, there are scenes in which the central characters appear aware that
they are being watched by figures inside and outside of the diegesis without
quite acknowledging our presence – the manner of playing is something more
than 'performative'. (This is more striking in the case of Fellini's film because
the actual direct address does not come until the final shot, consummating a
sense of 'to-be-watched-ness' that has been previously present, while, in *High
Fidelity*, the hero talks to us throughout, often in public places where other
characters seem oblivious to his monologues.) 'To-be-watched-ness' in musicals has a specific resonance because, not only is the objective of extra-diegetic
(that is, real-world) musical stardom to be the subject of the public's awe and
adulation and for the recognition and reward of one's musical talents, but also
this is often an objective within the film's narratives themselves. The recurrence of musical narratives that stress 'folk' values does rather soften and / or
disguise the commercial imperative behind this desire for fame and adulation;
also, as I have suggested, actual direct address, might sometimes be *de trop* in
confirming the performers' awareness of their audience, especially as the presence of the audience is played to through so many other formal means. Nadine
Hale as performed by Ann Miller represents a most obvious and extreme
example of 'to-be-watched-ness'. Far from passive, she is highly active in the

narrative (though often for ill, as she attempts to manipulate Don and Jonathan [Peter Lawford]) and her spectacular on-screen musical numbers see her gaze boldly out at us. It must be said that Mulvey's essential point about the subjugation of women in mainstream narratives holds true because *Easter Parade* does present this ambition for fame, adulation and desire to be watched as, at worst, a threat and, at best, an unattractive quality. Nadine contrasts with the more sympathetic character of Hannah, who is more ready to define herself through her relationship with a man – Nadine, in contrast, is defiantly a solo performer.[22]

The above analysis may appear peculiarly conflicted because I have argued, contrary to Mulvey, that the diegetic and extra-diegetic lure of musical spectacle may be brought together by an 'active' look at the film spectator and that the musical is particularly 'direct' in its address to the external audience – both these aspects make direct address seem more suited to this genre than any other. At the same time, I have suggested that direct address is less prevalent than one might expect and, rather, 'nearly-direct address' is a more significant mode of performance. However, this acknowledgement may, ironically, prepare us to underline the specific resonance of *music* for direct address.

Richard Dyer's essay, 'Entertainment and Utopia', is one of the best-known accounts of the Hollywood musical and helps suggest the specific affective power of musical performance. The model it offers also provides further justification for treating musicals in Hollywood as a part of a much larger comedic mode. To return to Deborah Thomas's table (which is included on page 57, above), we can see a number of links with the table that Dyer uses (1992: 20–1). Both cite community; Thomas contrasts it with melodramatic 'hierarchical power', while Dyer sees 'community' as a quality of musical numbers in which characters sing and / or dance together as a response to the problems of 'fragmentation' (ibid.: 24) in the real world and in the worlds of the narratives. More broadly, Dyer sees musical numbers as transformative, as offering 'the image of "something better" to escape into' (ibid.: 18), while Thomas contrasts the comedic mode with the melodramatic in similarly utopian terms: 'melodrama shows us a version of the world in some sense as it is, rather than as it might be' (2000: 72) – showing the world 'as it might be' is the domain of comedy. Thomas and Dyer's schemas are by no means interchangeable, however. While Thomas is describing two broad modes predominant in Hollywood cinema (and the tertiary category of 'romance' crossing into both), Dyer's account focuses specifically on the utopianism of the musical genre.

Dyer's model for musical utopianism has two main dimensions: first, he says something of the way different kinds of musicals integrate music due to the nature of their fictional worlds and, second, his utopian categories describe specific affective structures. First:

The three broad tendencies of musicals – those that keep narrative
and number separated (most typically, the backstage musical); those
that retain the division between narrative as problems and numbers as
escape, but try to 'integrate' the numbers by a whole set of papering-
over-the-cracks devices (e.g. the well-known 'cue for a song'); and those
which try to dissolve the distinction between narrative and numbers,
thus implying that the world of the narrative is also (already) utopian.
(Dyer 1992: 26)

The second two categories of musical, and especially the last, are in their
underlying structures more comedic. The second category – where numbers
are 'integrated' – is transformative, at least for the duration of the song and
dance, while the third (the example Dyer uses is *On The Town*) is fully utopian
and generally sees narratives set 'in places where it can be believed (by white
urban Americans) that song and dance are "in the air"' (Dyer 1992: 29). The
fictional worlds of the latter such films are thus generally continuous with the
comedic qualities Thomas stresses: 'safety, expression, satisfaction, mutual-
ity, community, improvisation, spontaneity, benevolent magic' (2000: 92).
Conversely, the first category is more susceptible to melodramatic inflection
– indeed, though musical-melodrama is rarer in Hollywood, the example cited
above was *A Star is Born*, which is, effectively, a 'backstage musical'. Direct
address may appear in all three, though being more obviously grounded in the
theatrical narrative settings of backstage musicals, it is perhaps less striking
there.

One of the most valuable and most distinctive aspects of Dyer's account
is that he shows the five utopian categories of Energy, Abundance, Intensity,
Transparency and Community to be the genre's underlying structures of
feeling, not simply things that the musical numbers, narratively speaking,
'mean'. He talks of the utopian aspect of musicals as representational and as
non-representational, noting that the non-representational has been widely
neglected in film studies (1992: 22). Dyer draws upon the work of American
philosopher Susanne K. Langer:

The tonal structures we call 'music' bear a close logical similarity to the
forms of human feeling – forms of growth and attenuation, flowing and
stowing, conflict and resolution, speed, arrest, terrific excitement, calm
or subtle activation or dreamy lapses – not joy and sorrow perhaps,
but the poignancy of both – the greatness and brevity and eternal
passing of everything vitally felt. Such is the pattern, or logical form,
of sentience; and the pattern of music is that same form worked out in
pure measures, sound and silence. Music is a tonal analogue of emotive
life. (Langer quoted in Dyer 1992: 19)

In quoting from Langer, Dyer shows his determination to locate the utopian aspect of musical numbers not only in terms that can be deduced as their literal meaning but also in their qualities as analogies for 'emotive life'. Thus, for example, 'community' in a musical number – visible in having a large number of performers collaborate on stage or in a narrative space – can mean, in literal terms, 'we'll overcome this obstacle if we all work together.' However, communal musical numbers also create a space in which the music conveys relationships that are 'phatic' – 'i.e. those in which communication is for its own sake rather than for its message' (Dyer 1992: 21). It is notoriously difficult to describe affective structures clearly, certainly within the discipline of film studies.[23] This difficulty is behind the irony that the *musical-ness* of musicals is often neglected – musicality is liable to be overlooked because we are more accustomed to analysing narrative meaning and deducing the effect of a film's visual signs.[24] Indeed, here, there is only the space to point to these abstract issues rather than examine them in anything like the required depth. However, at a minimum, it is worth pointing to the emotive structures behind music because, as we shall see in the later case studies, even when the film is not *a musical*, it seems as if music is needed or, at least, is felt apt for the performance of direct address and for the emotions it can express. The emotionality of direct address – that is, the impact of facial expressions and eyes delivered straight to the viewer – is one of its unique capacities. My analysis of direct address will show its capacity to act as a metaphor or metonymy of wider meanings, but it should be remembered that the material for this metaphor is the human face, and one of the face's key functions is the expression of emotion. The wider meanings that are expressed are, indeed, often emotional ones.

Earlier, we cited Feuer's comment that 'when performers in musicals turn to face us directly, we do enter another register' (1993: 36). I would not want to suggest that music is this other register but music is *another* affective register in some respects analogous to direct address. As Claudia Gorbman's work has shown (1987), music occupies a special place in film form. In almost all films, regardless of genre, it communicates emotive structures directly to the audience, though, of course, this communication should generally go unnoticed by the spectator / auditor (Gorbman's book is called *Unheard Melodies*, after all); while film often seeks to move us by having us observe the interactions of characters in and with their environments generally 'unaware of our presence', extra-diegetic music frequently guides and shapes our reactions to what we see in more 'direct' way. However, this perhaps gives undue emphasis to the 'directness' or otherwise of a particular means of communication and there is something more specific – though still very difficult to define – that may be seen to connect music with direct address in terms of affect.

Richard Dyer's category of 'intensity' perhaps suggests what is not literally interpretable both in music *and* in direct address. 'Intensity' is the least susceptible of Dyer's terms to literal understanding and most analogous to music's capacity to convey, in Langer's terms, 'everything vitally felt'. It is perhaps Dyer's most evocative but most slippery category:

> It is hard to find a word that quite gets what I mean. What I have in mind is the capacity of entertainment to present either complex or unpleasant feelings (e.g. involvement in personal or political events; jealousy, loss of love, defeat) in a way that makes them seem uncomplicated, direct and vivid, not 'qualified'; as day-to-day life makes them, and without intimations of self-deception and pretence.
> (Dyer 1992: 23)

The drive to interpret the meaning of facial expressions performed to the camera should not neglect the essential ambiguity of many of these gestures – the next chapter focuses on a final shot remarkable for its ambiguity. In this context, Dyer's notion of 'intensity' is worth dwelling upon because the language used stresses vivifying affect over representational meaning. The way Dyer describes 'intensity' chimes with the way direct address may express themes and / or feelings present elsewhere in a narrative but make them seem more 'uncomplicated, direct, vivid and unqualified'. This suggests that, in its affectivity, direct address may have a 'utopian' function.[25] Clearly, this is by no means always the case; the camera looks in *Funny Games* and other 'confrontational' examples of direct address throw our engagement with fictional characters back in our faces – though Dyer is clear that the utopianism of 'intensity' is far from being its capacity for cheeriness (he stresses rather 'negative' emotions), *Funny Games* sets itself up against the 'emotional manipulation' of conventional fictions. The crucial point, however, is that 'intensity' is affective and, though by no means incompatible with narrative meaning, its ambiguity provides a useful point of reference. The next chapter sees the analysis of a complex, ambiguous moment of direct address. *Le Notti di Cabiria* shows that direct address can reveal something *in combination with music* that the normal register of representational performance perhaps cannot.

NOTES

1. I thank Alex Clayton for providing me with the text of his essay. I am informed that Clayton's essay is to appear in 2012 in Aaron Taylor (ed.), *Theorizing Film Acting* (Routledge). However, because of potential changes to format and pagination, I shall refer to the earlier version Clayton sent me. As such, I have used the year in which the essay was completed (2010)

and indicated the page numbers present on the manuscript Clayton sent me.

2. *Mabel's Strange Predicament* (1914) was made first but released afterwards. *Kid Auto Races* is easily viewable in its entirety online.

3. Many of the scenes between Brydon and Coogan were apparently improvised, helping to inspire a further collaboration with the director Michael Winterbottom – the TV series, *The Trip* (2010), in which the two actors again play versions of themselves.

4. Print reviews were not (and certainly are by no means now) necessarily the primary means of getting such story information but it is notable that most contemporaneous reviews compiled at imdb.com mention the show being signed up by a commercial station.

5. A further study focused on the use of direct address in teen film and television might find the recurrence of direct address and its more common cousin, voiceover narration, as a marker of authenticity and honesty. I have suggested that this is a common function of direct address regardless of genre. However, in teen texts, this has added resonance, for they are often concerned with demonstrating the 'phoniness' (that is, hypocrisy) of the adult world – see, further, *Ferris Bueller's Day Off*, TV programme *Malcolm in the Middle* (2000–6) and, more ambiguously (for its direct address is, at least partly, diegetically motivated through the use of a webcam), *Easy A* (2010).

6. *Wayne's World* is not strictly a spoof in the manner of, say, *Airplane* (1980) but, aside from the multiple endings, other scenes spoof famous films and TV shows – for example, Wayne and Garth recreate the opening of long-running US sitcom, *Laverne & Shirley* (1976–83). The comedy of *Wayne's World 2* (1993) is based more consistently on spoofing.

7. Dirk Eitzen counters the Bordwellian model of classicism within the context of screen comedy by suggesting that such films are 'emotion machines' (1997). This account of comedy is far more compatible with direct address.

8. Animation might be pointed to as an exception because it does not maintain the ontological connection with the real in the same way. (Though it is interesting how the convention of the 'blooper reel' has found its way into many recent animations, where, of course, it is entirely artificial.) However, I would not seek to labour the documentary aspect of the cinema in such general terms but rather indicate the *specific* documentary resonances of comedies, musicals and what is brought out by Jean-Luc Godard's techniques. I consider the particular ontology of photography as enormously significant to cinema but not *determining* of what cinema 'is': 'the vocation of the cinema that corresponds to its technical possibilities is one that *uses all the resources of the image* in order to extend the field of representation to the

dimensions of the world' (Dufrenne quoted in Yacavone 2008: 95; emphasis added – Yacavone chooses to add emphasis to the final part of the sentence instead). I would consider the specific ontology of photography to be *one* of these 'resources of the image', though a particularly significant one.

9. There is clearly a much larger body of comedy theory. However, as Clayton discusses, much of this work is primarily concerned with theorising the effect of comedy. I have subscribed to Clayton's emphasis on intention because I ask, 'what is the effect *sought* by direct address rather than what is the actual effect of direct address on audiences?' (which would be very difficult to measure, in any case).

10. The other film scholar whose work is most central to this chapter also debates the definitions of the terms 'comic' and 'comedic', partly in relation to questions of the *intention* to make us laugh (Thomas 2000: 17–18).

11. Clayton's emphases are appropriate for his purposes, as he seeks to nuance his thesis through more subtle or, rather, less immediately clear instances of the duality of actor and character. However, we see, as seems often the case, that the 'obviousness' of direct address blocks its further consideration (see Vernet 1983: 32).

12. For example, three minutes into *Perfect Day* (1929), when Stan is hit on the head by Ollie and realises this was no accident, he looks at us much more insistently than is usual.

13. This is part of a contrast Perez draws between Chaplin and Keaton: 'Buster seems to have no thought for us, occupied as he always is with some demanding task at hand – and convinced, we surmise, that soliciting anybody's sympathy, ours included, is not going to make any difference' (1998: 117). The actor Keaton, like the actor Chaplin, looks at the camera, but his characters do not: 'his eyes appear directed not at the camera itself but at some point past it that claims his attention. We never get the feeling that he's looking at us: the effect, instead, is of our looking into him' (ibid.: 120). Here and in his other work (2008), Perez demonstrates the expressivity of a wider range of camera looks than are my concern here.

14. I shall leave discussion of the 'world-ness' of fictional worlds until Chapter 6. This broad and rather abstract issue is best discussed in relation to a specific fictional world.

15. This is potentially a gross simplification. From other angles, James Mason might be seen to lend the schoolteacher a 'star power' appropriate to the characterisation of his inflated ego. James Walters characterises the actor–character relationship more elegantly, with reference to Judy Garland in *The Wizard of Oz* (1939):

> On screen, actress and character are always there, but are like the separate colours in an iridescent fabric, where each shade emerges

more clearly only as the light plays on the material's surface. It becomes impossible to say what singular colour such a material is, as it is made of the two shades. (2008: 58)

To follow Walters's metaphor, I would suggest that, in the PTA scene at least, the light catches the 'Ed Avery' shade of the fabric rather than James Mason because the close-up of his face is so powerfully metaphoric (it is perhaps, almost, onomatopoeic; see Brown 2008: 168–9 for a discussion of onomatopoeic as a descriptive term) of the character's situation and sense of himself: the 'too-close' shot on his face vivifies a worldview that has become self-regarding to the point of delusion.

16. They are referred to simply as 'Ma' and 'Pa' from the first scene and are generally defined by their children as such throughout much of the film. However, their proper names are more appropriate here given the space and romantic identity they finally manage to assert for themselves in the scene on which I shall focus.

17. According to a DVD extra presented by Gary Giddins, the film was released the year Roosevelt's reforms finally kicked into effect.

18. The term 'aggregative' is used by Martin Rubin (1993) in order to resist the too-great emphasis on integration into narrative of most written histories of the genre. 'Integration' implies a self-effacement of narration, a disavowal of the act of presenting the story, whereas stressing the aggregative structure of musicals is more compatible with understanding their highly presentational style.

19. Though *Easter Parade* is set in 1912 and the magazine covers referred to are painted ones, the stance of the models is identical to that found in later fashion photography – the film clearly refers to 1948 trends at least as much as those of the 1910s. The opening number of *Funny Face* (1957) also employs camera looks to suggest the vacuity of the fashion industry – a vacuity, strangely, to which the films seems to believe its heroine (played by Audrey Hepburn) should aspire. (Richard Dyer notes the profound ideological and aesthetic contradictions of this film – 1992: 28–9). 'Think Pink' sees Kay Thompson's Maggie Prescott and various employees of the fashion magazine of which she is editor strike poses reminiscent of fashion photographs. Kay Thompson / Maggie Prescott often looks at the camera in this number but, I would suggest, there is a deliberate blankness to her gaze that does not seek a human connection. In contrast, Ann Miller / Nadine Hale's gaze does seek a connection but it seeks it *too* hard. This brief comparison further underlines the fact that the meanings of camera looks and direct address are extremely varied and often complex.

20. The narrative about making it big in Hollywood involves the character changing her name, but Esther (this is her original name) ends the film by

calling herself 'Mrs Norman Maine' as a gesture towards the memory of her dead husband (played by James Mason). The film, a musical remake of a 1937 film of the same name, is much concerned with the sexual politics of twentieth-century fame.

21. Further proof that direct address is less appropriate to the theme of romantic longing as played out in the specific medium of musical performance can be found in the fact that, as Jim Collins indicates (1981: 144), the look at the camera does not appear in the 'private' dances that take place between Fred Astaire and Ginger Rogers. These numbers often concern the formation of a romantic couple, something too 'private' for direct address.

22. These issues are nothing if not complex and the film is far from 'unconscious' in subscribing to gendered discourses – one of the climactic integrated numbers sees Hannah tell Don how 'it's different with men' and sings to him 'I never saw you look quite so pretty before' as she dresses him up.

23. Phenomenological film theory could be seen as a contemporary response to this lacuna. However, it is notable that having focused its attention primarily on the affect of the human body on film (see Sobchack 1992 and Marks 2000, for example), the object of study has been relatively concrete.

24. Rick Altman is a leading scholar of the musical, who often talks about the significance of musical structures – his *The American Film Musical* remains the most comprehensive study of the genre. However, his analysis is notable for its literalness (the musical is actually defined, according to Altman, by its narrative focus on romance) and the important 'phatic' or affective qualities of the genre are here rather neglected.

25. This analysis appears to have moved to suggest that direct address *is* particularly attuned to melodrama in the sense that many scholars acknowledge its historical root being musical (*melos*) drama. Clearly, the heightened emotionality of melodrama is a key characteristic. However, the influence of melodrama on wider film form is huge and the relationship is tremendously complex (see Gledhill 1987) and I have deliberately drawn upon Thomas's narrower definition of melodrama (already a large area of concern) in order to explore the issues of fictional worldhood that are more urgently relevant to the analysis of direct address – these issues are further discussed in the *La Ronde* chapter. Direct address remains less compatible (but by no means *incompatible*) with the heaviness and oppressiveness of the melodramatic fictional world as defined by Thomas.

CHAPTER 4

Le Notti di Cabiria (1957)

At the edge of a cliff, robbed, abandoned, nearly killed by a man who had promised to marry her, Cabiria (Giulietta Masina) pulls herself up from the ground as if waking from a deep slumber. She picks up a bunch of flowers (flowers she had earlier gathered with the man) and begins to walk screen-left. A dissolve takes us to a shot of her continued movement left to right, back through the woodland that borders the cliff. Even away from the light (moonlight? dusk?) shining off the lake beneath the cliff, and within seemingly thick woodland, strong shadows are cast; they seem to point in the direction Cabiria walks. She wanders up a gradual incline as if in a trance, seemingly unconscious of where she is going. However, music begins to suggest a destination, its qualities (it gradually gets louder, there is some echo) hinting at a source within her world, that it is diegetic. For a few moments more, the source remains unseen, but, as Cabiria meets a road and turns left to follow its path, we see some figures behind her, further down the road. One calls out, the voice of a young woman: 'Maurizio, hurry up! We're leaving!' A group emerges from behind some trees, rising voices now singing along with the music, leaving us in no doubt now that they are the source of the music. However, Cabiria appears oblivious to them. She moves as if she were sleepwalking, her gaze fixed blankly ahead of her. Her isolation from the merriment of the teenagers is further underlined with three cuts showing separate members of the joyful procession – these closer shots reveal well-dressed young people, some wearing party hats, some playing instruments (guitars, harmonicas, accordions), and two couples on scooters. In one of these shots, a girl, presumably the same one who had earlier called out to 'Maurizio', exclaims happily, 'We're gonna lose our way home.'

In the fourth shot after Cabiria has joined the road, we see the group dancing around her. Some of them look at her, but she does not meet their gaze; her head remains partially bowed and she continues her trance-like walk. Then, one of the guitar-playing boys manœuvres himself in front of Cabiria. Playing as he walks or almost skips backwards, he smiles at her yet she does not look at him and her gaze remains blank. He makes a playful barking noise and, briefly, their eyes meet. Though there remains a gulf between her emotions and those of the group now surrounding her (the light catches the tears in her eyes), Cabiria at least now seems cognisant of where she is. This awakening coincides with the beginnings of the song's climactic section, the notes of Nino Rota's theme rising in the first of two upwards-moving gestures. (I use 'gesture' in its musical sense, but it is appropriate that this is what we might also call the performer's acknowledgement of the camera.) In rather wonderful harmony, the second musical gesture accompanies the physical gesture towards the camera, the moment of its acknowledgement that will be described shortly. What is more, Cabiria's weak smile accompanies a transition from a minor to a major key, just one of the ways in which music prepares us for the shift that occurs in the film's final shot.

Then follows one of the longest takes of the sequence; to be precise, it is the third-longest, the longest being the shot that shows Cabiria's walk through the woods to the road, the second-longest being the final shot of the film, which contains the moment this chapter is focused towards understanding. Whereas the longest take establishes Cabiria's movement towards the road, the introduction of the 'travelling players',[1] and the former's isolation from the latter, the final shot's duration enables a heightened sense of connection, a connection that is consummated and stretched outwards from the film's world in the moment of direct address. However, in this, the third-longest take, Cabiria looks around at the teenagers who now seem focused on rousing her from her melancholy. She has become the audience for their playful and intimate performance, though perhaps this description implies too great a distance (performers–audience) than is achieved in this moment. Towards the end of the shot, Cabiria is often largely hidden behind foreground members of the group; she has, to some extent, been absorbed into them. In the penultimate shot of the film, one of the young women, who, throughout, has been walking arm in arm with a young man, turns to Cabiria and warmly greets her: 'Buona sera' (see Figure 4.1). The young woman – more a girl, really – is perhaps fifteen, her dark hair falling to just below her shoulders. The impact of this greeting is rendered visually and aurally by the cut to the final shot, a close-up of Cabiria and the beginning of the score's second climactic gesture. Significantly, the music shifts from the diegetic (the sound matching the instruments we see played on screen) to the extra-diegetic (an orchestral, scored rendition of the same piece of music), a transition from one level to another matched by the final look at the camera. This movement between levels is aided by the rising scales and lilting cadence of the song's climax.

In the film's final shot, Cabiria looks around her, smiling at different members of the group. The lighting of the actress's face highlights eyes that

Figure 4.1 *Le Notti di Cabiria* (Dino de Laurentiis Cinematografica & Les Films Marceau, 1957): the young woman (uncredited) wishes Cabiria (Giulietta Masina) '*Buona sera*'.

glisten with tears. Her smile is brave but modest (for the most part her mouth remains closed), her expressions towards the players delicate – she gives gentle nods and, at one point, lowers her gaze. There is an unmistakable resemblance to the sad and lovelorn clown, Pierrot – a mascara-coloured teardrop sits next to her left eye. Masina / Cabiria then looks at us twice. This acknowledgement of our presence is akin to Cabiria's acknowledgement of those occupying the diegesis with her (we receive a nod much as they do). However, this is no point-of-view shot – the camera does not occupy the position of one of the teenagers. For one, the smooth tracking shot fixed on Cabiria's face makes no attempt to mimic the movement of the teenagers (they circle Cabiria) and the look into the camera is given an added 'extra-diegetic' emphasis in the way performance and framing combine with Rota's score. Cabiria's gaze moves from left to right, at one moment looking downwards. The first time Cabiria looks at the camera (Figure 4.2), it is followed immediately by a nod of the head, a glance away, a bashful smile. She then glances at us again. The delicacy of Masina's gestures is matched by the delicacy of the scoring. The second climactic musical gesture, as with the previous, lilts slowly before reaching a more rapid climax. The first look at the camera occurs precisely at the brief transition between the two tempos. The beat Masina / Cabiria takes

Figure 4.2 Cabiria looks at us.

before looking combines with the music to produce something of the feeling of an intake of breath. The swelling music adds to our sense of this moment as a powerfully emotional one, though much work still needs to be done before understanding the particular emotions involved.

None of the details described above is incidental, yet, as in much of the film, the feeling is primarily one of encounter. In writing about the final moments on the road and, indeed, in writing about the film as a whole, there is a particularly acute problem of balance: that is, balancing respect for the film in its unfolding present (and the sense of 'encounter' it produces) with unpicking the function of each moment within an intricate and highly structured network of filmmaking decisions. For this reason, I began with the final scene of the film, indicating some of the steps (physical, visual and aural) that move us towards one of cinema's most famous instances of direct address. This final moment is one I will return to at various points but it must be returned to in the context of other scenes from the film whose sense of unfolding sits in productive tension with the containing structure: a structure, I suggest, that leads inexorably towards the final acknowledgement of us as audience. Because of the film's structure and its particular style, the structure of this chapter has been dictated more urgently than is usual by the film's chronology. But this chronological structure is not a negation of argument. Indeed, my argument about the film is precisely that the free-flowing, in André Bazin's terms, 'phenomenological realism' of *Le Notti di Cabiria* disguises a narrative trajectory that is determined to the extent we might call it 'fated'. Moreover, the chronology of the scene recounted above can help us list a series of issues that will organise our thinking about the film and the role of direct address within it. We have encountered some of these issues already, but now, an extended case study enables us to give them more nuanced shape.

NARRATION VERSUS PERFORMANCE, DESTINY VERSUS AGENCY

Cabiria's movement from cliff-side to road feels pre-determined. She does not appear conscious of her movements and proceeds as if guided by some unseen force. Of course, films regularly need to combine a narrative trajectory with the appearance of spontaneity but, due to what I identify (through Bazin) as the particular relationship between the 'vertical' and the 'horizontal' in the film, this tension is here especially pertinent. The horizontal designates linear narrative, the vertical the highly 'spontaneous' performance offered by Giulietta Masina. Direct address is, by definition, a declamatory gesture but different kinds of declamation form a pattern throughout Masina / Cabiria's performance within the film. Moreover, the relationship between horizontal and vertical axes is key to acknowledging the film's debt to the aesthetics of Italian 'neorealism'; on a more ethical level, it lies at the heart of the film's at one time controversial relationship to that 'school' of filmmaking – that is, the degree to which Cabiria / Masina is invested with the sense of an independent spirit conflicts with the emphasis on material determinants in much post-war Italian film realism. The framing of Cabiria / Masina's performance takes us, in Bazin's words, 'to the end of neorealism' and then 'out the other side'.

Self-consciousness, irony

The reference to Pierrot in Cabiria's tear-stained face reminds us of Federico Fellini's love of quotation and allusion. Masina's performance also recalls her earlier performances for Fellini (who was also her husband) and she carries with her a performance style that cites Charlie Chaplin. Direct address is a facet of the self-consciousness of a number of films and its appearance is often linked to a level of irony in the film's narration – the look at the camera can be ironic in the sense of being 'knowing', the character / actor appearing to admit their place within the film *as a film*. In *Le Notti di Cabiria* 'dramatic irony' (a character's lack of awareness of a fate the audience may perceive) is also suggested in the gathering of flowers in the final scenes of the film, an action that recalls another, earlier scene of romantic illusion (which I examine below). I will highlight other aspects of the film's tone and structuring that reveal their irony as the film progresses.

Awakening, transcendence, grace

In the final scene, Masina / Cabiria is awakened from an almost somnambulist state by the young players she encounters on the road. In particular, the young woman who greets her offers an image of youthful purity and hope for the future at the same time as recalling Cabiria's own past. The final look at the camera can thus be considered the ultimate point of Cabiria's awakening. Thus one considers the relationship between direct address as a facet of the film's self-consciousness *and* what it suggests of a consciousness, an awareness, emerging from *within* the character. Following on from the discussion of the film's irony, I will assess the apparent sincerity with which the film invests notions of redemption through 'grace'.

Diegetic and extra-diegetic

In the latter moments of the film, the shifts the music undergoes from the diegetic to the extra-diegetic parallel what direct address represents in terms of shift from a normally self-enclosed filmic world to one that performs connection with our world, the world of the spectator. By indicating the particular role of music throughout the film, I will suggest that Masina / Cabiria's final address of the audience is part of a subtle but still evident trajectory towards a recognition of her place within the film.

The above provides something of a roadmap through the meanings of the film but, as the summary implies, the route is in many ways circular – the horizontal–vertical distinction introduced above is intimately connected with the diegetic–extra-diegetic distinction which, in this film, is tied to the character's awakening to the fate / narrative trajectory in which she is caught. To continue the analysis, it is necessary to step back from the immediacy of the film and consider the broader significance (for the director and for the cinematic traditions in which he worked) of this gesture towards the film audience.

> Fellini's art is, above all else, a struggle to overcome the dangers of falling. It is committed to the transcendence of gravity, of matter, of all that weighs down the spirit . . . At its best, it dreams Fellini and us anew, in a shared revolution of sensibility that brings us somewhere closer to the angels; Fellini said 'It is the no man's land . . . the frontier

between the world of the senses and the suprasensible world, that is truly the artist's kingdom.' (Burke 1984: 5)

In writing on the director, *Le Notti di Cabiria* (known as *Nights of Cabiria* in some Anglophone countries), Fellini's sixth film, receives less attention than many of his later works and is often valued, it seems, for demonstrating a director on the cusp of the greatness of *La Dolce Vita* (1960) and *8½* (1963).[2] This evaluation is not surprising, given the famous idiosyncrasies of the director's style; in their stylistic extremes, the films from *La Dolce vita* onwards cannot help but be more 'Fellinian'. If Fellini's art is seen to be defined primarily by its commitment to the 'transcendence of matter', then *Le Notti di Cabiria* does not appear to go far enough; it becomes a minor work. However, to my mind, his 1957 film is not to be valued as a precursor to supposedly more fully realised artworks, but as the peak of Fellini's output in its balancing of the wider material concerns of post-war Italian cinema with his more 'spiritual' preoccupations. As 'matter' and 'spirit' are held in tension in the above quotation, I want to suggest that they are held in perfect balance in the film's final sequence. To develop this argument, it is necessary to explore aspects of *Le Notti di Cabiria*'s relationship to the sensibility, aesthetic or movement (as the debate goes) known as 'neorealism'. It is my contention that the address of the audience in the final moments of Fellini's 1957 film is best understood in relation to what André Bazin identified as the director's voyage to 'the end of neorealism'. Seen in this way, the breaking of the 'fourth wall' not only crosses the frontier between 'the world of the senses and the suprasensible world', but that between two aesthetic sensibilities, two attitudes to fiction that exist in tension in Fellini's work of this period.

Scholarship on the best-known Italian cinema of the 1940s and 1950s is often burdened with the task of defining neorealism.[3] The term describes a body of films (often seen as running from *Roma, Città Aperta* [1945] to *Umberto D.* [1952]) and filmmakers (Rossellini, De Sica, Zavattini, Visconti and so on) concerned with exploring the socio-economic realities of Italy in the years after World War Two. The methods used by these filmmakers are characterised primarily by a relatively unobtrusive 'realist' style that may show a preference for some of the following: location shooting, long-takes, non-professional actors, narratives that eschew 'classical' causality. The more sensible accounts of these films have avoided narrow delineations of their neorealist characteristics without neglecting the ethical, political and aesthetic dimensions that initially excited interest in the films. Gilles Deleuze's account of neorealism's central place in a shift from the 'movement image' to the 'time image' (1989) has been very influential because, as well as properly acknowledging historical context, it offers a fluid model for understanding the relationship between attitude (towards the real) and aesthetics. Deleuze's account owes a clear debt to André Bazin's contemporaneous writing on the post-war Italian cinema, which, for my purposes, is more useful in its greater sensitivity to the appreciation of the detail of films' moments than Deleuze's grander theoretical (and notoriously jargon-laden) project. Bazin's writing on neorealism culminates in his account of *Le Notti di Cabiria*.[4]

Bazin was key to neorealism's rise. Whether one considers it a legitimate term for a distinct body of work or merely a critical construct, he could be said to have been the first either to notice it or to have invented it.[5] Roberto Rossellini was so grateful for the French critic's role in raising the profile of his and his contemporaries' films that he dedicated two consecutive Venice film festivals to Bazin's memory (Andrew 1978: 3). After neorealism gained currency as a term in critical debate, Bazin sought to rescue the concept from the dogmatism of certain Italian critics who disparaged the later work of Rossellini and others for having abandoned their commitment to the plight of the working class of contemporary Italy. From *La Strada / The Road* (1954) onwards, Fellini was, like Rossellini, often attacked by critics on the left. Guido Aristarco, the Marxist editor of the Italian film journal *Cinema Nuovo*, rounded on Fellini for his apparent political disengagement (see Bazin 1999: 347–57). Aristarco and his colleagues saw Fellini's films increasingly as a betrayal of his neorealist training (Fellini was one of the scriptwriters on Rossellini's *Roma, Città Aperta*) because they were seen to rely on an excessively spiritual (and specifically Catholic) understanding of character, and because his picaresque narratives abstracted his characters from contemporary material concerns.[6] Bazin's response to this was to try to shift the terrain of neorealist discussion from ideology (in a narrow sense) to aesthetics, frequently turning to Fellini's films as demonstrating a more fluid but more profound notion of realism. In these essays, Bazin offers some of his most fully realised accounts of the neorealist attitude and approach to character construction and narrative, seeking, for example, to defend *Le Notti di Cabiria* not by pointing to its socio-political relevance (something not to be discounted entirely) but by suggesting that it achieves a fuller understanding of the reality of individual human experience through its narrative construction.

As Millicent Marcus notes, 'Bazin gives the apt description of "neorealism of the person" to [Fellini's] holistic approach, which considers the problematics of human existence apart from its sociopolitical determinants and unbound to the particulars of historical context' (1993: 88). Bazin even states, 'what I am not far from thinking is that Fellini is the director who today goes the furthest in the neorealist aesthetic, so far that he crosses it and finds himself on the other side' (1999: 341). At times, he overreaches in his claims for the film's radical, 'phenomenological' approach to characterisation. However, Bazin's account of the structure of the film provides a starting point for understanding the retrospective 'inevitability' of Cabiria's final look into the lens:

The beauty and rigour of its construction is . . . a product of the perfect economy of episodes. Each of them . . . exists by and for itself, in its singularity and in its vividness as an event, but each participates in an ordering that always reveals, in retrospect, its absolute necessity. From hope to hope, on the way plumbing the depths of betrayal, derision and destitution, Cabiria follows a path, each halt preparing her for the next. When one thinks about it, there is nothing . . . that does not reveal itself as subsequently necessary to the catching of Cabiria in the trap of trust. (1999: 340)

In order to assess Bazin's claims, a brief account of the key 'halts' of Cabiria's story is useful, in order to point to moments of foreshadowing and echo.

1. The film begins as it ends, with the heroine taken to a water's edge by a lover, Giorgio (uncredited), who robs her and, in this case, succeeds in pushing her in. She is nearly drowned but is eventually fished out of the Tiber; still in shock and initial denial at her betrayal, she is not exactly grateful and berates her rescuers. One of the local boys recognises her as Cabiria, a prostitute.
2. Later, when we see her on her favoured patch, Rome's Passeggiata Archeologica, a prostitute and her pimp pull her away from a fight with one of the other women – the fight is provoked by the latter's mocking of Cabiria's betrayal by Giorgio, her gullibility in matters of love and the woman's predictions of a destitute future. Cabiria is driven away and dropped off on the upmarket Via Veneto.
3. Here, she is picked up by movie star Alberto Lazzari (played by real-life Italian movie star, Amedeo Nazzari), who, at his lavish and overblown mansion, offers a more fantastical though, paradoxically, more authentic vision of romantic possibility than the film otherwise presents. Their meeting is cut short with the return of Lazzari's girlfriend.
4. Back on the Passeggiata Archeologica, her fellow prostitutes mock Cabiria's claims of meeting Lazzari, and the scene ends with the sight of passing pilgrims and the women discussing visiting the shrine of the '*Madonna del Divino Amore*' ('Madonna of the Divine Love').
5. In the subsequent scene, a client has abandoned Cabiria in the wastelands of Rome's environs (he told her of a non-existent 'shortcut'), where she encounters 'the man with a sack'[7] (uncredited), who distributes food and clothing to the destitute living in the caves, including a former prostitute Cabiria recognises as 'Bomba' (the 'Bomb').
6. Next, Cabiria goes on the pilgrimage with her friend Wanda (Franca Marzi) and the other women from the Passeggiata Archeologica, where they are

bombarded by merchants selling candles and trinkets, wailing crowds and a level of hysteria which produces in Cabiria an emotional turmoil.

7. This scene of empty spectacle and false promises (the debauched and crippled uncle of one of the pimps crashes to the floor when seeking a miracle) is followed immediately by a scene in a tawdry vaudeville hall, where Cabiria is tricked by a vaguely sinister hypnotist (Aldo Silvani) into enacting a tender love scene for the amusement of the rowdy audience. The hypnotist leads her through an imagined meeting with a rich, sensitive young man he calls 'Oscar', Cabiria revealing a desperate yearning for love as she enacts the picking of flowers on the stage. After being jolted from this waking dream and subsequently sheltering from the jeering men who wait for her after the show, a man (François Périer) introduces himself to her. She is initially sceptical of his claims of seeing a kindred spirit on the stage but finally agrees to meet him later that week. He tells her he was especially touched because his name is, in fact, Oscar.

8. A series of meetings culminates in the pair's engagement, the sale of her house and her departure for a new life with him. As a presage to their elopement, he takes her on a romantic walk through the woods (he tells her it is a 'shortcut'), where she picks flowers. They reach their destination – a cliff beside a lake[8] – where, though he cannot bring himself to kill her, he robs her of her life's savings, leaving her wailing on the ground. After the afternoon light gives way to dusk, she rouses herself and wanders to the final encounter with the young players.

In this synopsis, there are links worth particular emphasis. The circularity of the narrative is clear (the parallels between the betrayals at the beginning and end) but costume also links 'Giorgio' and 'Oscar' – we are asked to doubt the veracity of the latter's name, but it is also likely that 'Giorgio', who disappears after the opening minutes, is an assumed name (indeed, Wanda suggests as much). In the opening few minutes, which otherwise maintain Cabiria and Giorgio in extreme long-shot, an abrupt cut to the sunglass-wearing Giorgio, just before he pushes Cabiria into the river, asserts his villainy. Later, in a moment Bazin regretted for a similar over-assertiveness (1999: 339), Oscar will lead Cabiria to her final fall while wearing sunglasses. Her romanticism, her vulnerable social status and her susceptibility to romantic betrayal are core to our assessment of Cabiria as a character, and so too particular moments within the film cue us to the likelihood of her ultimate impoverishment: for example, the mocking words of the prostitute she fights as well as the sight of 'Bomba'. On a different level, a series of major sequences link thematically in their exploration of fantasies or illusions. Though we may never entertain the possibility of a lasting romance, the meeting with Lazzari offers the fleeting possibility of a real connection, but only after his home has been constructed as highly artificial (his mirrored wardrobes play music as they open and close mechanically), as something akin to a movie set (the white telephone recalls the 'white telephone films' and are thus a prop associated with luxurious, escapist Italian film melodramas), and as a space in which Cabiria can only be a fish out of water. Further elements of foreshadowing will be uncovered as we delve in more detail into moments of the film, noting, for example, the film's relationship to Christian notions of redemption and grace, and the important role the scene with the hypnotist plays in Cabiria's journey towards a final betrayal.

For the moment, I wish only to point to the fact that what I have described, if not 'classical' in its structuring, possesses a unity, a constructed-ness that sits uneasily with claims for the film as pursuing the 'neorealist aesthetic'. To approach this from another angle, the film's determinism tends towards a sense of the fated, whereas the determinism of neorealism is more readily associated with naturalism's emphasis on the material conditions of the immediate environment. However, stylistically speaking, *Le Notti di Cabiria*'s 'neorealism' might be said to lie in what Bazin emphasises as the sense of the existence of the films events 'by and for [themselves], in [their] singularity and in [their] vividness as . . . event[s]', the sense of encounter earlier noted:

> The primacy of the event over plot has driven for example De Sica and Zavattini to substitute for the latter a micro-action, which is based on undivided attention to the complexity of even the most banal events. By the same token, any hierarchical organisation of events based on psychology, dramaturgy or ideology is condemned. Not that the director must therefore renounce any choice as to which event to show us, but that this choice no longer operates with reference to a pre-existing dramatic organisation.
>
> But nonetheless, even with *Umberto D.*, which represents perhaps the extreme in the experimentation into this new type of dramaturgy, the development of the film follows an invisible thread. Fellini appears to me to have perfected the neorealist revolution in innovating a script without any dramatic linking [*enchaînement dramatique*], one based exclusively on the phenomenological description of characters . . . It is when they do not act [*agissent*], that fellinian characters best reveal themselves to the spectator, that is through their agitation [*agitation*]. (1999: 344)

For Bazin, in this 'fellinian system', events no longer occur in the horizontal plane of linear narrative, but fall vertically into the field of character (1999: 338) – thus the emphasis is on the ostensively disconnected events that *befall* characters. However, Bazin is being contradictory in combining these claims with the earlier-cited description of *Le Notti di Cabiria*'s 'perfect economy of episodes'. Indeed, I would suggest that what Bazin claims is absent from *Le Notti di Cabiria*, an '*enchaînement dramatique*', is precisely the phrase that best describes the narrative to which its heroine is submitted. Yet Bazin's contradictions hit upon a central tension within the film, between what is characterised as the 'vertical' (a way of conceiving performance and its framing) and the 'horizontal' (the organisation of story). These combine, I will argue, to construct a causality that is so binding, so inexorable, that all Cabiria can do is, finally, recognise her place in it and gaze outwards at us. This can only be plotted with renewed sensitivity to Cabiria / Masina's performance, particularly the 'agitation' that Bazin suggests is so revealing.

This particular kind of performativity is introduced in the film's first scene and the sense of play and playing it creates. In an opening long-take that follows Cabiria and Giorgio as they run to the river's edge, Cabiria seems to be throwing herself into the role of young lover (after playfully pushing Giorgio over, she embraces him with a highly theatricalised girlishness) while, in retrospect, Giorgio's actions seem simply to play along (he allows some space between their bodies during the embrace and his gestures as he points her towards the river are stiff). After the highly determined left-to-right movement of the opening shot, Cabiria's turmoil after her rescue from the river is expressed facially but also in her chaotic running about – she appears highly disoriented, moving in several directions, looking for Giorgio. Here, the film's relationship to neorealism may be noted. The wasteland location is consonant with many of the canonical neorealist films but Masina / Cabiria's 'agitated' movement around the space connects with a central characteristic of this strand of filmmaking in a more peculiar way. Amongst the films commonly grouped under the heading of neorealism, the frequency of narratives organised around the wandering of the lead characters is striking. The films of De Sica and Zavattini (as director and scriptwriter respectively) are apposite cases (the desperate search for the bicycle in *Ladri di biciclette* / *Bicycle Thieves* [1948] and the search for the dog, Filke, in *Umberto D.* both involve much walking around Rome). In this, neorealism's famous interest in the conditions of urban deprivation combine with the aesthetic associated with long-takes and a focus on, in Bazin's words, the 'micro-action'. Fellini's films share this perambulating approach to narrative; for example, *I Vitelloni* (1953) is focused primarily on following the listless wanderings of its young protagonists and *La Strada*'s title underlines the centrality of journeying to its story. *Le Notti di Cabiria* follows this tradition by beginning and ending many of its scenes on Cabiria's movement through the landscape, and by beginning on the heroine's movements through a Roman wasteland with Giorgio, and ending with her on the move once more, this time without the home which had once given her a modicum of rooted-ness. In a more idiosyncratic way, the film makes movement through the space of each scene particularly expressive, taking us perhaps to the limits of the neorealist comparison. With her running about after her near-drowning (the first close images we are given of the central performance), the register we enter into is not a naturalistic one. It has not yet shifted into the comical (the film is, importantly, often very funny) but there is this evident potential in the highly theatrical performativity of the film's opening.

In the next scene, Cabiria rushes home to what resembles a sparsely populated shanty town. After climbing through the window of her house (Giorgio stole her handbag containing her keys), Cabiria finally comes to a stop, if not a rest, on her bed. Her restlessness is conveyed by the tapping of her hand and foot, but also by her expressions. Masina's extraordinarily mobile and highly mannered performance relies on her facial agitation as much as on the movement of her body. Her eyes are used strikingly throughout the film (the effect of these being key to the final direct address, of course) and especially so in this scene. As she sits on the bed, she stares into the distance. By refusing to look at Wanda, whose supportive comments are not welcomed, her eye-line also helps feign a degree of nonchalance. When Wanda's concern becomes unbearable to her, Cabiria aggressively stares her in the eyes and tells her to mind her own business.

Wanda is driven away by Cabiria's aggression. However, it becomes clear to us that the latter's stance is mere bravado. Once Wanda has left the room, intense anxiety unfolds on Cabiria's face. This time, her eyes move from (screen-)left to right, finally looking towards the door and holding her hand nervously to her mouth. She then runs out to her front steps to call after Wanda. Wanda's suggestion that Cabiria call the police is rejected with an excessive force – Wanda is walking away from Cabiria by this point and, we presume, cannot see her hand waving and her shifting from front to back foot. These gestures are followed swiftly by even more revealing ones, as Cabiria looks from side to side with a smile that says she is pleased with a performance clearly given for the benefit of her neighbours – the neighbourhood children are often glimpsed in the background in isolated pools of light.

This illustrates the particular importance of declamation to Cabiria's performance as much as to the actress who incarnates her. Cabiria is a character keen for approval but one who, at times, seems also to strive for conviction – that is, to convince herself of what she is feeling – through a highly declamatory acting-out of emotions (this facet of her declamation is especially evident in other scenes examined below). This develops through the scene in a series of dramatic shifts in emotion. For example, Cabiria goes inside, looks at Giorgio's picture and sheepishly smiles in a way that suggests she would be ready to forgive him. She then goes back outside and sits on the steps. A 'cheat' cut (there is continuity in the performer's movements but not the angle at which she sits) demonstrates Fellini's recourse to subtle abstractions in this film. The strong lighting of Masina / Cabiria's face cannot be realistically motivated, but heightens the sense of her isolation. She again looks around her, now more slowly and with less confidence than before. She touches her face as more morbid thoughts invade her soliloquising. (Of the scenes in which she is effectively alone, this is perhaps the most loquacious.) This realisation engenders more shifting emotions. She moves to retrieve a chicken from a small coop beside her house. Holding the chicken tightly, she strokes it, looking down at it with a yearning for comfort. However, her emotions change once more as she looks upwards and outwards in what seems to be a dawning realisation. The dark eyebrows against her fair skin and bleached hair give her a cartoonish quality.[9] She throws the chicken in the air and runs inside, gathering numerous objects associated with Giorgio, while verbally listing the many things she bought him – here, as in many scenes, material concerns are intrinsically linked to emotional ones. She also declaims a bitter, mocking (of herself and of Giorgio) determination to be rid of him, before throwing the clothes and photographs on a fire started by one of the local boys.

These actions are followed, as before, by a look around her that suggests she seeks approval for her forcefulness. However, finding herself amidst a group of young boys whose stoking of the fire has none of the emotionality of her own, Cabiria's tenuous self-satisfaction (her eyes glisten with tears throughout) quickly crumbles. She looks to the fire and then around her as before, pain overcoming her face. Now, in one swift movement, she turns till her back is to us and she walks away. Withdrawing from the camera is a way of conveying stifled pain with a long provenance.[10] Here, its impact is particularly strong because it provides the full stop to a scene in which declamation and a frontal relationship to the camera have had several functions.

Declamation has (at least) three different facets in the above scene. There is the declamation of the character Cabiria, who, after her declaration that she is 'no stool pigeon' and after the burning of Giorgio's belongings, is revealed as someone keen for approval. Second, there is the declamatory style of the actress Masina. Clearly, this is designed to convey something of the character, but it also lends itself more generally to the comical as well as the performance of pathos. Broadly speaking, comic performances are often characterised by a frontal performance style and, as we have seen, are often willing to acknowledge the act of filming; more specifically, Chaplin's performance style and relationship to the camera are a touchstone I return to below. Third, moving back towards character alone, there is the final withdrawal from the camera's attention, a gesture that turns in on itself and turns away from us. This is a momentary refusal of declamation, but by refusing the attentions of the camera still, on some level, hints at its presence. This scene shows a clear accumulation of a sense of 'to-be-watched-ness'. These distinctions rest on the slippery relationships between character and actor, performer and camera, relationships that are particularly important to this film and to understanding the final look at the camera, which overtly acknowledges the relationship between the world of the film and the world of the filming.

The scene examined above reveals much of the interior life of the character through, in Bazin's terms, its intense focus on a single character's 'agitation'. It also arguably helps establish a tone in which the camera may become active in the fiction, a possibility only fully consummated at the end of the film. The scene that follows further develops the importance of declamation to its central characterisation. Cabiria's distraught walk away from the camera dissolves to the feet of the unnamed prostitute who will provoke a fight with Cabiria – I shall call this prostitute '*grande dame*' (uncredited), a title she gives herself (her claim is clearly ironic, but the irony is the film's, not hers). The fight ensues from *grande dame*'s cruel impersonation of an elderly Cabiria. 'Look how you'll end up, you lousy whore!' she shouts. Then, hunched over, holding out her purse, she performs: "'Please be kind, have a heart. Please, for my Giorgio's sake!'" It is these last words (and the screamed emphasis they are given) that lead Cabiria to fly at the *grande dame*. The latter is an incessantly aggressive presence, and Cabiria's attack on her understandable. However, in the patterning of the film, the scene is also significant as the first time in which Cabiria is doubled (the meeting with the destitute prostitute Bomba is the second occasion, but only this later encounter seems to be recognised by Cabiria for what it is: a presentiment or at least warning of the future).

Grande dame's impersonation of Cabiria is the literal facet of this doubling but, seeing the film in its totality, there are other links between the two prostitutes' performances. The *grande dame* is a figure whose eccentricities isolate her from the rest of the prostitutes, but so too is Cabiria. When Cabiria arrives on the Passeggiata, the *grande dame* is framed (as often in the scene) against a proscenium-like archway and given a huge shadow by unnaturally strong front lighting. However, when she declares, 'Here comes the psycho again!', she offers a description of Cabiria not without foundation – Wanda called Cabiria a 'nut' in the previous scene and, on the Passeggiata, the others observe her with a mixture of interest and wariness. Like Cabiria at a number of moments of the film, *grande dame*'s performance is also characterised by a kind of verbal diarrhoea. Masina / Cabiria's declamatory style is taken to grotesque theatrical extremes by the older woman. However, *grande dame* is, arguably, a nightmarish vision of what Cabiria could become, and certain shots hint at the parallels between the two women – for example, Cabiria holds forth in the foreground while the constant commentary of *grande dame* intrudes from the distant background. Indeed, one of the prostitutes, referring to *grande dame*, tells another 'That's how you'll end up,' a line that would more aptly be delivered to Cabiria.

Cabiria is far more sympathetic than *grande dame*, yet both characters evince a disparity between the presentation of the self and its exterior reality. When

Cabiria's rival calls herself '*grande dame*', one of the other prostitutes retorts, 'You look more like Moby Dick to me!' But a similar effect ensues from Cabiria's name, which recalls a famous overblown, historical epic (Giovanni Pastrone's *Cabiria* of 1914). The name thus combines with the diminutive stature of the woman who inhabits it to comic effect. More broadly, as Phillip Kemp (1999) notes, 'Much of the film's comedy derives from this gap between aspiration and achievement.' This is the first link we might make to Charlie Chaplin. To cite James Naremore, on Chaplin, again:

> One reason he is a comic hero is that there is usually a disparity between his grand actions and humble 'essence'. In every way he is what Leo Braudy describes as a 'theatrical character' – a figure who *acts* and who lets us see the artificiality of his performance. (1988: 123–4)

It is a commonplace of Fellini criticism, and particularly that focused on the films in which his wife, Masina, starred, to note the many echoes of Chaplin – indeed, Chaplin gets a whole entry in Sam Rohdie's *Fellini Lexicon* (2002). It is especially to the fore in *La Strada*, where the performance and costuming of Masina's simple waif, Gelsomina, makes conscious reference to the Tramp. For example, there is a scene where Gelsomina's brutish husband Zampanò (Anthony Quinn) gives her a costume for their circus act, one item of which is a bowler hat. Out of sight of Zampanò, she wrinkles up her nose, pulls a dopey smile, and waddles on the spot as she looks up at her hat (see Figure 4.3). It is a small expression of joy, playfulness in her new role and costume. It is also marker of the self-consciousness characteristic of Fellini and Masina's performances for him. The relationship between Masina as a performer and Chaplin is pertinent because of the latter's famously 'direct' relationship with the camera and, by extension, the audience beyond it. However, one risks subsuming the particularities of each performer into vague notions of 'connection' through pathos and / or comedy – it is particularly tempting to lapse into such discussions of Chaplin, whose Tramp persona is so powerful an icon. For now, I wish only to remark upon the tendency towards this kind of referencing in Fellini's films.

The director's work is, of course, known for its self-consciousness; he famously made a film about not being able to make a film (*8½*). It should also be noted that *Le Notti di Cabiria* is not the first time Cabiria had appeared in a Fellini film. Fellini's first film as solo director, *Lo Sceicco Bianco* (1950), contained a brief cameo by his wife as a winsome prostitute called Cabiria. She and another streetwalker appear to the dejected hero (Leopoldo Trieste) from around a corner. Cabiria appears to be discussing the scene from a film she has just seen, a scene of romantic climax that was accompanied by a dance which she proceeds to re-enact. In his 1957 film, Fellini's tendency towards

Figure 4.3 *La Strada* (Ponti–De Laurentiis Cinematografica, 1954): Gelsomina / Masina does her Chaplin shtick.

inter-textual reference is also evident just before Cabiria's fight with *grande dame* in her arrival in a vehicle that clearly recalls Zampanò's in *La Strada* (both Zampanò and Cabiria's client drive three-wheelers with trailers on the back).

Fellini's allusions to his earlier film could be dismissed as self-mythologising. However, the connection to *La Strada* is more profound if we look at *Le Notti di Cabiria* with some aspects of neorealism in mind. As mentioned earlier, the film shares with many neorealist narratives an emphasis on walking. This is partly because material deprivation means neorealism's heroes are typically forced to walk and, in many of the films, this material deprivation is a central theme. Access to transport or owning one's own means of transport thus becomes a source of anxiety or aspiration for many of the characters, and in *Le Notti di Cabiria*, transport and transportation (in both their prosaic and more metaphoric connotations) take on considerable significance. This can be seen in the passage around Cabiria's arrival, in which the conversation of the pimps and their 'protectors' revolves around the new Fiat 500 of the pimp Amleto (Ennio Girolami) and the prostitute Marisa (María Luisa Rolando), earned, *grande dame*'s acerbic chorus informs us, by drug dealing. The pimp mocks one of the other young men who sits on his motorbike, 'You're always on two wheels!'; Cabiria then arrives on three. Cabiria's eccentric form of transport marks her out from the others as a figure of considerable independence yet, also, vulnerability. Her fierce independence, asserted in her refusal of Amleto who, as he drives her to Via Veneto after the fight with *grande dame*, tries to recruit her, contrasts with Marisa's dependence on the pimp to drive the car she supposedly owns.[11] At other points, however, including the ending, Cabiria's vulnerability is linked to her isolation from transport – at the end of the film she must walk home and the meeting with the man with a sack occurs because a truck driver trick has left her to walk home via a non-existent shortcut. To return to Bazin's vertical–horizontal model, independent transport would allow Cabiria simple passage through the spaces of the film. As it is, events befall the heroine as she walks through Rome and its environs. At street level, on her own two feet, her potency within the narrative rests upon the highly theatrical business one might designate with Bazin's vertical line. However, this command of the performance spaces of the film always suggests vulnerability as well as potency as a performer.

Aside from Bazin's conceptualisation of Fellinian neorealism, descriptions of cinema in terms of horizontal and vertical axes have been used to describe the genres of Hollywood filmmaking discussed earlier, comedies and musicals, the two genres in which direct address is most at home. In musicals and comedies, performance 'numbers' exist, to paraphrase Bazin, 'by and for themselves', in seeming tension with the forward movement of linear narrative. Given such correspondences, and given the importance of declamation to Cabiria / Masina's performance earlier noted, I wish to devote some attention to a series of musical / comic 'numbers' in which Cabiria dances. The three examples come within the space of twelve minutes of screen time: first, Cabiria dances a mambo to the Fiat 500's radio just before she attacks *grande dame*; when dropped off on Via Veneto by Amleto and Marisa, she dances on the street in what is, arguably, a reference to a Hollywood musical; this comes just before her meeting with the movie star Alberto Lazzari, who takes her to a club where she will dance another mambo.

In the first example, Cabiria draws one of the young men who hangs around on the Passeggiata Archeologica into a lively dance at odds with the rough setting. The other prostitutes watch, and for the moment the space becomes something more joyful. However, the constant invective of *grande dame* undercuts any transformation: 'Now she's found another dead beat to say "I love you." One who'll send her off begging.' The romantic associations of dance are thus greeted acerbically. The second dance sees Cabiria alone on a street outside what appears to be a nightclub. She moves to a window, leans into it so her bottom points towards us and wiggles her hips in time to the music. The music is, in effect, the film's main theme – numerous variations

Figure 4.4 Cabiria dances on the street to music whose 'diegetization is weak or ambiguous'.

of it occur throughout the film, including the music played by the travelling players at the end. In this instance, it appears to have a diegetic source (heard through the window). Cabiria, smiling, then breaks out into a little dance on the corner, at one point kicking her legs out as if she were in a chorus line (see Figure 4.4). Though a highly declamatory bit of business, this is a private moment, which ends as Cabiria notices a doorman round the corner. A cut to a reverse angle shot of her modifying her performance to a sweet and demure appeal to the doorman (this remarkably sexless prostitute is, of course, supposed to be looking for business) is accompanied by a change in scoring that seems to 'Mickey Mouse' the change in action. As so often in the film (and in Nino Rota's scores more broadly – see Dyer 2007 and 2010), the relationship of diegetic to extra-diegetic music becomes open to question – in Claudia Gorbman's evocative description, the 'diegetization' is 'weak or ambiguous' (1978: 86).[12] At this moment, this serves what I take to be a reference to another uniformed authority figure in the title number of *Singin' in the Rain* (1952). Faced with the attentions of the policeman, Don Lockwood (Gene Kelly) will briefly continue his performance, whereas Cabiria will stand in static defiance of the doorman's disapproving glare. The way music is used outside the night-club establishes the permeability of the diegetic–extra-diegetic boundary in a way that reminds us of how Hollywood musicals seem not to worry over the distinction. However, the permeability of this boundary is activated to more singular effect by the musical shift that occurs as Cabiria / Masina prepares to acknowledge the viewer in the film's final moments.

Cabiria now encounters a movie legend from her own world, 'Alberto Lazzari', who, following an argument with his girlfriend (the actress's name is 'Dorian Gray'!), will pick up the heroine. Lazzari's motivations do not appear to be primarily sexual (they scarcely threaten to become so), and he takes her to a luxurious nightclub, principally, it seems, to serve as a buffer against the irritating attentions of numerous glitterati. Without much enthusiasm, he asks her to dance along to a mambo; now performed live, it is in fact a slightly different version of the mambo that earlier emanated from the car radio. Cabiria breaks off from the relatively staid dancing to perform a lively solo number that includes a couple of the same kicks earlier performed on the street. Her movements are intercut with a series of reaction shots of generally warm and amused smiles. Then, when a vampish young woman looks over towards her unsmilingly, Cabiria moves back to her partner – she appears to sense a threat to her hold on Lazzari.

In such moments, Masina / Cabiria's vivacious performativity suggests the utopianism of the musical and the classic comic disparity ('between grand actions and humble "essence"') noted by Naremore (1988: 123–4). The ability of a lower-class character to transcend the more rigid etiquette of the wealthy nightclub patrons is only reined in by the comedic gap between her over-the-top performance and the insecurity of her social standing (expressed partly in her sense that Lazzari might easily be stolen from her). The film's intertextual games demand a consideration of external frameworks; we are reminded of Cabiria's dancing entrance in *Lo Sceicco Bianco* and Gelsomina in *La Strada* (dressed with her Chaplinesque bowler hat and cane, Gelsomina does some dancing kicks in much the same manner as Cabiria when she and Zampanò are hired to entertain a wedding party). Moreover, such associations ask us to question the boundaries of the film world in much the same way as direct address itself asks us to reconsider a number of the cinema's 'rules' and boundaries. It is the balance between being inside and outside of a particular film moment that will be central to my ultimate appreciation of the ending.

To return to the comparison with Chaplin, it is pertinent to draw attention to the relationship sometimes noted between Chaplin and Brecht. For example, James Naremore quotes Brecht's qualified praise for Chaplin (1988: 114–15). Naremore suggests that this is:

> not surprising . . . because the *verfremdungseffekt* has a good deal in
> common with the standard techniques of comic alienation . . . By its
> very nature, comedy undermines our involvement with the characters,

barely maintaining a dramatic illusion . . . [and] invites us to observe
plot machinery *as* machinery. (ibid.)

To make this link carries two main risks: first, to perpetuate the 'Brechtian
assumption' about direct address that predominated in classic film theory;
and, second, to perpetuate the misconceptions about what 'Brechtian' means.
As noted earlier, the German playwright and theorist is often called upon
in the name of anti-realism and to illustrate antagonism towards the notion
of character. However, as Richard Dyer suggests, Brecht's practice did not
constitute anti-realism so much as propose to 'reinvent realism according
to historical-materialist principles'. Formally, this involved a 'rejection of
actors because they "looked right"'; 'second . . . a rejection of psychological,
rounded character construction in favour of characters seen as . . . an inconsistent bundle of conflicting motives and interests' (2001: 105); and third, most
famously and most relevant for this study:

> there was an emphasis on 'showing' or 'presenting' a character rather
> than embodying it, so that the actor sometimes steps out of character,
> comments on it, plays it a different way, etc . . . The stepping out of
> character is not intended to destroy the reality of the character, but
> rather to give the performer / audience the opportunity of seeing the
> character in a new light, discovering a new contradiction, analysing the
> character's social, historical or political significance, etc. This breaks
> novelistic realism, but does not throw the baby of character out with the
> bathwater of psychologism and individualism. (ibid.: 106)

Dyer's conception of the Brechtian is pertinent to understanding Masina /
Cabiria's final acknowledgement of the camera because this moment of direct
address asks us to consider where the boundary between the character and the
performance of that character lies. Some may object to this as a false opposition by emphasising that character or personality is always already performed,
or by pointing to the ease with which film audiences commonly accept the
co-presence of individualised characterisations with ostentatious performative
business (as with 'the standard techniques of comic alienation'). However,
the point is valid here because of the way 'Masina' may be seen to interpose
between us and 'Cabiria'; the ending, paradoxically, promises us a glimpse
into the character's 'essence', while drawing attention to the mechanisms (of
movie-making) through which such an essence is performed.

The ending is not the only moment that may be described as 'Brechtian' in
Dyer's sense of the term. In reminding us of her performance of Gelsomina in
La Strada and an earlier version of Cabiria in *Lo Sceicco Bianco* (and remind-
ing us of Chaplin more generally), Masina's dancing shtick does not quite

step out of character, but it raises this possibility. Yet this self-conscious bit of business also reveals something of her character. The dancing she performs in the street outside and in the nightclub and the reactions of others (the doorman and the nightclub patrons) suggest Cabiria's unconventionality (showing her in 'a new light'), at the same time as hinting at considerable insecurity (showing 'a new contradiction') rooted in her fundamental sense of social inferiority (her 'social, historical or political [in]significance'). Thus, one finds oneself in the uneasy territory where to describe a degree of stepping out of character is to understand its consonance with aspects of characterisation. But as we move towards a better understanding of the effect of its direct address, one should be mindful of Dyer's plea not to 'throw the baby out with the bathwater'. Further attention to the comic elements of the film's 'vertical' focus on its central performance will underline the potential power of direct address as a form of 'stepping out of character' which can reveal further truths about that character.

Cabiria's status as a fish out of water on the upmarket Via Veneto and the expensive nightclub is revealed through her dancing (more specifically, the interruptions to her dancing). The comedic shift from un-self-consciousness to self-consciousness this entails is then especially to the fore when Lazzari takes her home. Cabiria is full of wonder as she is led through the movie star's mansion to his bedroom – this is scarcely surprising, given the ludicrous luxury of the apartment (Cabiria must walk through his well-stocked menagerie before she gets to his chambers). She is initially ill at ease and Lazzari responds by commanding her to 'Sit down. You're making me nervous.' She obeys but, lounging on his chaise-longue-like bed, he remains a remote figure. He waves his hand as if languidly conducting the classical music he has just put on (Beethoven's Fifth Symphony). 'You like it?', he asks her. She responds in a drawn-out series of statements: 'Beh. Kind of. It's not really my thing. It's not really my thing, but, yes.' The disparity between the length of her answer and the import of the question is amusing in revealing her nervousness. The music reaches a rather bombastic crescendo as the valet wheels in their supper. Cabiria rises to her feet but remains rooted to the spot for a few minutes – this is striking in a performance generally characterised by its considerable mobility. Lazzari continues to question her, Nazzari's performance only now beginning to suggest genuine interest. He asks her where she lives and she seems to answer honestly (later, she will try to give the stage hypnotist and his audience a more upmarket address):

Lazzari: You come to Via Veneto?
Cabiria: Via Veneto? Me? I work the Passeggiata Archeologica. Much
     more convenient.
Lazzari: Why?

Figure 4.5 Cabiria / Masina's performance is marked by excessive declamation . . .

> Cabiria: Subway takes me right there. There's another girl, my friend
> Wanda. She lives there too. But I don't bother with the others. The
> others sleep under the arches in Caracalla. Mind you, I have my own
> house . . . With water, electricity, bottled gas, every convenience. I
> got everything. Even a thermometer. See this one here? She never,
> ever slept under an arch. Well, maybe once. Or twice. Of course, my
> house is . . . nothing like this. But it's enough for me. I like it.

Lazzari switches off the music and gently implores her to eat, his pompous
behaviour and bad humour vanquished. Cabiria's speech is filmed in one of
the longest takes in the film (it is certainly longer than any of the shots earlier
remarked on for their duration). However, recourses to the conceptions of
a 'neorealist' style are patently inappropriate here, more liable to obscure
than enlighten. Though the content stresses the ongoing concern with material possessions, the delivery (characterised first by excessive declamation
[Figure 4.5] and then crumbling self-assurance [Figure 4.6]) is both comic and
pathetic. Cabiria's assertions of material prosperity are, faced with Lazzari's
home, revealed as insecure, and the comedy is of the 'digging-yourself-a-hole'
variety, the camera fixed on her as confidence unravels and she increasingly

Figure 4.6 . . . and by crumbling self-assurance.

contradicts herself ('Well, maybe once. Or twice.'). While this performance, and the camera's refusal to cut away from it, invite us to laugh at Cabiria, we also feel intense sympathy for her. Masina's extremely mobile performance (the early scene in and around her home and the sudden shifts that punctuate her dancing are prime examples) asks us to observe Cabiria as a figure eager to break out of the restraints imposed by norms of behaviour and social perform-ance; yet her economic and social vulnerability is such that this breaking-out is only ever short-lived. The moments of stepping out of or presenting her character thus actualise her *character*'s stepping out of the bounds forced upon her. In this, the excessive, then curtailed declamation of some of the moments examined above are a step towards the more enlightened, more mature, more modest and more *graceful* declamatory act of addressing the camera in the film's final scene.

The circuitous route from and back to direct address has been necessary in order to chart Masina / Cabiria's performance in its particularity, in its rela-tion to notions of both neorealism and comedy, and as a part of a structure of containment and occasional release. 'Containment and occasional release' seems apt because of the irony of much of the film (a facet of which is the gap opened up between Cabiria's forcefulness as a performer and her vulnerable status), an irony often disclosed when the heroine breaks out to do some comedic business. The final look towards us, the viewers, seems to admit this irony and the constricting structure that has produced it. But while irony may often suggest a 'knowing' superiority to character, direct address in *Le Notti di Cabiria* suggests an awakening of knowledge from *within* character. However, before returning to the final scene, what remains is to understand its other resonances because, as an 'awakening', it needs to be understood in relation to two scenes that deal with thresholds and with the attainment of grace or enlightenment: the scenes of the pilgrimage and the stage hypnosis.

The authentic, humble Christian qualities of the man with the sack scene give way to the crass artifice of the religious festival. Cabiria's earlier decision to attend was presented much like her speech about her home to Lazzari: 'What would I ask [the Madonna] for? I've got everything. I'll even be done with the mortgage soon. But I might go anyway. I haven't said no . . . We'll see.' Cabiria's lack of assurance continues into the visit itself. She is overwhelmed by the enormous crowd, rows of stalls hawking religious artefacts and a loudspeaker directing the pilgrims, and what seems to be at stake in the scene is the relationship of her experience of the pilgrimage to that of the other prostitutes and the rest of the crowd, and her struggle to find the appropriate response. In a performance in which thought is played out so strongly on the performer's face, this search for an appropriate response is important to the characterisation of Cabiria throughout, and visible at numerous points throughout the film (for example, with Lazzari in the club, she does not know what to make of a dance act, and looks to him for confirmation of how to feel, modulating her facial response accordingly).

At the pilgrimage, Cabiria seeks out Wanda and tells her that she too will ask the Madonna for grace (the sub-titles repeatedly translate '*grazia*' as 'mercy', but the more literal translation is needed here). Wanda protests at the presumption, claiming that she has changed her mind and might ask for 'a villa in Peripli'. Cabiria is upset by this change of heart and, as they mount the steps towards the church, tugs at Wanda's coat like a child. There exists a gulf between Cabiria's aspirations for this experience and those of Wanda and the other characters from the Passeggiata – while Wanda considers what riches she will ask for, two of the other prostitutes go to get novelty photographs taken and Amleto's uncle, a crippled drug dealer and pimp, speculates as to how much money the church is making. The heavily made-up faces of the prostitutes stick out in the crowd, but Cabiria appears to be the only one truly anxious about her belonging. She moves amongst a singing crowd but only joins in after a few verses. All eyes are fixed towards the altar, apart from those of Cabiria, whose restless gaze conveys continued anxiety and self-consciousness (contrast the way Marisa and another prostitute call out '*Viva, Maria. Grazia Madonna*' without a hint of self-consciousness). The camera pans from

Cabiria's troubled looking around her to a line of wailing women, who, running from right to left, provide a spectrum of increasing hysteria – the one furthest to the left collapses to the ground. When Wanda comes over, Cabiria tells her, 'I feel so strange, Wanda.' Wanda now looks around her, but there is little sense that the experience is affecting her as deeply as it affects Cabiria.

The script then offers what might be taken as a literal anticipation of the ending of the film and the encounter with the young players. Over a loudspeaker, the priest calls to the worshippers: 'Look into Her sweet eyes, and in Her glance, each one of you will feel the light of hope turned on in your heart.' Cabiria advances to the altar, struggling to maintain her composure. On her knees, she looks up to the icon of the Virgin and implores, 'Madonna, help me . . . to change my life. Bestow your grace on me too. Make me change my life.' In retrospect, the priest's words have considerable resonance for the film's moment of direct address, but it is unclear whether they describe Cabiria's experience or ours as viewers during the final encounter on the road; at the end, we look into her 'sweet eyes' and, though what kind of hope it evokes is ambiguous, hope is certainly at stake in the final look into the camera; yet, there are also the sweet eyes that belong to the young woman whose 'buona sera' instigates the shift from diegetic to extra-diegetic music.

Moreover, the development in Cabiria's prayers from asking for help to pleading the Virgin to '*make*' her change her life is answered in the final betrayal by Oscar that leaves the heroine shorn of all property save the clothes she is wearing. Thus, if the ending were taken literally (that is, if we were to take its relationship to the prayer to the Madonna as crassly literal), it would endorse a particular Christian notion of redemption through the abandonment of all material possessions (of course, what Cabiria owns has been earned through prostitution). For now, one can at the minimum assert that, for Cabiria, the experience is authentic, vivid, that she has undergone a realisation that has taken her from asking why she would attend the pilgrimage (a question framed in relation to the things she owns – 'What would I ask for? I've got everything') to a sense that she needs to change her life. That Cabiria feels this, but is alone amongst the prostitutes in feeling this, is further apparent as the scene dissolves to a picnic outside the church where Cabiria's increasingly drunken turmoil is contrasted with the uncomprehending, festive behaviour of the others. How one relates Cabiria's prayer to the ending depends on how one assesses the irony of the pilgrimage scene and the film as a whole. For while Cabiria's experience may be 'authentic', its setting is not. The irony of the juxtaposition between the humble, 'Christian' qualities of the encounter with the 'man with a sack' and the crass commercialism of the festival is exceeded by the cut from Cabiria's prayer to the debauched uncle abandoning his crutches only to crash to the floor. Irony has not yet become the problem it presents in Fellini's next film, *La Dolce Vita* (it does not stand as a barrier to engagement with the character) but it does provide a particular challenge to understanding the ending and to situating direct address more widely.

In making his claims for the neorealism of *Le Notti di Cabiria*, Bazin suggested that 'the choice [of which events to show us] no longer operates with reference to a pre-existing dramatic organisation' (1999: 344). Against Bazin's claims for the film's condemnation of any 'hierarchical organisation of events', one must point to its recurrent irony (a kind of organisation that is both 'dramaturgical' and 'ideological') – that is, irony as a facet of structuring (the juxtapositions I have already noted[13]) and other aspects of narration that create irony (including 'dramatic irony'). The stage hypnotist scene, for instance, which immediately follows the pilgrimage, is ironically juxtaposed because, like the pilgrimage, it promises to transport the heroine to another level, to enable her to transcend her normal, lived reality. Both scenes promise, in different ways, to satisfy her deepest desires, though the ostensible cultural values of the settings could not be further apart. The pilgrimage provides a seemingly authentic experience for Cabiria, which is in stark contrast to the hypocrisy and artifice of the surrounding event. The stage hypnotist's show plays out her innermost longings for the amusement of a paying crowd. There are also further aspects of the scene whose irony is later revealed as Oscar betrays Cabiria.

Cabiria's arrival at the music-hall is shown in a dissolve that turns a religious procession of children passing the disconsolate Cabiria to the heroine alone arriving in front of the down-at-heel 'Lux' theatre – the fantasy enacted under hypnosis will make the link clearer. She enters to catch the end of a magician's act being watched by a rowdy, overwhelmingly male audience. As Cabiria takes her seat, she is picked out by the magician who, for his next act ('experiments with magnetism, hypnotism and auto-suggestion'), needs a female volunteer to join the five males on stage. Initially reluctant, she is cajoled into accepting the invitation by the magician-hypnotist and by the men in the audience. After the men have been hypnotised into believing they are the victims of a shipwreck, Cabiria tries to leave the stage but the magician is not yet done with her. He asks her a series of questions, the first being whether or not she is married, and when she tells him she lives in an upmarket area of Rome, a 'hypnotic' wave of his hands forces her to tell where she really lives – her answer is met by laughter and whoops of recognition by the men in the audience. Breaking her trance, the hypnotist's questions return to the question of marriage, to which she responds, 'Why should I [get married]? I've got everything.' She reveals, after some prompting, 'I own the house that I live in.'

Then begins the conjuring of a meeting with 'Oscar', a wealthy young man who, through the voice of the hypnotist, tells Cabiria he has long desired to meet her. The hypnotist places a garland of flowers on her head. In combination with the white coat which reflects the spotlight shining down on Cabiria throughout the imagined encounter, this costuming reminds us of the vision of youthful purity that was so remote from Cabiria at the end of the previous scene (young girls, perhaps in confirmation dresses, pass by Cabiria's rowdy post-pilgrimage party). The religious associations are carried through the hypnotist's performance of 'Oscar': 'I often see you standing by your window, and at Sunday mass. Your eyes are always lowered. You're always with your mother.' Unprompted, Cabiria then crouches down, miming the picking of flowers – the hypnotist congratulates her, suggesting that it reveals a 'gentle soul'. 'Oscar' then thanks her for the flowers and asks her name. She tells him, 'Maria'. This is the only time that anything other than 'Cabiria' has been offered as her real name, though Italian viewers (to whom Pastrone's 1914 epic was very well known) would have recognised it as likely something akin to a 'stage name'. Though nothing explicit is made of it, 'Maria' must surely have been chosen for its religious associations. Cabiria begins to enact a dance with 'Oscar'.

In response to the hypnotist's cruel invocation of a wealthy admirer (he appears untroubled by the irony of his words: 'What good are fancy cars, long journeys and luxury hotels? Smoke! Illusion!'), she tells him, 'When I was eighteen, that's when you should have known me! I had long black hair. To here' – she mimes shoulder length. Again, what is at stake is the incongruity of Cabiria's genuine emotions in a space of illusions, as she halts her dance and implores, 'Then it's true? You really love me? . . . You're not trying to fool me?' The memory of Giorgio's betrayal is clearly still alive in Cabiria's mind, and the hypnotist is momentarily flustered. He ends the hypnosis, but rather than wake up, Cabiria seems to faint. He then picks her up (handling her somewhat roughly) and the camera assumes Cabiria's point of view as the audience (cheering, clapping, laughing) come into view.

The scene ends with a dissolve to Cabiria, inside the foyer of the theatre, sheltering from the jeering men in the audience who have clearly been waiting around after the show. The cleaning lady forces her outside, where she meets D'Onofrio – he does not disclose that his first name is 'Oscar' for a few minutes yet. Distancing himself from the other spectators, he expresses his distaste at the deceptions of the stage act and Cabiria's exploitation: 'We can all pretend to be cynical and scheming. But when we're faced with purity and innocence . . . the cynical mask drops and all that is best in us awakens.' He remarks how cold it has become and, so he can put on his coat, he hands Cabiria his bag. This prop gives weight to his claims to be an accountant (his profession, a marker of financial stability in the tumultuous world we see in neorealist films, is one of the first words he addresses to Cabiria). In a revealing gesture, Cabiria appears, unconsciously, to weigh the bag as if this would give some clue as to the figurative weight of his words. Aside from the irony of his words (evident only in retrospect), like the priest's earlier invocation of the encounter with the Virgin Mary, Oscar invokes the experience of Cabiria's closing encounter on the road. Faced with the 'purity and innocence' of the young players, the look at the camera has the feeling of a mask dropping.

Thus begins Oscar's courting of Cabiria, where he seems to speak to the deepest desires of her soul. Though the more intuitive viewer might be alerted to Oscar's villainy by a brief view of him waiting for Cabiria with a toothpick clenched in his teeth like some Hollywood gangster, their romance seems to offer genuine hope. However, any premonitions of the disappointment to come are given definite shape in the moment which Bazin regretted for its lack of ambiguity. As Oscar and Cabiria sit after a lunch at the start of their elopement, Oscar's sunglasses (something we have not seen him wear previously) and Périer's shifty performance combine with Cabiria's handling of a huge wad of cash (her life savings and the proceeds of the sale of her house) to tell us this will not end well. The costuming choice may be crude,[14] but what we now sense as the inevitability of Cabiria's betrayal enables the film to explore better the dream-like qualities of the final scenes ('trance-like' perhaps better maintains the links to the scene of hypnosis) and leads us towards the moment of awakening on the road.

After Cabiria has bid goodbye to Wanda, Oscar takes her to a rustic restaurant, a *trattoria*, to begin their elopement. This *trattoria* offers beautiful, romantic views of the lake below. In shot-counter-shot images of Oscar and Cabiria, shots of the latter contain more background views of the water (as yet, we are unaware that Oscar's glances towards the lake suggest his plans to kill Cabiria, but the framing anticipates this). Their conversation (or rather Cabiria's speech, for Oscar is unusually quiet) revolves around the money Cabiria has in her possession. In spite of Oscar's protestations, she seems to want to discuss how she earned it: 'Because you never asked if I had money. You, you're an angel a saint! If you knew what I went through to end up with this money . . . The beatings I took.' Any discussion of the film's 'realism' would belie the extent to which the film has rendered Cabiria's life as a prostitute remarkably unthreatening, unsexual even – she is pushed into a river by Giorgio, certainly, but we have no sense that he was ever a 'trick'. The worst that happens to Cabiria on the job is that she is left to walk home through Rome's wastelands and, in one scene, is forced to hide in the bushes from the police who raid the Passeggiata Archeologica. For Cabiria, the scene at the *trattoria* is the start of a new life with Oscar and she feels a need to unburden herself, revealing more of her past than had previously been offered – this also gives Oscar's visible discomfort an apparent source within their conversation. As Oscar leads them off on a 'little walk', Cabiria continues her near-monologue: 'I don't even remember how I started. I was a child, that's all I remember . . . You shoulda seen me at 15 . . . with my long black hair . . . down to here. Who understood anything?

My mother just wanted the money.' When Cabiria mentions her long black hair, she points to somewhere near her waist (the framing makes the gesture indistinct). Though the age and length of hair are an inexact match (earlier it was 18, and the hair was shoulder-length), Cabiria is clearly recalling memories (or perhaps fantasies, the distinction is unimportant) of her younger self that were brought out under hypnosis. As the hypnosis brought to the surface a depth of yearning for love, the promise of fulfilment with Oscar awakens both conscious memories and unconscious presentiments in Cabiria.

The scene at the *trattoria* ends with Oscar leading them off on their walk. He wonders aloud, 'what's the name of that song?' Throughout the scene at the *trattoria*, a guitarist has played a slow, dreamy, folk-like version of the film's main theme.[15] The scene began with Cabiria singing along to the song, and now ends with Oscar drawing attention to it. The ontological status of theme music that is played diegetically, where elsewhere it is presented extra-diegetically, is too broad in its implications to be resolved here. However, Oscar's words alert us to a question we might ask of the film at numerous points: to what extent are characters 'aware' of the film's music, and what does this awareness tells us of their relationship to the narrative of which they are part? The parallels between the beginning and end of the film have already been noted (the robbery and betrayal of Cabiria by a lover at the water's edge), but the role of the music asks us to note other correspondences.

For example, the film begins (as others do) with variations of its main themes played over the credits. A musicologist could describe more fully the relationship between the four pieces of music – with a fluency I cannot recreate here, one described to me the close harmonic, rather than melodic, relationship between them. What I can say is that the very fact of repetition within the variation of music, combined with repeat performances of snippets of the melodies, contributes strongly to the sense of pre-determination in Cabiria's trajectory. After a soft, tinkling waltz prelude beneath the Paramount insignia ('*La Paramount Presenta*'), we hear a lush orchestral arrangement of the two rising gestures that later accompany the final moment of direct address. The lilting tempo contrasts with the initial rigid waltz to give this section of music an almost improvised, or at least spontaneous feel – but this sense of improvisation is only consummated when we reach the travelling players in the film's final moments. The music then transforms seamlessly into a rendition in a swing-era jazz style, before returning to one of the lush orchestral gestures. The latter is then cut short by a more abrupt shift into an up-tempo piece of music. Melodically, but more so harmonically, it resembles what precedes it, but it has a much more sinister feel. Its tune is also the closest to the *canzone* that accompanies Cabiria and Oscar's meal towards the end of the film, but it will be repeated before then. The more 'sinister' piece of music is cut short with the effect of ending the credits as if with musical continuation points, creating anticipation for what is to follow. The film then fades from black to show (in long-shot) Cabiria and Giorgio's run to the river's edge.

There is no music anywhere over the opening scene, except when Cabiria stands on the bank swinging the bag around her. Just before Giorgio grabs her bag and pushes her in, she sings a few notes of the sinister piece of music we have just heard. If not suggesting that somehow she has 'heard' the credit music, it at least suggests a link between her subjectivity and that music. Moreover, given the role music later plays in moments of foreshadowing, the film does seem to suggest a link between character awareness of music, diegetic or otherwise, and their awareness of their narrative trajectory or fate. For example, as Cabiria wanders with Oscar through the woods towards the cliff-side, she bends to gather flowers, much as she did with the imaginary 'Oscar' during the hypnosis scene. As she does this, she sings the theme – in fact, almost exactly the same snippet of the theme that was briefly sung with Giorgio. It is, of course, a possibility of *Le Notti di Cabiria*'s world that 'Lia ri lli rà' is a well-known song that is covered by the singer at the *trattoria* and that Cabiria would have been aware of prior to that particular performance, thus explaining her singing of it at the very start of the film. However, it is not a compelling possibility. She does not answer Oscar's question, 'What's the name of that song?', and the question instead alerts us to the music's indeterminate status within the film world. Like Cabiria's 'awareness' of the music, the song has a name or a function we cannot quite put our finger on. One might tentatively suggest that the music forms part of the film's 'subconscious', and it is, finally, questions of consciousness (self-consciousness or otherwise) that direct address asks us to consider.

As with more recent examples, direct address at the end of *Le Notti di Cabiria* suggests a coming to consciousness, a coming to a greater awareness of one's self and one's place in the world. This has particular resonance in the Fellini ending, whose dream- or trance-like qualities never entirely resolve themselves. As Cabiria walks out into the cliff-side, she responds to the view: 'What a strange light.' Indeed, the luminousness of the point-of-view shot Fellini offers suggests the dream is not yet quite over. The pair stand by the cliff's edge, Cabiria again calling Oscar an 'angel'. Otherwise, the setting is as silent as the wasteland at the start of the film; here, silence is created through the soft sound of wind. It feels as if they are standing on the edge of the world. In his silence and in his looks (see Figure 4.7), Cabiria finally discerns his purpose. She drops to the ground, then, kneeling, turns towards him in a supplication even more desperate than her prayers to the Madonna: 'I don't want to live anymore! Enough! Kill me! Throw me off the cliff!' Guilt roots Oscar to the spot, until, struggling at the cliff edge (Cabiria tries to make him push her off), he falls and runs away with Cabiria's bag. Her screams are all the more upsetting for the silence that precedes and succeeds this moment at the cliff edge.

Figure 4.7 The intentions of Oscar (François Périer) are revealed as he stares into Cabiria's eyes.

Thus we return to where we left off: Cabiria's rise from the ground and her sleepwalk towards the road and the young players. If the address of the camera, the acknowledgement of our 'presence' marks her final awakening, her attainment of consciousness, it is by no means a coming to terms with any simple 'reality' of the world of the film. This ultimate awakening is cued by the '*Buona sera*' of the young girl who walks arm in arm with her young male friend (see Figure 4.1 again). Is this girl fifteen? Certainly her dark hair is down to about the length Cabiria had indicated, unwittingly, to the theatre crowd (Figure 4.8 shows Oscar's recollection) and close to her invocation of her young self at the *trattoria*. This 'young player' offers more than simply the symbolism of future hope (encountering the young people moving along a road clearly has this about it); this young woman is a vision of Cabiria's past, before the weight of the world (and Cabiria's mother's desperate poverty) had taken its toll. In some examples of the device, direct address seems to aspire to turn the screen into a window between the characters' world and our own world. But it is important to note that here Cabiria's looking outwards only follows a moment of looking inwards; the shot-reverse-shot of Cabiria and the girl can be understood as akin to her looking into a mirror. Thus the priest's words from earlier in the film retain their rich ambiguity: 'Look into Her sweet

Figure 4.8 Oscar recalls what Cabiria revealed under hypnosis.

eyes, and in Her glance, each one of you will feel the light of hope turned on in your heart.' If the final moments of the film conjure for Cabiria both a mirror and a window, these words can address both our and Cabiria's experience of the reawakening of hope.

A reading of the above moment should not seek to destroy the final indeterminacy of the gesture towards the camera. For this reason, by way of conclusion, I should like to say some more of its threshold status: that is, the sense of it as a threshold within one particular fictional world, and as a threshold in Fellini's œuvre. One threshold is not so easily divorceable from the other, as a brief account of the ending of Fellini's subsequent film will illustrate. Like *Le Notti di Cabiria*, *La Dolce Vita* ends with the acknowledgement of the camera, but in this case it serves to express the protagonist's failure of recognition, the opportunity for redemption missed. In the 1960 film, the dawn following a debauched party sees Marcello (Marcello Mastroianni) on a beach, momentarily separated from the other revellers. From across an inlet, he is greeted by a girl we recognise as Paola (Valeria Ciangottini), a young waitress he had met earlier. Like the young woman who greets Cabiria at the close of her film, she is unmistakably a figure of innocence and hope for the future. Yet, though we may recognise her, Marcello appears unable to. Space (the expanse of water

Figure 4.9 *La Dolce Vita* (Riama Film et al., 1960): the 'Umbrian angel' (Valeria Ciangottini) looks at the camera as the film ends.

between them) and sound (the crashing of waves drowns out their attempts to communicate) separate them and Marcello wanders off disconsolately. Once more, Fellini makes recourse to direct address, but the performance and effect of the gesture are here very different. As Marcello wanders off, we are left with Paola held in close-up. She continues to smile as her gaze follows the hero's movement away from her. Ciangottini's smile then fixes into something more mechanical, and the actress's head turns very gradually to her right until her gaze is just below that of the camera. She then looks up and, for the briefest of moments, looks at us. The film then immediately fades to black and the credits roll (see Figure 4.9; though it may not be visible, the image has already started to fade, such is the brevity of our contact with her eyes).

The previous use of the actress's name is deliberate, for it underlines the extent to which this moment takes us away from character into a more straightforwardly symbolic register. The movement of her head makes her little more than a marionette. Where the ending of *Le Notti di Cabiria* is generous, *La Dolce Vita*'s is mean-spirited. This is not a criticism of their respective meanings (it would be churlish to criticise *La Dolce Vita* for the clarity of its cynical, disappointed view of Marcello and his choices in life), but the means of their expression. Where Bazin was enraptured by the indeterminacy, the ambiguity of Cabiria's gaze towards us (1999: 345), the fade to black feels like an authorial imposition, a false and forced striving for a similar kind of ambiguity (we are not allowed to see clearly that Paola looks at us[16]). Crucially, Paola is no longer a character, she is a symbol. She was never more than a very minor character, and in Marcello's one previous meeting with her he described her as an 'Umbrian angel'. Her appearance at the end thus continues Fellini's interest in angels and the attainment of grace. However, like Marcello's failure to grasp it, this film's performance of direct address appears to me ungraceful.

This contrasts with the ending of *Le Notti di Cabiria*, which, in its generosity, does not sacrifice a consciousness that appears to emerge out of the character to a more overarching self-consciousness emerging from the film. In a letter to a Jesuit priest, Fellini himself evoked the way the final moment of direct address seems to 'speak for itself', without destroying the ultimate ambiguity of what is being said: 'in spite of everything Cabiria still carries in her heart a touch of grace; it is kinder to leave Cabiria the joy of telling us, at last, whether this grace is her discovery of God' (in Keel and Strich 1976: 66).

The ending of *La Dolce Vita* sees Fellini having crossed a threshold into the more wholesale abstractions for which his later films are known. This is not to deny the importance of abstractions to *Le Notti di Cabiria*, but pointing to its consonance with aspects of neorealism has sought to underline the film's and its ending's extraordinary achievement of balance.

I would like, tentatively, to describe Masina's performance of Cabiria as an example of 'transcendent' characterisation. It is transcendent because, throughout, Masina has referred us to her own particular performativity (the business with dancing, the references to Chaplin and the references to her earlier references to Chaplin), and because it has been woven into a narrative of subtle but inexorable pre-determination, in which the permeability of the barriers between diegetic and extra-diegetic hints at a move from unconscious to conscious realisation of her narrative trajectory and / or fate (ultimately, the distinction is immaterial). All she can do, finally, is look out of the film with a gaze that performs the reawakening of hope for the future, a recognition of how events repeat themselves and an acknowledgement of the camera. In light of this, Masina / Cabiria's look seems to say to us, 'the show must go on.' It seems to say this because of the self-reflexivity noted above, but also because we know where Fellini as a filmmaker is headed – the ending of *8½* trumpets this maxim with much more bombast or brio. Crucially, however, in *Le Notti di Cabiria*, the self-reflexivity of this statement in no way undermines the emotions involved.

Thus, the interactions between the horizontal and vertical planes, and the sense of *enchaînement dramatique* this creates, extend Bazin's understanding of the film in ways he did not anticipate. Moreover, because of the relationship to long-standing traditions of comedic and pathetic performance, this sense of 'transcendent characterisation' need not be isolated from more 'mainstream' practices. Finally, the sense, earlier cited, that spirit and matter are in perfect balance in this film is evinced by an exclamation by one of the young players, 'We're gonna lose our way home.' Halfway between a warning and a wish (she is smiling as she says this – losing one's way home can be fun, after all), it reminds us of Masina's material vulnerability (she has no home to go back to), as well as a more spiritual desire to find a place of belonging.

My claims for the film rest, still, on this notion of Fellini's work on a cusp, on a threshold. Contrary to the conventional notion of thresholds generally adopted in aesthetic histories, in this case it is the threshold itself that it is the height of achievement, not what the threshold gives way to. The road is the symbol of the threshold (one Fellini returns to again and again) and *Le Notti di Cabiria* ends on the road. Direct address enables us to imagine what lies in store for her; the ending's 'marvellous ambiguity' (Bazin 1999: 345) means that is where she remains.

NOTES

1. 'Travelling players' captures something of their function, though Gilberto Perez (2008) has referred to them evocatively as being like 'elves'.
2. To be precise, *Le Notti di Cabiria* is his sixth film as sole director – *Luci del varietà* (1950) was co-directed with Alberto Lattuada. *Le Notti di Cabiria* was received as a return to form after the (unjustly) critically disparaged *Il Bidone* (1955), winning the year's Oscar for best foreign language film. Moreover, Giulietta Masina won various awards around the world for her performance.
3. There is a great deal of scholarship in this field but Marcia Landy (2000) provides a very useful introduction to the films and the debates.
4. In Bazin's anthologised writing, his essay on *Le Notti di Cabiria* appears as the last sustained analysis of neorealism he wrote. Because of divergences between English versions of the essay in circulation (and the existence of some very 'free' translations), subsequent references are from a French language edition of *Qu'est-ce que le cinéma* (1999). Translations are my own.
5. At a conference at the University of Warwick in June 2008 ('Beginnings and Endings in Films, Film, and Film Studies'), Geoffrey Nowell-Smith suggested to me that he had ultimately come to the conclusion that 'neo-realism' is a product of Bazin's imagining, a case of a critic's wishful thinking. I am in no position to refute this claim. However, if it is 'only' a critical construct, I have found neorealism a tremendously useful one for my discussion here. This is perhaps because *Le Notti di Cabiria* is such a vivid threshold example. If my intention were to define Fellini's film as being neorealist or not (rather than to suggest its 'on-the-cusp-ness'), the construct might become hopelessly reductive.
6. For an example of the key attacks on Fellini, see Aristarco (1978a and 1978b). Bazin's essay on *Le Notti di Cabiria* seems to be conceived as a response to Aristarco and *Cinema Nuovo*'s Marxist critique. For a useful account of these debates and a look at neorealism and its 'transcendence' in *La Strada*, see also an essay by Millicent Marcus (1993).

7. In complex negotiations with the censors (effectively the Catholic Church), this scene was sacrificed and did not appear in versions of the film until its re-release in the 1990s. The church objected to the film's apparent celebration of amateur acts of charity, which, juxtaposed with the subsequent scene (the religious festival), must have appeared to them as a reproach (see Bondanella 1992: 130–1).

8. Real-life influences on the story include the newspaper reports of a waitress whose headless body was found in the actual lake pictured in these scenes. It was believed that she had been conned out of her life savings and murdered by her lover (Kezich 2007: 181). This illustrates that the film's complex relationship with the real, and with neorealism more particularly, resides largely in its use of its locations – for a further discussion of this, see Bondanella (1992: 101).

9. Fellini began his career as a cartoonist and many of his film characters were first sketched in this form. See Bondanella (1992: 3–29) for a discussion of the importance of cartoons to Fellini's formation as a filmmaker.

10. I am reminded again of Tom Gunning's analysis of D.W. Griffiths Biograph work, in which 'actors seem at moments to hide from the powerful camera, as if from a sense of shame'. This is illustrated by Gunning's reading of Lillian Gish's performance in the 1913 *A Timely Interception* (Gunning 1991: 263). Seen from this historical perspective Gish's interactions with the camera in Charles Laughton's 1955 *The Night of the Hunter*, as analysed by V. F. Perkins (2005: 34–8), take on added resonance.

11. A facet of the film's singular relationship to neorealism is its worrying over property, felt more strongly in relation to Cabiria's ownership of her house.

12. Though furnishing some useful vocabulary, Gorbman's essay on the film is, unfortunately, rather imprecise; she mistakenly suggests there is no visible source for the music accompanying the 'honeymoon' meal with Oscar (1978: 84–5, 90), when, in fact, we glimpse the singer with his guitar more than once.

13. Though Bazin had seen the film with and without the man with a sack scene (he comments on the merits of its exclusion, seemingly unaware of its censorship – 1999: 337n2), its absence may partly account for the tone of Bazin's claims. However, Bazin sets out his agenda as being to counter criticisms of the film as being 'too well made', in which 'nothing is left to chance' (ibid.: 337). In my emphasis, which runs counter to Bazin, on the film's clear '*enchaînement dramatique*', I do not, however, wish to negate the sense of encounter, the sense of events *befalling* Cabiria to which Bazin's essay is so sensitive.

14. The sunglasses are crude in the sense that they help tell us Oscar is 'bad'. However, in the light of Oscar's earlier speech outside the theatre, perhaps

we underestimate the consistency of the film's ambiguity. Oscar's change in costuming erects a mask that signifies that he is 'cynical and scheming', but normally a mask signifies artifice, whereas this moment seems to suggest what he's 'really like'. If we gave closer scrutiny to the details of Périer's performance (for example, the hints he gives of Oscar's feelings of guilt), we might need to question our assumptions of what is the 'truth' of his character. We know nothing of his background, his motives for conning Cabiria, and it remains a possibility unexplored by the film that after his betrayal of Cabiria, he may meet the fate of the conman hero of Fellini's earlier *Il Bidone* and achieve a type of redemption. (Bondanella 1992: 114–21 provides a compelling reading of the Christian elements of the latter film and goes as far as to call these films – *La Strada*, *Il Bidone* and *Le Notti di Cabiria* – Fellini's 'trilogy of grace and salvation'.) This digression is merited particularly because Cabiria's look into the camera asks us to think about the 'essence' of characters, and the extent of our access to them. In this sense, one might contrast our 'direct' access to Cabiria's 'windows to the soul' as against Oscar's use of sunglasses to mask his – significantly, the final revelation of his villainous plans (but perhaps not his villainy) comes with the film's most emphatic close-up: his eyes from Cabiria's loose optical point of view (see Figure 4.7 in the main text).

15. Though the chorus is of the 'tra-la-la' variety ('Lia ri lli rà', the title of the song, to be precise), the song's lyrics echo beautifully the realisation experienced by Cabiria and the film spectator in the final sequence. I am grateful to Louis Bayman for having translated the Neapolitan dialect in which the song is sung:

> One love goes another comes
> No-one loves you any more
> Don't think about it, your eyes are dry
> Go back to singing like me
> Love passes like the wind
> Get on with life, don't suffer
> Don't complain if you want to understand
> Don't think about your crying eyes.
> Love has betrayed you
> It wasn't like you'd dreamed
> Love . . . you can enjoy
> It's no use if your eyes cry
> Time goes on, you need to forget
> always sing la ri li la.
> Love passes like the wind,
> and like the wind, it can't be stopped.

The melody has multiple meanings throughout the film (it is clearly performed in very different humour by the young players), but in this case, the resignation and mournful tone (which, I am told, is perfectly in tune with the characteristics of traditional Neapolitan *canzone*) help establish the passage from dream to realisation (or realisation from within a dream) that the *trattoria* sequence sets in motion. More broadly, the very fact of the melody's repetition and variation throughout the film echoes the '*enchaînement dramatique*' of Cabiria's experience.

16. When I have discussed and shown this moment in presentations, it has been striking how few people remember and / or have noticed this look at the camera before.

CHAPTER 5

High Fidelity (2000)

The surrounding chapters examine films in which declamation takes on profound thematic significance, and in which a moment or moments of direct address contribute to systematic explorations of the theatricalisation (in various senses) of romance. I wish also to consider an apparently matter-of-fact use of the device. With *High Fidelity*, we encounter a more recent film in which direct address plays a constant but seemingly casual role in the narration; the film's hero, Rob (John Cusack), talks to us throughout, often speaking directly into the camera, sometimes addressing us via voiceover (a form of audience address related to the 'direct' kind examined here). Though I wish to stay true to the 'matter-of-factness' of the fourth wall's permeability in the film (direct address in *High Fidelity* never feels transgressive), there remains much more to be said. *High Fidelity* demonstrates further ways in which, in the context of romantic relationships, direct address can articulate the attendant problems of knowledge (of one's self, of the motivations and subjectivities of others). The film also shows that direct address can create a peculiarly intimate link between performer / character and audience *at the same time as* helping to open up a kind of critical distance in the characterisation. As already seen, direct address has been valued as a distancing (or even 'distanciation' device) but its capacity for intimacy is only very occasionally noted. There is never an acknowledgement (as far as I am aware) that these supposedly opposed effects can work together. In addition, *High Fidelity* further underlines the particular role music can play in the questions of point of view and perspective that direct address is apt to explore.

Some of the commentary by the filmmakers involved underlines the apparent straightforwardness of *High Fidelity*'s direct address. In a DVD extra entitled 'From script to screen', director Stephen Frears tells how the script had initially been greatly driven by voiceover. As the adaptation of a book

(Nick Hornby 1995) so oriented around the central protagonist's musings, one can see why voiceover would have been an initial response to the material. However, one often hears how filmmakers are warned off relying heavily on voiceover, and perhaps direct address was subsequently chosen as a way of making the highly personal narration more interesting. In any case, what we are told is that voiceover was abandoned:

> We very, very soon invented the device of talking to the camera.
> Once you did that, then you get at all the good stuff, because the good
> passages in the book were really his thoughts. So once you invented a
> character talking to the audience you stopped having to try to find a way
> to get the good bits in. You could simply take the good bits and say,
> 'Let's just shoot them' and that was a tremendous relief.

Frears goes on to express a general preference for scripted dialogue that possesses a 'literary' quality, and the decision to make direct address a central part of the film is presented, primarily, as a way of preserving the novel's particular voice. There are major changes in the novel's adaptation (particularly the transplanting of the action from Hornby's north London to John Cusack and his fellow writers' native Chicago[1]), but the changes I wish to examine here result from more fundamental differences between literary and filmic narration, and direct address's particular place within the latter.

Hornby's novel does possess an intense introspection that seems to fit with the self-consciousness of direct address as a cinematic device:

> It's only just beginning to occur to me that it's important to have
> something going on somewhere, at work or at home, otherwise you're
> just clinging on . . . You need as much ballast as possible to stop you
> floating way; you need people around you, things going on, otherwise
> life is like some film where the money ran out, and there are no sets,
> or locations, or supporting actors, and it's just one bloke on his own
> staring into the camera with nothing to do and nobody to speak to, and
> who'd believe in this character then? (Hornby 1995: 59)

Rob is a thirty-something record shop owner whose emotional immaturity and problems with commitment (Hornby's title is a play on words) lead him to a painful break up with his girlfriend, Laura. Faced with what he perceives as yet another rejection, the novel begins with his compilation of his 'top five breakups' (various such compilations are key to the way music geek Rob narrates his worldview[2]) and, later, the mission to track down each of the women involved. Though the film is a relatively close adaptation, the extract above was not chosen for cinematic rendering – the extent of its reflexivity would have undermined the essential wholeness of the film's fictional world. By coincidence, it seems, the filmmakers did choose to rely on a bloke talking into the camera. However, this decision has the effect of intensifying the isolation and (at times) loneliness of the main protagonist, and of vivifying the sense of his self-obsession. While literary narration is commonly introspective in the manner of Hornby's book, it is certainly more unusual (though not unheard of) for filmic protagonists to narrate their own experiences incessantly to the audience. And, indeed, of all the three films I examine, *High Fidelity* is the most loquacious in its direct address.

In writing about the role of the master of ceremonies in *La Ronde* (examined in the next chapter), Deborah Thomas (1982) divides his role into its 'ethical', 'epistemological' and 'aesthetic' dimensions. These divisions are similarly useful for considering the function of direct address in *High Fidelity*. As we shall see, the ethical is important because of the judgements we are invited to make about what the hero expresses to us. Direct address must walk a tightrope here because the film largely succeeds or fails on its ability to make us 'identify' with Rob as the film's guiding point of experience[3] at the same time as making us laugh at his extraordinary insensitivity and immaturity. Rob's relationship to his story is complex too in terms of its epistemology. The story turns on his (in)ability to know himself and understand the viewpoints of others ('others' in this case being women; the men he works with – 'Barry' played by Jack Black and 'Dick' played by Todd Louiso – are practically his doubles). This may rather stretch what is meant by epistemology; however, there are other moments of the film that, because of the interweaving of subjective flashbacks and, for want of a better word, fantasised sequences, ask us to question the epistemological relationships between what Rob says and what the film shows. Rob's aesthetic role is of a very different nature to what Thomas identifies in *La Ronde*'s master of ceremonies (in *High Fidelity*, it is primarily in the choice of music as a part of modern taste cultures), but it is just as important. Rob's trajectory towards a greater degree of enlightenment involves an accommodation to difference in musical taste, much turning, as we shall see, on the distinction between 'credible' and 'cheesy' popular music. Given the particular role diegetic versus extra-diegetic music plays in *Le Notti di Cabiria*'s movement towards a 'transcendent' moment of direct address, it is interesting to note music's very important function in the more recent film. The ethical, the epistemological and the aesthetic meld together in sometimes complex ways and the opening of the film is (unsurprisingly) a good place to begin our examination of their inter-relationship.

Rob's viewpoint is articulated as a topic of the film from its very first moments, specifically in exploring the distinctions between his interior perspective and the external world, the relationship between what is inside and what is outside his head. The film begins with the precise synchronisation of the Touchstone Pictures logo to the sound of the crackle that begins a vinyl disc. The animation of the company's logo features a flash moving left to right. It completes its movement in time with the start of the opening chords of the 13th Floor Elevators' 'You're Gonna Miss Me' (a rock song with a proto-punk tempo and fuzzy guitar sound). The credits then roll (quite literally) in front of an image of a spinning record held close enough for us to observe its grooves. The camera movement along its surface threatens to move us away and out from it but instead a cut shows us a hi-fi amplifier as the song's lyrics, 'You didn't realise' (most apt in the context) repeat themselves. The camera pans along a cable running from the amp to headphones atop a head that faces away from us. As the camera moves, there is a gradual change in the acoustics of the song. As we move further away from the source of the music (the record playing through the electric amplifier) the song becomes less loud, more 'tinny', until the source of what we hear has clearly become the headphones. Like an over-loud iPod on a commuter train, we experience the music from the outside; the music is 'embodied' (one feels its physical presence in the space), but the body is not ours.

This transition is something like that from the extra-diegetic to the diegetic, though the position of the spinning record in the diegesis is ambiguous (the filmmakers abstracted the spinning disc from its surroundings; it may or may not be the same record being played by this man in this room). Fixing this distinction would be fruitless here. What is important is the distance this auditory and visual movement initially sets up. We are introduced to Rob in a way that asks us to observe rather than share his viewpoint – consider the difference made if the filmmakers had chosen to have Cusack facing towards us rather than away from us in the opening shot ('opening' at least what follows the credits). Here, however, one should be mindful of the visual chauvinism Claudia Gorbman warns against (1987: 2), as sound is at least as important as image; we are also invited to *hear rather than share* Rob's 'point of audition'. Other aspects of the framing convey a downbeat mood: the droning music, of course, but also the lighting that combines with the dark hair and dark blue shirt of the faceless figure; his posture also suggests slouching, but for the moment he is slouched away from us.

The distinction between intimacy and distance is activated in the cut to the next shot. With a 180-degree cut, Rob's face is revealed in close-up (see Figure 5.1). The lighting is diffuse, but Cusack's fair skin still reflects more light into a palette that has, up to now, been sombre; his eyes are especially highlighted, their reflectiveness suggesting they are close to tears. His look passes from screen-right to the centre and the camera's lens. As he looks at us, he asks, 'What came first: the music or the misery?' He then compares social concerns about violent videos with the emotional effect on kids of 'thousands of songs about heartbreak, rejection, pain, misery and loss'. He wonders, 'Did I listen

Figure 5.1 *High Fidelity* (Touchstone Pictures et al., 2000): our first view of Rob (John Cusack).

to pop music because I was miserable? Or was I miserable because I listened to pop music?' This questioning is accompanied by two glances away from the camera, the second performed with brow scrunched up in a way that suggests a search for an answer inside himself. However, already the self-pitying terms of the questioning make an enlightened discovery seem unlikely. From the film's opening moments, the tone of the performance (particularly in Cusack's voice and the movement of his eyes) has demanded emotional involvement with Rob, as well as encouraging preliminary judgements about the character's self-indulgent attitudes – I would take this combination to be fairly typical of a number of strands of screen comedy. Audience judgements of Rob become more pressing with the introduction of another perspective within the film.

The film cuts to the actress Iben Hjejle (who will be revealed to be 'Laura') putting on a coat as she walks towards the camera. Her entrance disrupts (though in an unassertive way) what has already been constructed. First, the filmmakers choose to have her walk into focus rather than remain in sharp focus throughout the shot; her hair colour (light blonde, the wispy edges of which are emphasised by rear lighting) and light-coloured clothing offer a strong contrast to Rob; though the continued music tells us we have not changed locale, the exact spatial relationship of this shot to the previous is initially unclear – it upsets the very ordered set-up of amplifier, lateral movement along headphone cable, and 180–degree cut from the back to the front of Rob's head. That these two occupy the same space (at least physically) is clarified as Laura leans down screen-right and we cut to her hand pulling the headphone jack from the amp. A rapid cut shows Rob grab the headphones and throw them to one side; he looks over his left shoulder upwards, creating an eye-line match with Laura that reveals anger as well as upset. The cumulative effect of Laura's entrance suggests incompatibility with Rob's central point of experience; her slightly out-of-focus entrance achieves this visually, and her cutting-off of the music, *his* music, does this aurally.

We have clearly entered *in media res* into a breakup, in which the woman is the active and the male the passive-aggressive participant; Rob asks Laura to stay in a tone of petulance rather than genuine entreaty. After she has awkwardly walked out the door, direct address further separates their viewpoints – that is, it demands that we intimately observe, if not entirely endorse, his, and further separates us from her. Rob slams the door and walks towards the camera with a hyper-masculine, aggressive gait. The fingers of his right hand spread out, and the rapid movements of his arms threaten a violent assault on the walls or the banks of records lining the corridor. He glares around him angrily before he looks at us, his arms adding emphatic emphasis to his words: 'My desert island, all time top five most memorable breakups, in chronological order, are as follows. . .'. Rob's pain and anger are channelled into his delivery of this line. He uses his left hand, in combination with furrowed brow and a bobbing of the head to add emphasis to 'desert island, all time'. Then, he raises his right arm and again spreads the fingers of the hand to indicate the 'top five' – Rob's compiling of lists is his way of fighting back against what he perceives as rejection.

Cusack's performance is highly mobile and undergoes a number of shifts. It is a delicate balancing act, for this opening must manage the expression of Rob's pain and indignation (his dishonesty is hinted at, but only truly revealed in retrospect) through charm – the film's direct address will succeed or fail on Rob / Cusack's ability to balance charm with comedy (laughing at him *and* with him at different moments) and pathos (sometimes 'pathetic' in all the senses of the word). As he says 'in chronological order', he performs pedantry with a hint of self-deprecation – he looks down and away from the camera and moves his right hand (index finger partly extended) as if miming leafing through a filing system. As he starts to move in another direction, he looks at the camera again, but only from the corner of his eye (Figure 5.2). Accompanying 'as follows', it suggests self-deprecation because it hints at Rob's awareness of the pomposity of his posturing and he seems slyly to be checking we are still on board.

This briefest of glances illustrates one way in which Cusack's performance constructs the matter-of-factness of *High Fidelity*'s direct address and negotiates the potential rupture it could represent. It would seem apt to talk of a 'confessional' quality to Rob's audience address, or to discuss its 'honesty', were its honesty not so hampered by failures of insight; Rob's to-camera discourse is, rather, 'ingenuous' in its appeal to our agreement or complicity. Both in terms

Figure 5.2 Rob checks we are still on board.

of narrative theme (an emotionally immature and / or shallow man's relationships with women) and the seemingly casual execution of its direct address,
the terrain resembles that of *Alfie* (Lewis Gilbert). The 1966 British film has
the eponymous hero (Michael Caine) address the audience as if expressing his
thoughts directly. In the manner of the theatrical aside (*Alfie* was an adaptation
of a play), Alfie's to-camera discourse is apparently invisible / inaudible to the
narrative's other characters and, like *High Fidelity*, this device is central to the
particular strategies of audience 'identification'[4] that the film sets up.

    As already noted, intimacy versus distance is often central to evaluations of
the role of direct address in different kinds of film practice but the two co-exist
in a film like *Alfie*. That film's central character seeks our complicity by appeal-
ing to common male fantasies of sexual conquest but, as the film progresses,
the harder he tries to justify himself and seek our acceptance, the further *the
film* distances Alfie's values from our own (that is, the values *Alfie* presumes of
its viewer). This develops not only through the increasingly vile misogyny of
Alfie's words and actions but by the film's opening up of a space between what
Alfie says about his actions and the what the film shows of their effect. In *High
Fidelity*, on the other hand, and in sly glances (such as that shown in Figure
5.2), a more ironic, self-deprecating complicity is sought. As we shall see, the
film does open up gaps between Rob's verbal narration and the film's wider
narration (that is, the images and sounds it presents to us), but these disparities
are, more often than not, papered over by this self-deprecating tone.

    Returning to the scene, Rob then moves to his right in a semi-circle that
brings him towards the camera, listing the women who make up his top five.
This closer position gives his subsequent claims added emotional weight, Rob

/ Cusack again furrowing his brow and tightening his mouth to suggest a barely contained well of pain: 'Those were the ones that really hurt.' Then a 180–degree cut moves the camera back towards the door, as he runs – almost skips – towards it: 'Can you see yourself on that list, Laura? Maybe you'd sneak into the top ten . . .'. The first line is shouted, so too the second, but its volume tails off. Rob turns away from the camera and walks back into the room (the camera tracking behind him). With his next line ('. . . but there's just no room for you in the top five'), his performance has returned to a register that is clearly delivered for himself and us alone.

At this stage in the film, Rob's shouting after Laura begs a question inherent in this kind of direct address: even if she had been present in the room while he was telling us about his top five breakups, would she have heard what he said? That is, does his speech to us, the audience (who, according to the 'worldhood' of most films, should not be accessible from the fictional world), take place in a realm occupied by the other characters? The answer is not simple, though there are enough instances of Rob addressing us in crowded public spaces in which his monologues go unremarked by passers-by for it to seem that Rob's direct address is the expression of 'private' thoughts (much like in *Alfie*) – I shall examine one such a moment below. In Frears's terms, direct address is simply a device for getting at his thoughts and nothing in the execution noted so far demands that we question his summation. What seems important is what Rob's direct address reveals about him as a character. Indeed, implicit in my choice of this film (and the two films examined either side of this one) is the fact that direct address is consistent with wider strategies in complexly 'rounded' characterisations. Unless Laura has been lingering on the stairs outside the apartment (and what we glimpse of her departure gives us no cause to suppose this), there is no way she could hear or even possibly understand his question, 'Do you see yourself in that top five, Laura?' If we keep alive for a moment the ambiguity of the external 'reality' of his direct address, one might go as far as to suggest that Rob shows evidence of a psychological disorder. Like a small child who might believe covering their eyes means they cannot be seen, this thirty-something male shows little grasp of the difference between what is going on inside his head and what exists outside of himself. However, this would be a grotesque characterisation of Rob, out of step with the tone of his presentation and the weight that direct address gives to his *self*-presentation. Rob is no sociopath; his actions, rather, demonstrate an immature understanding of self–other relations.

Back with the scene, Rob continues as if talking to the absent Laura, '. . . Sorry! Those places [in the top five] are reserved for the kind of humiliation and heartbreak you're just not capable of delivering.' He moves over to the amplifier and with one swift, petulant gesture turns up 'You're Gonna Miss Me' very loud. He runs to the window, an exterior shot looking up at him as a change in acoustics tells us the music is now blaring out into the street. He screams down at her (and, here, the delivery is unambiguously aimed at her), 'If you really wanted to mess me up, you should have got to me earlier.' This reveals a self-indulgent obliviousness or lack of interest in her feelings, actions or motivations – the effect on him is always the focus of his speech in this part of the film. It is also an example of the kind of pathetic actions that are often funny in the film – we see him at a number of points screaming after women (often in the driving rain) with a comical absence of dignity. Rob is a lovable loser, and he even fails to perceive the irony in the element of his life over which he has most control: his music collection.

'You're Gonna Miss Me' seems to have been chosen for its defiant tone, one constituted from the punkish style of the (male-performed) vocals and guitar sound, but particularly by the lyrics:

> You're gonna wake up one morning as the sun greets the dawn.
> You're gonna look around in your mind, girl, you're gonna find that I'm
>   gone.
> You didn't realize . . . [repeated several times]
> Oh! You're gonna miss me, baby [also repeated]
> I gave you the warning,
> But you never heeded it.
> How can you say you miss my lovin',
> When you never needed it?
> Yeah! Yeah! Ow!
> You're gonna wake up wonderin',
> Find yourself all alone,
> But what's gonna stop me, baby?
> I'm not comin' home.

Not all the lyrics are as audible as others and I have been selective as to which ones to transcribe, in order to highlight certain links between music and action. For example, as Laura pulls out the headphones, the song is stopped just before the word 'stop' in the penultimate line – the word is never heard, so presumably only music aficionados like Rob might be expected to appreciate the timing of its deletion. As he turns it back on and up loud, and then runs to the window, 'I'm not comin' home' blares out. With this song, initially listened to through headphones, Rob seems to have sought temporary escape from the immediate situation. Indeed, we have seen that Laura's bags were already packed and ready by the door so his petulant entreaty for her to stay really is textbook passive-aggressive behaviour (the recourse to psycho-babble seems apt for such a modern kind of navel-gazing as Rob's). Presumably, like many of the lovelorn souls who seek solace in the 'thousands of songs about heartbreak, rejection, pain, misery and loss' he earlier mentioned, Rob has chosen to wallow in one that he feels echoes his own thoughts and feelings. Ironically, however, he has chosen a song that could be said to see things from Laura's point of view, something of which he is, for the moment, incapable. Clearly, the song is presented from the perspective of one who is leaving, but some of the less emphasised lyrics seem remarkably clear-sighted about Laura's motivations. In retrospect, we understand that he was the one that failed to 'heed the warning'; he is the one who will realise, despite the exclusion of Laura from his 'top five breakups' (which he will later admit was dishonest), that he misses her; he is the one who, via the monologue of his direct address, will incessantly 'look around his mind'. This meaning is divorced from the spirit in which Rob intends it, and it is only once he has consciously come to terms with Laura's feelings (an imagining of another's position hinted at by the song, but unavailable to Rob in the opening scene) that their relationship will find a hopeful future.

The scene is concerned with epistemology only to the extent that it suggests narcissism, a mode of being that impairs one's ability to know what is outside of one's self. More cinematic issues of epistemology arise from the film's combination of straight-to-camera testimony with dramatised visualisations of that testimony – that is, flashbacks, fantasy sequences or dramatised representations of 'what really happened'. Such a structure inevitably raises questions of narrational 'reliability', particularly when the insight, honesty and thus *emotional reliability* of the film's narrator are as central as they are here. However, rather than pursue these issues theoretically, I want to approach them through the film's concrete detail.

The first thing to note is the patterning of the 'top five breakups' listed in the opening scene and the flashbacks that visualise the events Rob / Cusack recounts to the camera and / or microphone (if he is not seen on screen, his voiceover is regularly heard during this passage of the film). These breakups provide a structure for the subsequent twenty or so minutes of screen time, though he never reaches the fifth woman he had listed at the start (he eventually admits Laura's place in this elite pantheon: the fifth breakup 'had no effect on my life whatsoever, it was a casual thing . . . I just slotted her in to bump Laura out of position'). Each breakup is presented in a flashback sequence, the first image of which is always the female seen in long- or extreme long-shot. The woman or girl (the first breakup recounted was that with Alison Ashmore [Shannon Stillo], the focus of his six-hour-long love affair when Rob was fourteen) is thus presented as a somewhat remote and awe-inspiring figure, and Rob's voiceover always suggests a fundamental incomprehension of female subjectivity. Starting with the woman might, in another context, be seen to ascribe her particular force within the narrative, but this is clearly mitigated by Rob's 'editorial' or narrational role; the top five list obeys chronology but is, primarily, a facet of Rob's music geek way of ordering the world. He is, moreover, the only character with direct 'access' to the audience.[5]

A different piece of music is used for each flashback, another way in which Rob's worldview is echoed (visual chauvinism or not, the term 'view' is sometimes unavoidable). The development of the soundtrack hints at the imposition of this view, but this begins to take on ironic proportions. For example, the sequence showing the second of his breakups, a high-school romance with Penny Hardwick (Joelle Carter), is preceded by Rob's direct address on the platform of a railway station in which he lists her 'nice' musical tastes: 'her top five recording artists were Carly Simon, Carole King, James Taylor, Cat Stevens and Elton John'. The film's hero shares enough with the book's (for whom Elton John is 'mildly awful' – Hornby 1995: 49) for us to imagine Elton John is far from entering one of Rob's 'best of' lists, but his nostalgic hit, 'Crocodile Rock', accompanies the introduction of sweet-natured, pretty, blonde Penny. However, as Rob recounts (and we see) his incessant sexual advances (the refusal of which leads to the breakup), a much harder, rougher-sounding rock song (Joan Jett's 'Crimson and Clover') is heard. Thus the young Rob's aggressively sexual pursuit of Penny is echoed in the opposition of two different and, perhaps, incompatible styles of pop music.

But neither the visuals nor the soundtrack straightforwardly endorse Rob's perspective, and the music takes on a more strongly ironic dimension around the narration of his breakup with Sarah Kendrew (Lili Taylor). By this point, Rob has become increasingly depressed, and he returns to his apartment to continue his 'autobiographical' reorganisation of his record collection. He puts on Bruce Springsteen's very melancholy record, 'The River' and narrates his and Sarah's perfect 'match'; they matched principally because they were both depressed at having been recently dumped. The images that ensue are ironic in their romanticism and in the comic literalism of the match between music and visuals. Rob's dark, mainly black clothes, leather jacket and bandana, and Sarah's hooded jacket over checked shirt situate them firmly within the depressed white working-class milieu of the Springsteen song. 'The River', a lament about a love lost to harsh reality, in which the river is a symbol of redemption (but one which we learn is now 'dry'), accompanies their walk along Chicago's coast, waves crashing behind them. One of the film's funniest moments, these two depressives agree they want to be on their own for a while, before, rather quickly, deciding to embrace. Their clinch, caught against a dramatic, very pictorial backdrop, coincides perfectly with the breaking of waves behind them (Figure 5.3) – something about the sublime combining with the ridiculous springs to mind.

In the flashbacks, we appear to see the objective reality of Rob's past, though, clearly, the tone of its presentation is coloured by Rob's musical and romantic sensibilities. The film does offer two notable fantasy sequences, but

Figure 5.3 Ironic romanticism – the sublime and the ridiculous.

their exaggerated qualities authenticate rather than question the veracity of Rob's memories. The first is the Barry White-accompanied sex scene Rob imagines between Laura and her new boyfriend, Ian (Tim Robbins), which begins with a close-up of Ian's name tattooed on Laura's buttock. The second, also a product of anger and jealousy, is when the film shows us four successive versions of Rob's meeting with Ian, which visualise Ian's humiliation with increasing violence, before, finally, revealing the reality of Rob's impotence. Thus sex and violence, and the male anxieties upon which they are attendant, are shown to be particularly susceptible to imaginative distortion. A more ambiguous, boundary example comes when Rob imagines a meeting between Laura and their mutual friend, Liz (played by John's sister, Joan Cusack) – Rob's direct address tells us, 'I get the feeling that Liz talked to Laura'. This is offered to the audience as a means of explaining why Liz has just burst into Rob's record store and called him a 'fucking asshole'. We then see the meeting intercut with Rob's shame-faced to-camera testimony. Following the previous pattern, the woman concerned (here Laura) provides the starting point for the visualisation, but, in this case, her actions have a stronger sense of Rob-style organisation: 'She would have revealed at least two but maybe all four of the following four pieces of information . . .'. The film cuts between each of Rob's four baldly despicable acts and Laura's recounting of them to Liz. We see Laura using her hands to count off the relevant details much as Rob had done in the opening scene. This highly self-conscious mode of narration thus expresses a battle that commonly ensues amidst the recriminations of breakups – that is, the battle over the ownership of the facts of that breakup. Ultimately, however unwittingly, Rob reveals the inherent problems in his own means of organising his life story (a list of five or, in this case, four things) by giving further information (visualised by the film in a series of flashbacks) of the circumstances that go a long way towards mitigating his being an 'asshole'. Moreover, the reliability (in a loose sense, the 'realism') of the visualised meeting between Laura and Liz is upheld (or, at least, is not undercut) by the filmmakers' choice to visualise Laura stopping Liz from rising from their meeting in anger; had we seen Liz storm out directly, the connection between this and her shouting at Rob (she is wearing the same outfit in the meeting as she is wearing when she enters Rob's shop) would have underscored the subjectivity of Rob's 'I get the feeling . . .' narration.

More broadly, Rob's framing consciousness imposes limits on his – and, to some extent, our – understanding of the events that his direct address and voiceover narrate. For example, the narration of his relationship and then breakup with Penny presents her subjectivity at a remove: as already noted, we first see her, like all the other women, in long-shot and Rob's voiceover is almost ever-present. However, the film suggests the limitations on his and our vision and the possibility of a perspective outside of his immature view. As the adolescent Rob abandons Penny on the steps of her home, the film cuts from him walking away to a close-up of her distraught face – she says, 'Rob', her voice cracking in a tone that must be barely audible to the departing hero. Then a shot of Rob walking towards the camera (his past, flashback selves are never 'aware' of it) sees her, out of focus, in the background, slumping dejectedly on the steps. The performance of Penny and her placement in space remind one of the opening presentation of Laura as disruptive of, and largely excluded from, the film's visual and aural creation of Rob's central 'point of experience'; importantly, though, they both none the less represent *potential* subjectivities. The sequence then cuts to the young Rob faced with the obnoxious machismo of 'this asshole, Chris Thomson' (Jonathan Herrington), who, the voiceover informs us, told Rob he had sex with Penny after a couple of dates.

We do not see Penny again for nearly forty minutes of screen time when, now grown-up, she takes her place in Rob's quest to track down his ex-girlfriends. Over dinner, he rapidly and stutteringly addresses her: '. . . and you wanted to have sex with Chris Thomson and not me. And I was hoping you could help me understand why this keeps happening? Why I'm doomed to be left? Doomed to be rejected? Do you understand?' Rob raises his eyebrows with child-like entreaty, before Penny reveals that it was he who rejected her. She also tells Rob how sex with Chris Thomson fell only just short of rape, and after which she was unable to have sex till after college: 'That's when you should be having sex, Rob. In college! And now you want to have a little chat about rejection?! Well, fuck you Rob!' Penny then storms out of the restaurant.

Rob's incomprehension and insensitivity are played for laughs: 'That's right. *I* rejected *her*! That's another one to strike off my list! I should have done this years ago! Can I have the check, please?' Throughout his exchange with Penny, Cusack performs Rob with mouth slightly open and eyes suggesting a gormless searching for answers. After she has walked out, he looks around himself, the performance of enthusiasm and excitement (he waves his arms about for emphasis, bobs backwards and forwards in his chair) and his speech offering no recognition of Penny's trauma. Moreover, the camera is acknowledged (he glances at it a number of times), but never fully addressed. The comedy of Rob's obliviousness to others is, for the moment, inconsistent with the ingenuousness of his to-camera discourse. What is potentially unpleasant about Rob's self-obsession and limited understanding is carried off by Cusack's skills as a performer and (even harder to pin down) his 'charisma' – were this not the case, Rob would be too loathsome for us to bear such 'direct' access.

As already suggested, performance and the subtle permutations of pathos, comedy and charm are crucial to the effects of Rob / Cusack's audience address. In light of this, one might sum up the film's flashbacks as being essentially reliable, from an epistemological perspective, though they are subtly inflected by Rob's subjectivity and are subject to the irony resultant from the limits on Rob's insight. 'Unreliability' is, instead, worked through in the performance of direct address; self-deprecation and Rob's gradual and tentative movement towards a degree of enlightenment ultimately render 'unreliability' as something more like comical 'insensitivity'.

The questions of epistemology broached here are clearly also questions of ethics, in the sense that we are encouraged to judge Rob. The key role music plays in presenting his subjectivity (giving us an intimate insight into his character) and framing it (at times distancing our perspective from Rob's: a reading available from close attention to the music in the opening scene, for example) is also a matter of aesthetics. Indeed, as I suggested earlier, it becomes increasingly evident that one cannot separate these three things. With *Le Notti di Cabiria*, I suggested that the film's music, in its frequent straddling of the diegetic–extra-diegetic divide, could be said to represent the film's 'subconscious'. According to this logic, the shift the music undergoes in *Cabiria*'s final shot echoes and expresses the dawning realisation experienced by the character. Similarly, in *High Fidelity*, the music at times hints at truths not yet consciously available to Rob (as in the opening scene). Music forms a crucial part of the film's overarching rhetoric that determines, to a large extent, the meanings and effects that Rob's direct address may have. I wish now to devote some more analysis to uncovering the place music takes in Rob's trajectory from a kind of emotional myopia to a much greater degree of clear-sightedness. Showing that direct address can express both these things is an answer to the device's general neglect in film theorising and a response to the privileging of a narrow sense of the 'Brechtian' in previous discussions. However, if direct address can express both, it seems that music, one the most powerful vectors of subjectivity in the cinema, is needed.

Some of the film's funniest moments occur in and around the record store and Rob, Barry and Dick's musical snobbery. Jack Black's 'Barry' is the most aggressive in asserting the primacy of his musical knowledge and taste and, at one point, mocks 'the middle aged square guy' (Brian Powell) who comes into the store looking for Stevie Wonder's 'I Just Called to Say I Love You': 'It's sentimental, tacky crap,' Barry tells the man. 'Do we look like the kind of store that sells "I Just Called to Say I Love You"? Go to the mall.' An argument ensues with Rob, who is resentful of the rejection of paying custom. Barry counters: 'Rob – top five musical crimes committed by Stevie Wonder in the 80s and 90s go . . . ? Sub-question! Is it in fact unfair to criticise a formerly great artist for his latter day sins?!' Later, we will be able to measure Rob's emotional development in relation to his attitudes towards Stevie Wonder but, for now, a rigid adherence to taste demarcations contributes to the inertia that characterises Rob as a human being. A revealing exchange between Laura and Rob turns on this point:

> Laura: Make yourself happy.
> Rob: So why am I not happy?
> Laura: Because you're the same person you used to be? And I'm not . . . And all I've done is change jobs.
> Rob: And clothes and hairstyles . . . attitudes and friends.
> [. . .]
> Laura: . . . You haven't changed so much as a pair of socks since I've known you . . . At least you used to talk about the future and now you don't even do that . . . All I'm saying is: you have to allow for things to happen to people, most of all to yourself. And you don't, Rob.

All of Laura's criticisms are borne out by Rob's narration of his life: the organisation of things into lists that precludes a more flexible account of human experience; a direct address combined with flashback / visualisation structure that is inherently inwards and often backwards-looking. Moreover, a music aficionado like Rob defines himself largely by his tastes, which, though they must respond to developments in popular music, are based on some fundamental and often rigid demarcations. One of the most basic (and most pervasive in wider cultural evaluations of popular music) is based on the opposition between musical 'credibility' and 'cheesy' music. Popular music is 'credible' when it embodies the values of artistic integrity, indifference (though often feigned) to commercial gain, and 'authenticity' (authentic emotions, the authentic lifestyle of the musicians – 'sex, drugs and rock and roll' and so on). 'Cheesy' music, on the other hand, is 'sentimental, tacky crap' like 'I Just Called to Say I Love You' – an inauthentic, unearned striving for emotional affect, commercialism and a style susceptible to becoming 'dated'. This opposition is part of a complex matrix of values well beyond the scope of this investigation, but the film does present ways of managing this opposition. For one thing, it appeals to and thus flatters the audience's ability to recognise the difference between the two and, indeed, in this way the film could be seen as styling itself, essentially, as a more than usually 'realistic', 'credible' rom-com (romantic comedy).

A figure who disturbs this opposition by injecting credibility into cheesy music is Marie de Salle (Lisa Bonet). Rob is taken to her concert by Dick and Barry. Rob initially groans as he recognises de Salle playing a song by a very corny artist: Peter Frampton's 'Baby, I Love Your Way'. However, when he enters to see de Salle performing, he is awe-struck and just manages to hold back tears. The three musical snobs then stare longingly at the attractive black singer. Rob: 'I always hated that song.' Rick and Barry together: 'Yeeaahh.' Rob: 'Now I kind of like it.' Dick and Barry together: 'Yeeaahh.' Rob: 'Yeah.' Aside from her physical attractiveness, de Salle's ability to invest a cheesy song with emotional authenticity wins them over. She takes the position of the three men's most vaunted object of sexual desire, and Rob is at his most self-satisfied when he later recounts to us how he manages to bed her. Though the significance goes unexplored, a brief glimpse of de Salle's CD, which Rob puts on his hi-fi to comfort himself, further suggests her peculiar place in the film's aesthetic and thus emotional preoccupations. The track listing is printed on the top of the CD and reads:[6]

1. Baby I Love Your Way
2. Patsy Cline Times Two [a song of her own about breakups that she mentions to Rob]
3. Ghostbusters
4. Beat It
5. Baby Got Back
6. 911 is a Joke
7. I Will Survive
8. Mmm Bop
9. My Heart Will Go On
10. You Can't Have It
11. The Time is Now

The list contains a remarkable amount of famously cheesy pop: a novelty rap record about large bottoms (Sir Mixalot's 'Baby Got Back'), nightclub dance-floor favourites (Michael Jackson's 'Beat It' and Gloria Gaynor's 'I Will Survive'), the theme to *Ghostbusters* (1984) by Ray Parker Jr, and, most saccharine of all, that for James Cameron's 1997 blockbuster, *Titanic* (the Celine Dion hit, 'My Heart Will Go On').[7] In the film, Rob's encounter with de Salle is certainly not presented as an epiphany (in the book, the 'Baby, I Love Your Way' moment is presented as much more affecting – Hornby 1995: 48–50). However, she does represent an important symbol of the accommodation of opposing styles – not only is Peter Frampton very cheesy, he is also a 'very white' musician, and de Salle's race thus negotiates difference in another way.

Following the death of Laura's father, Laura and Rob get back together. In the film's more 'authentic' (and 'credible') take on romance, the reasons for their reunion are presented as her being too drained and tired *not* to be with him. Importantly, though, Rob is also shown to have matured as a person and manages one heartfelt apology to Laura. This maturation has followed a sustained period of depression and alienation, a period in which Rob / Cusack addresses the camera *relatively* rarely. Between his boasts about seducing de Salle (at 54 and 58 minutes, intermittently) and his to–camera compilation of 'top five things I miss about Laura' (at 1:16), points which mark a trajectory from narcissism to greater realisation via his deepest depression, he only looks at the camera for a brief aside (at 1:05). Though Rob's voiceover still features during this sequence, this is the passage of the film in which direct address features the least. It is as if his emotions during this passage are too raw to be performed so directly; a withdrawal into himself and away from the camera marks his suffering more poignantly.[8]

Although Rob moves towards reconciliation with Laura and comes to realise the extent of his feelings for her, this does not mean that his views suddenly are straightforwardly endorsed by the film. The film's rhetoric maintains its combination of intimacy and distance, sometimes framing Rob's attitudes ironically. Music takes an important role in this. For example, sitting in a diner, Jackie Wilson's cheerful love song, 'I Get the Sweetest Feeling' playing extra–diegetically on the soundtrack, Rob addresses us, describing how their relationship has developed: 'We talked about the future . . . important stuff . . . issues.' His performance conveys sincerity, a modest pride in his achievements in the relationship. The film then cuts to a good–natured exchange between Rob and Laura about her musical tastes:

> Rob: How can you like Art Garfunkel *and* Marvin Gaye? That's like
>   saying you support the Israelis and the Palestinians.
> Laura [deadpan]: No, it's not like that at all, actually, Rob, because Art
>   Garfunkel and Marvin Gaye make pop records.

This exchange is worth citing, as it further illustrates how the film's comedy is framed by Rob's direct address but not necessarily controlled by him (that is, we laugh *at him* in the juxtaposition of 'issues' with his silly recourse to the Arab–Israeli conflict), as well as the opposition between 'cheese' (Garfunkel) and 'credible' music (Gaye). In the film's clever weaving of references around music, his dismissal of Art Garfunkel and celebration of Marvin Gaye can also be seen to anticipate the end of the film.

In the penultimate scene, Barry's band gives a triumphant performance of Marvin Gaye's 'Let's Get It On' at the launch party for an album produced and released by Rob. The song has emotional significance for Rob and Laura (he had earlier told Laura that it is 'our song'), the setting significance for Rob's personal and professional development (as Laura tells him, 'You, the critic, the professional appreciator, are putting something new into the world. Congratulations, Rob'). The scene ends with Rob and Laura dancing together and then kissing passionately. We cut to Rob, sitting in his armchair next to his hi-fi. He begins to explain to us the rules for the making of a 'great compilation tape'. This to-camera address references two earlier scenes: he had begun to explain the same rules to us while making a tape for a young music journalist (Natasha Gregson Wagner) he has been flirting with, a sequence in which he ultimately realises the vanity of his failure to commit definitively to Laura; also, as these are the final moments of the film, the scene harks back to his position next to the hi-fi at the beginning. This time, however, the shot opens on Rob's face looking directly into the camera. And his performance here contrasts with the morose, self-pitying tone of his introduction. Cusack uses his characteristic quick-fire, clipped delivery, in combination with rapid looks away and then back towards us. He gives us some detail about the intricate rules for compilations but then cuts himself short: 'There are a lot of rules.' With these words, he looks at the camera, then rapidly looks back and forth away to his left. It is a moment of self-deprecation, suggesting he realises this is not what is important. 'Anyway . . .', he pauses and looks away for a few beats. He then looks at the camera more insistently than at any other point in this passage: '. . . I've started to make a tape, in my head, for Laura . . . full of stuff she'd like. Full of stuff that would make her happy.' A smile has formed on Rob's lips and these last two points are also delivered with a raise of the eyebrows that helps emphasise the sincerity and warmth of his feelings towards Laura (Figure 5.4). He then looks to his left again, turns his eyes back towards us and, raising his eyebrows, says, 'For the first time I can see how this is done.' In this way, Cusack times his responses to the camera's looking to give emphasis to a revelation in vision – the looking away suggests a drawing on a new found knowledge of how to 'make Laura happy' from within himself. As he does this, Rob holds his headphones up towards his face, the camera beginning to pull back and away from him, a movement preparing us to leave Rob's world.

This leaving of the narrative is also achieved (as in many films) through

Figure 5.4 Rob's final, open, heartfelt direct address.

music. Given the important role of music in the performance of direct address we have seen previously, the development of the soundtrack has particular relevance here. A song begins to play just after Rob's words, 'I've started to make a tape.' Its volume gradually builds, but as this bears no correlation with any of Rob's physical actions, it is evidently not of the immediate diegesis. The mention of 'in my head' then suggests the song is emerging from Rob; 'in my head' had further significance because, when he had begun making a tape for the music journalist, Caroline, he had been making incessant scribbles on a piece of paper. The 'internal' source of the music now suggests a new degree of emotional investment, in contrast to the use of the headphones to place us 'outside' of Rob's head in the film's opening shot. As Rob puts the headphones on, the song continues to build. We begin to recognise Stevie Wonder's voice. The camera continues to pull back, Rob leans forwards to the hi-fi, hits a button on the tape deck, an action that coincides with a ranking up of the song's volume and the explosion of its chorus: 'I believe when I fall in love with you it will be forever.' The film fades to black, leaving Rob sitting back in his chair, looking up and into the distance, tapping his fingers against his headphones and moving his feet in time to the music.

The surface meaning of the music, the romantic optimism it embodies, its pure, unalloyed commitment, might be seen to be offset by situation – Rob is, after all, back (physically) where he was at the start, and he is still expressing himself through compilation tapes. However, to emphasise this would be ungenerous and contrary to the moment's tone. His performance and the choice of music are of overwhelming optimism. The music is optimistic also because, though it may not be one of Wonder's 1980s 'musical crimes' (it is from a 1972 classic album, *Talking Book*), it suggests a degree of accommodation to shamelessly sentimental (if not tacky) music; though Barry may not have, Rob has clearly forgiven Stevie Wonder for his latter-day sins. It should be noted that the song is also associated with Art Garfunkel (it appears on his second solo album, *Breakaway*, 1975), the artist that Rob cannot believe any self-respecting Marvin Gaye admirer could like.

Rob's final looks into the camera fulfil the gesture's potential to express openness, honesty and clear-sightedness. Throughout the film, this has always been *Rob's* tacit claim for his audience address. However, the wider rhetoric of the film has frequently framed Rob's direct address as a failure of openness, honesty and vision. It is difficult to imagine the expression of this shift without the use made of music in the opening and closing scenes, both in terms of the meanings of the chosen songs and in their acoustic and more abstract qualities. The embodied sound of 'You're Gonna Miss Me' ('embodied' in the sense of its existence in space: in this case, the private space of the headphones from which we are initially separated) contrasts with the disembodied clarity of 'I Believe (When I Fall In Love It Will Be Forever)' (the music may build in volume but it is 'disembodied' in the absence of any discernable acoustical qualities; its aural clarity places it outside the diegesis).

One is reminded of the ending of *Le Notti di Cabiria*, in which the only moment of direct address is experienced as a transcendence and a revelation of vision partly because of the shifts in scoring. Similarly, the music at the end of *High Fidelity* suggests that Rob has overcome his previous problems because of the harmony between his looking inside of himself and the way music is used. Perhaps music alone can match direct address's force as a gesture that crosses the boundary between the inside and outside of the film world. As Claudia Gorbman remarks, '[music's] ease at crossing narrational borders puts [it] in a position to free the image from strict realism' (1987: 4); 'the only element of filmic discourse that appears extensively in nondiegetic as well as diegetic contexts, and often freely crosses the boundary line in between, is music' (ibid.: 22). Of course, this kind of music is much more common than direct address but the latter derives its force partly from its place on the boundary that Gorbman evokes. We shall again see the harmony between music and direct address in the fictional world of the film examined in the next chapter.

NOTES

1. The star of the film adapted the screenplay with D. V. DeVincentis, Steve Pink and Scott Rosenberg. The DVD extras tell us that the writers (with the exception of Scott Rosenberg, who, it seems, was brought in at a later

stage) grew up together in Chicago. The DVD extras present the production as a space of male bonding much like the world of the record shop in
which Cusack's character works.

2. See the blog by Steven Wells (2008), which discusses the importance of
list-making to the sub-culture Rob represents and to music journalism
more broadly.

3. Claudia Gorbman uses the term 'point of experience' as a response to the
'visual chauvinism' of saying 'point of view' (1987: 2). It is apt for *High
Fidelity* because the lead character's identity is so bound up with the choice
of popular music on the soundtrack – the soundtrack often originates with
Rob materially (because he owns the central setting of the record store)
and, at other points, more abstractly. I shall deal with the music through a
discussion of Rob's 'aesthetic' role.

4. The important critiques of the notion of 'identification' in our experience
of film (see especially Murray Smith 1995) require the use of inverted
commas here. While I accept that the term is inherently problematic, and
that Murray Smith's 'engagement' (with the clarifying sub-categories of
'recognition', 'alignment' and 'allegiance') is generally preferable, I am
unwilling here to forego a term that is in such common usage. It is central to
the film's claims to say something about the (late twentieth- / early twenty-
first-century Western) male psyche that we are asked to 'identify' with
Rob through what he says to us and the choice of music on the soundtrack.
Popular music has a particularly strong role in such claims, though I can
only really touch upon this topic here.

5. The exception to this is Bruce Springsteen's cameo appearance as himself.
As Rob decides that he will call his ex-girlfriends to try to get to the bottom
of his many romantic failures, a guitar begins playing on the soundtrack.
Then, sitting in some recording studio, Springsteen appears on screen
facing the camera, sometimes looking into it, sometimes looking down
at the guitar he is playing. His words address Rob, not us, and echo the
thoughts Rob also narrates into the camera. This moment could thus be
seen as an example of an 'axial shot-reverse-shot', as discussed by Perez
(2008), as it presents a discussion between Rob and Springsteen rather than
a moment of direct address *per se*. It also visualises Rob's solipsistic view of
the world as he is shown to imagine a dialogue that is really only a monologue; moreover, the moment references a Springsteen song, 'Bobby Jean',
which features a phoned attempt to try and track down an ex-girlfriend
(this reference is taken directly from Hornby's book – 1995: 122). However,
this moment ultimately underlines the enormous complexities of looking
into the camera because Springsteen's stature as a star perhaps exceeds the
subjectivity of its framing. Also, given my discussion of direct address as a
facet of particularly privileged (or, at least, dominant) narrators, it is also

appropriate that 'the boss' (a sobriquet often used for Springsteen) should be the only other figure in the film permitted to look into the camera.

6. It should be admitted that the songs are only all readable with the help of freeze frame, making this something of an inside joke, but a revealing one none the less.

7. The one truly unfathomable entry is militant black hip-hop group, Public Enemy's '911 is a Joke' – a song from their 1990 album, *Fear of a Black Planet*. This may link somehow with the film's positions on race. In the film, Marie de Salle's exoticism and allure is linked to her racial identity (though very fair-skinned, Bonet has her hair in dreadlocks). In the London-based book, de Salle is exotic because she is an American; in the American film, it appears that she is exotic partly because she is black.

8. The same thing happens in the depressed middle act of *Alfie*, where the cocky hero has his confidence shaken by illness (this happens in both the original 1966 version and the recent 2004 remake, the illnesses being a 'shadow on the lungs' and impotence respectively). *Annie Hall* (1977) also sees the hero's direct address become less frequent during its middle section, suggesting there may be a pattern for direct films such as this – that is, that the device recedes as the narrating figure gets embroiled in the central dramatic conflicts and problems.

CHAPTER 6

La Ronde (1950)

La Ronde was Ophuls's first film in France after returning to Europe from Hollywood. It was his second adaptation of an Arthur Schnitzler play (the first being his 1933 filmed version of *Liebelei*). Schnitzler's 1897 *Reigen* (often known as *La Ronde*, due, in part, to the success of Ophuls's adaptation – Perkins 1982: 32) had scandalised the Viennese society whose sexual behaviour was the play's focus. The play comprises ten interconnected episodes, each centring on a sexual encounter. Seen by some as an allegory for the transmission of syphilis through all strata of turn-of-the-century Viennese society (see Marcus in Schnitzler 1982: xi), the play begins with the coming together of a prostitute and a soldier, and literally comes full circle with the final encounter between the same prostitute and a count. Between these points, from one episode into the next, one of the partners moves to the next. The film presents to us a pattern of interweaving couples that is waltz-like, an analogy Ophuls's film is explicit about, though a dance more traditionally characterised by the command to 'change your partners' is more apt to the content of the narrative – indeed, a *'reigen'* is just such a dance.[1]

Ophuls follows Schnitzler's structure precisely, though he renders this structure more self-conscious with the addition of a master of ceremonies, the *'meneur de jeu'* ('leader of the game'), played by the Viennese-born actor Anton Walbrook. The *meneur* wanders in and out of the fiction, guiding the viewer (and occasionally other characters) through a meta-fictional space that sometimes appears at the edge of the main, period-set space of the drama. A carousel is a key feature of the meta-fictional space, and a concrete embodiment of the circular trajectory of the interweaving narratives. The *meneur*'s interactions with the carousel suggest he is the only one aware of its ambiguous 'presence' and, similarly, the only one aware of the causality its circularity symbolises. As well as manning the carousel, the *meneur* assumes a number of roles within the central narrative, disguising himself as a waiter, a soldier and other figures. Otherwise, he is dressed in his uniform of top hat and tails (the film's introduction establishes this, too, as an assumed costume). Crucially, the *meneur* addresses the viewer throughout, both speaking to us and frequently looking directly into the camera; with one brief but notable exception, he is the only character to do so.

Already, it will be clear that direct address is once more intimately tied to questions of narrative causality and expresses one character's access to perspectives normally unavailable from within fictions. *La Ronde*'s eloquent self-consciousness makes it an ideal case study through which to bring together these issues, as well as to ask broader questions about how films construct their fictional worlds. Indeed, the role direct address plays in relation to the 'worldhood' of the film's world is something I shall focus on with reference to V. F. Perkins's defining essay on this topic (2005). I will begin with the remarkable long-take that Perkins describes as Max Ophuls's 'brilliant essay in film aesthetics' (ibid.: 34).

As the film begins, there is a clear continuity in tone between the credits and the film that follows. The Oscar Strauss theme (used at various points in the film), combined with the borders and calligraphy of the caption cards, situates us within an old-world register. (The continuity is noteworthy, given the calm, collected nature of the *meneur*'s presentation of events; contrast this with sudden shifts in scoring over *Le Notti di Cabiria*'s credits *and* in the performance of its heroine.) Given the *meneur*'s meta-fictional role already noted, a key question one might expect to ask of the opening is, does he create and / or shape the film's world or does it seem to pre-exist him? The choice of opening offers no clear answer to this, and the performance and filming maintain this hesitation, at least for a while. With the credits' completion on a fade-out and a rising series of harp notes, the film fades from black to a view of the *meneur* emerging on to a scene (the French *scène*, which can mean 'scene', 'stage' and 'setting', is most apt here). For the briefest of moments we hear his footsteps before we see him, their considered rhythm accompanying a new passage of the score. A slightly different choice for his appearance (we might have seen the space for a few beats before we saw him; a cut to him in the space might have added a stronger sense of him as focus) might have guided us towards determining his status vis-à-vis the film world more strongly. As it is, the camera movement (tracking left to right and forward) neither exactly follows him nor seems to lead him. He appears as if emerging *out of* the fade-in, appearing at the right of the frame as the image reveals a space lit, it seems, from in front of him, so that he begins the film as a silhouette, his features only becoming clearer as he reaches some stairs. He has crossed a different sort of threshold by the time he has reached this point (we are only about seven seconds in): floorboards have given way to cobbles and he appears to have reached an exterior setting. Or, rather, he has reached an 'exterior setting', for this set is still presented *as a set*. Throughout the film, though it always has a strong sense of being set-bound (at the very least, it always has that quality one feels in one of Ophuls's earlier versions of 'Vienna', *Letter from an Unknown Woman*, 1948), he is the sole character to occupy these liminal spaces – they are the 'meta-fictional' spaces, but are liminal (at the limits of things) because they bleed into other kinds of spaces.

He begins to speak. His eyes do not yet address us, only his words: 'And me? What am I in this story, 'La Ronde'? The author? The compère? A passer-by?' (my translation). As he talks, his ambling walk has taken him past a backdrop of baroque architectural splendour, and then a small stage. On completing the questions about his role, he pauses and, for the first time, looks up from the floor. However, he is not yet looking to the space around him for answers and the gesture is casual, resigned, as if he accepts he must offer some sort of answer: 'I am you. That is, I am someone, no matter whom, amongst you.' The pace of his speech is languid, the accent is softly Germanic. He pauses again, clearly searching for the words to define his role properly: 'I am . . . the incarnation of your desire . . . your desire to know everything. Men [*les hommes*] only ever grasp one part of reality. Why? Because they see only one aspect of things. Me . . . I see it all . . . because I see . . . in the round [*en rond*].' His choice of words (*les hommes* [men], rather than '*l'homme*' [man]) is perhaps significant and, at the very least, establishes a degree of distance between the *meneur* and other males. With 'because I see', the *meneur* looks up and outwards towards the camera, but he only looks directly at it with the words '*en rond*' (see Figure 6.1). Thus the claims for his particular vision are given weight with this look that breaks the normal bounds of film fictions.

The *meneur*'s eyes move away from the camera and upwards as he thinks out loud again. His speech continues, the tone bordering on the complacent: 'And that permits me to be everywhere at once. Everywhere.' The final, repeated word is accompanied by a kind of shrugging gesture, and is intoned in a breathy way that says, 'This is how it is Why deny it?' However, these claims of omniscience will be undermined at particular moments of the subsequent narrative, and the *meneur*'s delivery, though always characterised by a charming élan, will not always be so sure of itself. Indeed, in retrospect, the 'everywhere' is delivered (by Walbrook, not the *meneur*) in consciousness of its ultimate hubris.

The questions he asks as he continues his movement through the space become less rhetorical: 'But, where are we now? On a stage? [He walks along the stage] In a studio?' With the latter words he moves into a space screen-left previously unexplored. The delivery of the question suggests some genuine perplexity (he furrows his brow) and as he sees what is clearly a film lighting rig and a boom microphone (see Figure 6.2), he looks around himself as if

Figure 6.1 *La Ronde* (Films Sacha Gordine, 1950): as he looks at us for the first time, the *meneur* (Anton Walbrook) defines his vision '*en rond*'.

surprised. As he continues walking screen-left (previously his movement had been back and forth; the direction now suggests 'we are getting somewhere'), his perplexity continues. He says tentatively, '[we are] in a street'. But then the steady pace of his walk pauses for a moment, he raises his arms as if welcoming a revelation: 'Ah! We are in Vienna . . . 1900.' The words '1900' are drawn out (he says, '*dix neuf . . . cent*'), as if he is aware this is an approximation. As he makes this discovery (for it does have the feel of a discovery), he begins to remove some of the garments that initially marked out his contemporaneity (that is, their '1950–ness'). Without stopping, he takes off his raincoat and silk scarf, and tells us 'A change of costume'. He slips on a combination coat and cape (the costume conveniently ready on a hat stand) over his white shirt and bow tie, and dons a top hat. A cane and white gloves complete his formal dress. '1900 . . . we are in the past. I adore the past. It's so much more restful than the present . . . and so much more sure than the future.' 'Restful' and 'sure', descriptions of the time and place but also of the performance style offered to us by the *meneur* / Walbrook.

The *meneur* has taken us across a meta-fictional threshold that would be dizzying in its many *mise-en-abymes* if we were not guided with such sureness

Figure 6.2 A film camera and boom microphone enter shot.

of footing. We have passed a stage (in size, somewhere between full-sized and puppet show, depicting a more miniature version of the miniature background of the surrounding set), we have passed the technology of filmmaking (see Figure 6.2 again) and now we move more deeply into the fiction. The *meneur* seems happy with our trajectory. As he wanders along a '1900', 'Vienna' street, stronger shadows trigger his speech: '*Voilà*, the sun' (a light source behind the camera reflects off the background). He then tells us it is springtime, a fragrance 'that raises questions of love, does it not?' This, the last but one of the prologue's rhetorical questions (soon he shall have a companion in his world to address questions to), introduces the story's key theme, 'love'. He continues in his movement: 'So that love can begin its round, what is missing? . . . A waltz. Here is the waltz.' Then, as he moves into a large square, which contains the carousel he has designated as this particular dance, the score changes to the introduction of a waltz. His speech responds to the change in rhythm and suggests a move into song.

The first two lines of the song are spoken, but there are recurrent crossings and recrossings of the threshold between speech and song (throughout the film he often speaks melodically, and Walbrook's modest singing is only just raised above normal speech). The lyrics of the song are worth quoting in their entirety (but, it should be noted, the rhymes have been lost in my translation):

> [Spoken] The waltz turns, the carousel turns . . . and the round of
> love can turn also. [Now sung] Turn, turn, my characters. The earth
> turns day and night. The rainwater changes into clouds and the clouds
> return as rain. Honest woman [*femme*] or tender *grisette* [*grisette*[2] *tendre*],
> aristocrat or, even, soldier . . . When love comes to take them, everyone
> dances the same step. Now the round starts. It is the calm hour when
> the day dies. Look! Here comes the working girl [*la fille*] and, there, the
> round of love [*la ronde de l'amour*].

With the line, 'it is the calm hour . . .', the lighting fades to turn the scene back to night time. There was no particular reason to begin the film at night, take us through a spring morning and into the night again, except to show that such transitions are possible, but the very gradual lowering of the lights still refuses to endow the *meneur* with god-like omnipotence; 'Look! Here comes the working girl' maintains the sense of encounter between the *meneur* and the world.

The *meneur* has already assigned the carousel a range of symbolic functions, from the more ephemeral metaphor of '*la ronde de l'amour*' to the more concrete symbolism (thus something closer to metonymy) 'here is the waltz'. Moreover, the lyrics establish the carousel as a 'whirling allegory' (Masao Yamaguchi's description of the circus in *Lola Montès*: 1978: 65) for the passage of time, the cycles and rhythms of life and, especially, for love. However, the change in lighting also brilliantly but more simply turns the carousel, for a moment, into a night-time street, the proper setting for '*la fille*' (Simone Signoret; see Figure 6.3). She propositions the *meneur* but he responds, 'Ah, no. There's an error, *madame*.' She initially takes this polite address as mockery (the distinction between formal and familiar forms of address ['*vous*' and '*tu*'] runs throughout the film) but he responds, 'I never mock.' At her repeated invitation to 'join' her, he explains, 'I am not in the game . . . I lead the round [*Je mène la ronde*]. Do you understand? And it is with you that it starts.' He points her towards the street corner where, she is told, she must accost the sixth soldier she sees. She accepts his direction willingly enough.

It is significant that *la ronde* (and *La Ronde*) must begin with a woman, and the lowliest, most vulnerable figure in the film's class system. This enables its narrative to take not only a cyclical form (it begins and ends with her) but also to resemble a spiral moving upwards through the class strata (it begins and ends, respectively, with her encounters with a lowly private and a wealthy count, who is also a senior officer in the military). But more than this, seeing the film as a whole, women provide the characters with whom the *meneur* is

Figure 6.3 'La Fille' (Simone Signoret) appears on the carousel's 'street'.

most honest about his extra-/meta-narrative role; there is also a sense, often difficult to pinpoint, that his allegiance is with them. Though duplicity characterises all the relationships (it is inherent to the structure of *La Ronde* that each partner 'betrays' their previous), the men's romantic motives seem often the more suspect.

The sequence ends with the *meneur* giving a name to what follows: 'The prostitute and the soldier [*la fille et le soldat*]'. A wipe gives finality to what was a single take of almost five minutes (to be precise, four minutes, fifty-three seconds). This bald fact alerts us to elements of the filming and staging of the introduction not yet noted. The *meneur* is kept in long-shot for most of the sequence, presenting him as a part of his world, a world he sometimes seems close to conjuring but more often seems to encounter. The spectator has been held at some distance both spatially and in terms of the way the performance itself is constructed; as already noted, the *meneur* only briefly looked at the camera as he told of his vision ('*en rond*'), and for much of what follows, he wanders through the setting looking at the space around him, not at us. This distance has invited us to observe a measured, considered and, above all, elegant performance through which the *meneur*'s role and the relationship he claims to the spectator evolve. This relationship shifts to a more intimate

See, here come the lady of sin

Figure 6.4 The *meneur* sings to us.

register when the *meneur* begins to sing. Now, he looks at the camera more insistently (Figure 6.4; he looks at us again when he returns to this position to name the subsequent episode).

The presence of song amplifies the sense of knowingness evident in this introduction in some obvious and some less obvious ways. It is a cliché of the film musical (or a cliché of many people's reactions to the musical) that, in flagrant disobedience of the rules of realism, suddenly characters know the words to songs that spring forth as if out of nowhere. Here, this aspect of musical performance, and the more sustained intimacy with the camera it allows, add to the sense that the *meneur* has found his place, the role required of him within his world. From searching for the right words to describe his role and the space he encounters, his singing then communicates, 'I know the words. I know what this world is about.' In *La Ronde*, music recurs at various points and takes on a structural significance beyond this moment. At the very least, in light of the 'musical subconscious' of *Cabiria* / Cabiria, and the more prosaic obsession with music encountered in *High Fidelity*, one again sees that there is something about music (its often threshold status between different levels of narrative / narration; the diegetic versus extra-diegetic distinction) that resonates with the shift achieved by addressing the film audience 'directly'.

*

A brief detour via the film's critical reception will be instructive because the difficulty the film poses for some influential strands of film studies can be seen, in some ways, as a *mise-en-abyme* of the 'problem' direct address may pose. The first thing to note about the film's critical status is that it is rarely discussed. A relatively recent reissue of the film on DVD may, of course, change this but it is perhaps revealing that, in Susan White's book on Ophuls, the most sustained study of the director to date, her (broadly) feminist focus finds little space for the film. *La Ronde* seems to have been added as an afterthought and receives less than three pages of direct analysis in a 371–page book. White sums it up thus: 'This extraordinarily conscious, everyday work of leading women to the various humiliations and small triumphs of love has the painful clarity and inexorable quality of daylight' (1995: 241). 'Extraordinarily conscious' and 'everyday work' in this context seem to equate the film's formalism with the sense of the *meneur* 'just doing his job' (ibid.: 240; more of which later) but it also implies that the film is in some way self-evident; the fact of its extraordinary (self-)consciousness seems to dissuade further commentary. Indeed, via the *meneur*, the film may be said to 'speak for itself' and White's final evaluative point ('clarity and inexorable quality of daylight') sits in harmony with my emphases on making theoretical points emerge from the detail of the film. However, if this kind of self-consciousness were a barrier to analysis, it would prove a problem for the consideration of many Ophuls films, especially his later ones, and for direct address itself.

As suggested in the Introduction, '*Screen* Theory' offers the most immediate critical vocabulary for talking about direct address, but it struggles to account for the effects my analysis of a number of films has uncovered. For similar reasons, *Screen* Theory is, I think, inadequate when faced with the films of Max Ophuls. The Paul Willemen-edited booklet on Ophuls (1978) is the most sustained example of the 'problems' Ophuls presents and I would refer the reader primarily to Andrew Britton's (1982: 91–8) devastating critique of the collection and of the difficulty '*Screen* Theory' (and Colin MacCabe [1974] more specifically) have with an artist like Ophuls. It is a varied collection of works but many of the writers reach for a comparison with Brecht[3] (or, to be more precise, the narrow assumption we have encountered previously of what 'Brechtian' means) rather than engage with the film director in his particularity. Willemen's rather odd editorial commentary underlines, however, that the politics of Ophuls's relationship to the 'mainstream' is the crux of the matter, a fact further illustrated by Stephen Heath's rather impenetrable entry. Susan White astutely observes that the binaries in which Heath operates ('illusionistic mainstream narrative cinema' versus the avant-garde) make him incapable of dealing with the 'in-between-ness' of Ophuls's practice (White 1995: 7). If Ophuls presents a problem for the theory associated with 1970s *Screen*, it is because his films' 'exhibitionist' or 'theatrical' qualities were difficult to fit into the dominant paradigms for the popular cinema – Ophuls became either a mannered exception to the dominant style, or really an avant-garde filmmaker masquerading as the director of popular Hollywood, French and German films. As noted earlier, the work of Christian Metz became central to the theory that placed voyeurism at the cinema's heart, a medium defined by its projection of figures on to a screen who do not and cannot acknowledge the hidden spectator. The combination of Freudian and Lacanian psychoanalysis with a criticism *engagé* of industrial cinema's inherent 'illusionism' (a cause for which Brecht was often called upon) rarely acknowledged a place for exhibitionism in this model for the cinema, if not outright denied it. In looking at this theory through the particular lens of direct address, we can see the way the device was slotted into a schema in which psychoanalysis was called upon to uncover truths 'classical' cinema revealed *unwittingly*. In passing over the appearance of direct address in more mainstream cinema, direct address became associated with the more sophisticated *consciousness* expressed by avant-garde filmmakers through their films. Within such a relatively rigid framework such as this, the *meneur*'s to-camera discourse sits uneasily.

If the film theory associated with 1970s *Screen* finds difficulty accommodating Ophuls as anything other than a mannered exception, the film criticism of the journal *Movie* was the site of the most sophisticated investigations of Ophuls's style. The special issue on Ophuls and melodrama (1982) locates him within a much wider generic context, while tackling head-on the self-consciousness of many of his films. Douglas Pye's essay on *Le Plaisir* (1952), for example, makes repeated links to *La Ronde* in examining another film that dramatises the processes of dramatisation and, in the guise of an occasionally on-screen narrator, 'Maupassant' (*Le Plaisir* is an adaptation of some Guy de Maupassant stories), asks similar questions to *La Ronde* vis-à-vis narrational 'reliability'.[4] Like Pye's, Deborah Thomas's entry on *La Ronde* (one of the only published essays on the film I am aware of) examines Ophuls from the ground up and does not advance from so fixed a position on cinematic illusionism as was current in much film writing of the time. This is not, however, a negation of theory, but a re-emphasis, for Thomas draws upon aspects of Freud's writing in a way that, following Metz, the Freudianism of 1970s *Screen* generally neglected. Thomas notes how Freud himself understood voyeurism and exhibitionism as two sides (passive and active) of the same coin. Using this as a way of talking about the relationship between the *meneur*'s role as observer with our own, she notes:

> It is . . . precisely the 'sexual problems' of Schnitzler's characters
> which engross our voyeuristic interest and that of the *meneur de jeu*.
> Furthermore, our 'desire to know' is in some sense analogous to the
> patterns of sexual desire and pursuit of the characters in the narrative

itself, but it is less explicitly sexual in two respects: its aim is looking
rather than copulation and its object is not a person but a process, and
a representational one at that – that is, what we desire to look at is not
a person we desire, but a filmic depiction of the process of desiring.
(1982: 74–5)

Thomas indicates the complex layers of metaphor and metonymy made
concrete in the film's constitution of its narrative. She goes on to quote the
meneur's discussions with the count (Gérard Philipe), one of the narrative's
most knowing participants: 'I'm not a servant, Count. I'm here through love
of art . . . Through love of the art . . . of love!'

The object of [the *meneur*'s] visual desire is neither the unfolding of
the count's desire for the actress nor the representation of the actress,
but an amalgam of the two: the object of his visual desire is the
representation of the unfolding of the count's desire for the actress! His
voyeurism is above all theatrical, aestheticized. (Thomas 1982: 75)

The *meneur*'s role as observer thus moves from a relatively unsexual, artistic
form of voyeurism into exhibitionism through his role as an agent in the narrative. The *meneur* is seen adopting various 'disguises' throughout the narrative, clearly relishing certain opportunities to dress up. Thus, as a sometimes
agent within the narrative but more often a distanced orchestrator or observer
of events, his 'aesthetic' and 'ethical' roles mesh. Moreover, as we shall see,
these two terms (though with strong etymological links, often falsely opposed)
ultimately mesh via the role of direct address.

Thomas sums up the impact of Ophuls's choice to introduce this master of
ceremonies to Schnitzler's material:

Schnitzler's play is nudged from centre-stage, so to speak, by the extra-
narrative *meneur de jeu* . . . whose relationship to the Schnitzler material
– and no longer the material itself – is what the film is about. But this
relationship is a shifting and ambiguous one, further complicated by the
concomitant shifts in our relationship – as filmic spectators – to both
the narrative and the extra-narrative *meneur de jeu* himself. (Thomas
1982: 74)

Thomas provides a useful vocabulary for investigating the function of the
meneur and his relationship to the fiction – indeed, her division of the *meneur*'s
role into 'epistemological', 'aesthetic' and 'ethical' functions proved useful in
the analysis of *High Fidelity*. The 'shifting and ambiguous' relationship she
notes is evident not only when one investigates the structure of the narrative,

but is also visible in particular choices about the way direct address is presented and performed. Thomas's schema for identifying the *meneur*'s numerous functions within the text is intricate and provides a valuable response to Ophuls via Freud, one which respects the former's complexity without, crucially, neglecting the stylistic pleasures of *La Ronde*. However, there are limits to Thomas's approach to the film because divisions of the *meneur*'s roles inevitably neglect the insouciance of their combination. I hope to show that a more specific focus on direct address and the meanings it carries as a declamatory, 'outward' act help us uncover an even greater degree of thematic richness than Thomas acknowledges.

What is needed is a theoretical framework that treats the film holistically while finding a proper place for direct address within the whole. Such an approach is hinted at by Thomas but given more definite shape in the later writing of one of her *Movie* contemporaries, V. F. Perkins. Perkins's 'Where is the World? The Horizon of Events in Movie Fiction' sets out to address a long-taken-for-granted aspect of film narration and 'to show that the fictional world of a movie is indeed a world and, by means of a few concrete examples, to sketch some of the ways it matters that a fictional world is a world' (2005: 16).[5] This deceptively simple project considers the relationship between the world occupied by the viewer (our 'real world') and the world presented and created by the fiction. Thus the distance between a naturalist fiction and something in the genre of fantasy could be measured by the degree to and manner in which 'real' and fictional worlds overlap – in fiction, even in those works that aspire to the greatest 'realism', there would never be a perfect fit (for example, there is a 'Nana' in the world of Zola's 1880 novel, *Nana*, but not in the real world into which the novel was released, though there was a Franco-Prussian war in both). From this broad field of enquiry, there are three particular elements of Perkins's argument especially pertinent to *La Ronde*: first, the significance of knowledge to a film world being a world; second, the possible roles of artifice within a fictional world; and third, the particular significance within this implied for direct address.

First:

> The world of *Citizen Kane* [1941] is constituted as a world partly
> because, within it, there are facts known to all, to many, to few
> and to none. The phenomena of a world are independent of
> perception, though in principle and most of the time available to
> it. To be in a world is to know the partiality of knowledge and the
> boundedness of vision – to be aware that there is always a bigger
> picture . . .
> The camera's looking escapes some of the restrictions on our sight:
> those that follow from the fact that, for us, eye and ear always have to

go with body. The movie can explore the possibilities of unembodied
viewpoint but it can never escape the necessity of viewpoint itself.
So one of the arts of the movie is to turn this condition to advantage
– for instance, by articulating the condition as a topic within the film
– by dramatising the distinction between the seen and unseen, or the
relations between seeing and knowing. (Perkins 2005: 20)

This passage perhaps most succinctly underlines why a fictional world is,
like our own, a world. In any world, access to its facts is unevenly distributed
due to the necessity of viewpoint, individual positions within the world, and
other material and less visible factors that shape and / or limit that access.
To illustrate the significance of this to the movies, Perkins draws on films
that dramatise the boundedness of individual perspective and the distinction
between 'seeing and knowing' through novel narrational strategies. So, for
example, a shot inside the furnace at Xanadu (a viewpoint unavailable to the
human members of *Citizen Kane*'s world) reveals that Rosebud was a sleigh,
a truth missed by the film's characters (Perkins 2005: 16–19), while a simple
evocation of off-screen space in *You Only Live Once* (1937) forces the viewer
to assume knowledge in a film in which such assumptions are systematically
made problematic (ibid.: 22–6; see also Wilson 1986: 16–38):

> Since the film's characters are in a world their knowledge of it must
> be partial, and their perception of it may be, in almost any respect,
> distorted or deluded. But that applies to us, too, as observers of their
> worlds and their understandings. (Perkins 2005: 26)

Returning to the opening of *La Ronde*, one could say that the prologue, to
paraphrase Perkins, 'articulated the necessity of viewpoint as a topic within
the film'. The examples Perkins draws upon were films in which a *restriction*
on the characters' viewpoint served a particular narrational approach to two
different kinds of investigation (*Citizen Kane* and *You Only Live Once*). This
more idiosyncratic and explicitly reflexive film has introduced itself via a figure
who, embodying our curiosity as spectators, claims he can see everything; but
making this claim he contrasts himself with other men. The limitations on
viewpoint are 'articulated as a condition' of *La Ronde* also in the very fact of
the metonymic carousel. The *meneur* can see the carousel (he can also hear it)
but the other characters, it seems, cannot. This underlines his inhabiting of a
level of the fiction of which the other figures are, mostly, unaware. Following
Perkins's line of enquiry, we might say that, whereas most films constitute
their worlds in the three spatial dimensions, *La Ronde* possesses a fourth,[6]
what we might call the 'meta-fiction'. This meta-fiction is not a separate world;
it is merely a characteristic of the particular worldhood of *La Ronde*. While

most films shape our access to their world through standard elisions of time and space (dissolves and cuts move us from viewing one moment, one place to another), *La Ronde* often uses the meta-fictional carousel and the *meneur* figure to make literal the normally invisible chain of cause and effect such structuring underlines. The carousel is therefore a concrete metaphor for the narrative; more specifically, as a carousel, it is metonymic of the circular narrative, one that begins and ends with the prostitute.

The above underlines that this way of describing films is not limited to a focus on realism: 'worldhood is not primarily an issue of realism, and is a concept that should work to illuminate artifice, not to deny it' (ibid.: 34). Perkins underlines how artifice and a reflexive pointing to it are perfectly compatible with this notion of worldhood. In some of the most eloquent descriptions of the device, Perkins suggests the significance of direct address in all this. For this reason, it is worth returning to material touched upon in the Preface:

> The fictionality of the world is usually most marked in the characters' relationship to the off-screen zone which is the space forward of the frame – their unawareness of the apparatus through which their actions and images are relayed. Though the performers have to be aware of the camera's needs, their playing most often creates the camera's absence and thereby transforms the nature of the space in front of them. It is not that these characters are oblivious to the camera. There is no camera in their world. Their situation is interestingly contrasted with ours as spectators. We are aware of the mechanisms of presentation and have to be so to make sense of the movie's devices; if we could mistake the screen for a window, the world would have gone mad. There is a projector in our world. The projector is real and present; the absent camera confirms the fictional status of the movie image and the integrity of the movie world. (ibid.: 24)

He goes on:

> Note that the converse does not hold. The actors' occasional acknowledgment of the camera cannot be without effect. But the effect is not necessarily to break the fiction or to detract from the worldhood of the world. In their appeals to complicity or compassion, Oliver Hardy's camera-looks seem often to increase the sense of intimacy rather than produce a new detachment. (ibid.: 40n6)

The latter point is an important one. As we have seen, direct address has been most often discussed in relation to radical filmmaking, such as Godard's 1970s work, that seeks to attack standard 'visual pleasure'. Thus direct address's capacity to create detachment has been valued above its potential for intimacy, its presence in 'mainstream' fictional narrative films largely neglected. The example Perkins draws upon is the final moments of *The Night of the Hunter* (1955), where Rachel (Lillian Gish), alone in her kitchen, looks outwards towards the camera and speaks and smiles as if to us. Perkins wonders, 'how can it be that Rachel is smiling at us?' The answer lies in the reading of the film as a whole; as he suggests, 'If we insist too much on reason here we shall divorce criticism from experience':

> It is normal for a movie to stress and sustain the separation between the fictional world and the world of the viewer. Imagination allows the movie to work within that register. But imagination makes other registers available as well. In one such, a world may be suggested whose beings can respond to our watching. In another, the film may have its actors step aside from their character roles and move apart from the fictional world so as to appear to address or confront us in their own right . . .
>
> Yet within the film frame acknowledgement can only be performed, played, because it is without the essential condition for a real acknowledgment, the recognition of my presence and selfhood. When I respond to the invitation of the outward glance I engage in the fiction in a new way, by imagining contact rather than separation between my world and the screen world. By no means all outward glances carry this invitation. (ibid.: 35–6)

There is much to take on board here and to do so in isolation from a moment of *La Ronde* risks 'divorcing criticism from experience'. However, it should be noted that, with *La Ronde*, Ophuls has chosen another register of imaginative involvement from what Perkins describes as the usual. Indeed, in a sequence examined later in this chapter, the film discards the normal guidelines governing the characters' 'relationship to the off-screen zone'. As the *meneur* wanders through a 'backstage' space with Mademoiselle Marie (Simone Simon), the background reveals to us the filmmaking apparatus that framing would normally keep off-screen. The *meneur*'s easy attitude through this space suggests that he is aware of the 'apparatus through which their actions and images are relayed'. However, Marie does not fully comprehend what surrounds her. This foregrounding of artifice, rather than destroying the film's illusion, adds precisely to the film's revelation of the illusions of romantic liaisons. To put it rather clumsily, the film reveals truths about the lack of truth between men and women through means peculiar to the worldhood of its world.

The critical framework offered by Perkins's notion of fictional worlds seeks to bypass some of the problems encountered by other models of film narration that may, for example, rely on notions like an 'implied narrator' or an 'implied filmmaker' (Levinson [1996] provides a useful account of these positions).[7] In treating film narration in this holistic way, my intimations of the *meneur*'s role as like a surrogate, in some sense, implied filmmaker might seem to clash with Perkins's concerns. But if there is a clash, it is a superficial one. In turning now to the *meneur*'s 'directorial' function within the text, I wish to divorce the notion of director from the notion of authorship. It is important to stress that the *meneur* is a character who is a part of the fictional world that surrounds him, and his directorial functions take on meanings internal to that world. Indeed, my sense of his directorial role does not deny the shifts he undergoes nor the ambiguity of his status as noted by Deborah Thomas (1982: 74). It is central to my claims for the film's self-consciousness about the business of directing that the director's role is presented as, itself, a 'shifting and ambiguous one' – this is indicative of a humility about mastery felt in Ophuls work more widely.

Let us return to the end of *La Ronde*'s prologue. After the *meneur* has bid *la fille* good evening, he moves back towards the spot from which he sang to us. The musical passage on the soundtrack completes and then a bell rings. The *meneur* responds to the bell by turning to face us, tipping his hat and giving the title of what is to follow. The bell (of the kind one often hears at fairgrounds) is clearly meant to emanate from the carousel. However, no human hand has struck it – the *meneur* and the prostitute are now away from the carousel and we have seen no other person near it. Perhaps, then, rather than command the carousel, the carousel commands the *meneur*. This might appear to undermine the suggestion that the film presents the *meneur* as a director figure, some sort of surrogate for Ophuls himself. Nevertheless, a number of accounts or, at least, references to the film point to this relationship. For example, George Wilson notes that the *meneur* 'more or less explicitly stands in and speaks for the director' (1986: 124); Robin Wood repeatedly refers to him as a '*metteur en scène*' (2006: 148, 150); and Susan M. White's discussion of the film, though brief, emphasises this aspect of *La Ronde*. Indeed, the place and function of numerous directorial surrogates are a focus of White's book; the chapter containing the discussion of *La Ronde*, which is mainly focused on *Le Plaisir* (1952) and *Caught* (1949), is called 'Spectacle, Economics, and the Perils of Directorship'. I wish now to consider the *meneur*'s character in relation to the latter 'perils'.

Despite the presence of movie equipment, and the *meneur*'s direction of the prostitute to assume her mark, there is an evident paradox in his directorial role in the prologue in the way he points to the role of the spectator. When he addresses the viewer and tentatively concludes that he is 'someone, no matter whom amongst you' and the 'incarnation of your desire to know everything', he acknowledges the centrality of the spectator while stressing his own ability to satisfy spectatorial desire. This balance underlines a humility about his directorial role which is echoed in the disguises he assumes for his appearances within the narrative. Three times he masquerades as a worker in what we would now call the service industries; we see him as a coachman, a waiter and a valet. This humility neatly parallels that of Ophuls, who, though pushing self-consciousness about cinematic artifice to its limit in *La Ronde*, never abandons a commitment to the world and its characters: '[Ophuls'] work demonstrates his devotion to the possibilities of symbolic / realist film narrative, even as, in his last films, he pushes them to breaking point' (Pye 2002: 29). Moreover, there are numerous jokes at the *meneur*'s expense. For example, in his first disguise, a bugler, he apologises for playing a botched note. This sequence, his first appearance since the narrative has begun, also sees the *meneur* worry at the soldier's (Serge Reggiani) slowness in completing his business with the prostitute. When the latter arrives, the *meneur* says, 'One minute more and La Ronde would have stopped!' His appearance as a giant towering over Emma (Danielle Darrieux's 'the wife') and Alfred ('the young man', played by Daniel Gélin), filmed using forced perspective, is also something of a joke, for it comes after his power to keep the 'wheels of love' turning was for a while undone by Alfred's impotence, a moment that suggested that the *meneur*'s turning of the carousel is dependent on the success of the lovemaking, not the other way round. This cause for the carousel's breaking down is unseen by the *meneur*; it is understood by the film spectator alone.

There are other moments, however, when the *meneur* sees more than we do and when, in fact, he gets in the way of our voyeuristic desires. For example, during the episode with the actress and the count, the liaison threatens to break out of what is visually permissible. After the aggressively sexual actress has asked to hold the count's sword, the pair embrace and the camera pans up to reveal the couple's image reflected on the actress's mirrored ceiling. The image dissolves to the *meneur*, in some unidentifiable, liminal space, cutting a strip of film. As he does this, the music that accompanied the coupling is also cut, Walbrook's humming replacing it. He then sings, '*la censure*' ('censorship'). Here, a commonly indirect function of extra-diegetic music – to signify sexual intercourse – is made explicit and directly indicated by the *meneur*. Yet this moment of quasi-authorial intervention can also be read as a wry allusion to the control arrested from filmmakers such as Ophuls by real-world censors, and has been said to allude, especially, to his problems in America with the Production Code (White 1995: 240; see, further, Bacher 1996). Indeed, after the *meneur*'s second cut of the celluloid, the film returns abruptly to the actress and the count. Not only has their nascent understanding been undermined by the sex, but also the carefully plotted rhythm of their episode has been disrupted; post-coital depression (or, at least, malaise) meets with a joke about the destructive effect of censorship.

The *meneur*'s third appearance in the film develops his complex 'directorial' relationship with *La Ronde*'s world. It comes as the bridge between the sequence of the soldier and Mademoiselle Marie, the maid, and the subsequent episode, 'the maid and the young man'. Once the soldier manages to seduce Marie in a park (they struggle to find a space not already being used by other couples), he leaves her on the terrace outside a ballroom while he goes off to dance with another woman. Dejected and disappointed, she sits looking at the floor. The camera makes a track-and-pan movement around Marie, the high-angle framing her against the 'realistic' setting of a terrace. However, if we are alert to the space in the far distance of the shot (a liminal space that comes increasingly into focus through the subsequent sequence), we can see an electrical light that does not belong in Vienna, '*dix-neuf . . . cent*' but is the base of some sort of rig and a floodlight. The music emanating from the ballroom behind Marie comes to a completion and the *meneur*'s cane enters from the bottom left of the screen. He taps the back of her chair gently, like a conductor patiently requesting the attention of his musicians. This gesture is followed by a change in the score. The music that now begins is recognisably of another level; we could call it extra-diegetic if what follows did not make light of such distinctions. Then, almost immediately, the camera moves again to frame the *meneur* and Marie together. Marie asks the *meneur*, 'Who are you?' Clearly, his dress or some other aspect of his appearance means his role in this space is strange to her – just prior to this, she had responded to a soldier who approached her and said, simply, 'Mademoiselle' with 'I don't want to dance anymore tonight'; this new figure's role is clearly something different. The reframing also begins to extend the mystery of the background. Behind Marie, just visible above her head, there is an old-fashioned (perhaps '1900') photographic camera; as the *meneur* and Marie walk off stage-right, it is shown more clearly. His response to her question is 'Nobody. That is to say, anybody.' He invites her to take a '*petite promenade*'. She accepts without question (like the prostitute, Marie's sex and her youth, as well as her status, seem to make her especially open to direction), and the space they traverse is as indeterminate as is his description of himself.

As they walk, it becomes clear that the rigs in the background are electric lights mounted on stands. This space is, therefore, what was previously described as the fictional world's 'fourth dimension', and, indeed, its liminality is temporal as well as spatial. When Marie anxiously tells the *meneur* that she must get back to her employers, he notes that, regrettably, she will be sacked. He reassures her, however, that she will find another job: 'I know that two months from now, fate will be very kind to you.' She is a little perplexed but not alarmed. He tells her, 'We are making a little promenade in time.' A series of dissolves and superimpositions abstracts their movement through this space, but, if we look closely at the space around them, we might say that it resembles a studio or theatre prop warehouse (chandeliers hang next to more banks of lights, various cables and pieces of stage scenery are cluttered together). This is perhaps too prosaic a description but, as in many moments of the film, Ophuls finds a different, more visible way to render the normally self-effacing techniques by which movies compress space and time. Of all the many possibilities available, he chooses the dissolves accompanied by the following exchange to mark the transition in space and time:

> Marie: Two months? July is far off.
> *Meneur*: But, no. You're there already. Look at yourself.
> [He points to an apron she is suddenly wearing.]
> Marie: Ahh! It's true.
> *Meneur*: But, yes. There is the house.

With his cane he points screen-right and directs her out into a new space. As in the prologue, strong lighting effects and bird song on the soundtrack construct a bright, sunny morning. However, they have crossed no definitive boundary, for a facet of this world is its presentation of dynamic and shifting borders; and in *La Ronde*, these borders are as important as what they frame.

The self-consciousness of the shaping of the fictional world continues, but Walbrook's performance belies any self-satisfied celebration of directorial mastery. As he points Marie up a spiral staircase leading to the front door, he moves up behind her, both trying to reassure her and, it seems, hurry her along – he tells her '*Allez*' ('Come on') three times. His performance does not quite convey impatience but, not for the first time, there is a sense of urgency suggestive of some schedule to be met. Indeed, just as she has bid him '*Au revoir*' and disappeared from view, he says, as if to himself, 'Let's hope it won't be too late.' No sooner has he said this than the carousel's bell is heard once more telling him it is time to announce the next episode. A brief shrug and the *meneur* begins to sing, 'Turn, turn my characters . . .'. Seemingly extra-diegetic music accompanies him as he descends the spiral staircase – the staircase creating added harmony between his movements, the song lyrics and the unseen (but figuratively present) carousel.

In French, '*tourner*' also has a particular cinematic meaning, as in, '*tourner* [to make] *un film*', but the film makes a more obvious visual reference to movie-making. The *meneur* emerges from the stairs and moves further out into the right-hand space. He enters on to what appears to be a small stage (or the small corner of the stage that is visible), where an orchestra is playing the music we have been hearing. (Though the tone is distant, the content of this visual joke is not so far from Mel Brooks's spoofing of extra-diegetic music

Figure 6.5 The *meneur* cues the start of a new episode.

in his 1974 *Blazing Saddles*, when the sheriff [Cleavon Little] happens across
Count Basie's orchestra playing the film's theme in the middle of the desert.)
He bends down, leaning on a piano to write on something that seems to have
been left for him. It is revealed to be a clapperboard and the *meneur* brings
it forwards towards the camera (apologising to a harpist he almost bumps
into), announcing the start of a new episode (Figure 6.5). In delicious further
harmony, the clapperboard's crack is closely followed immediately by the 'cue
mark' (the spot at the top-right of the frame) that marks the end of *La Ronde*'s
first reel.[8]

This combination of elements is extraordinary in its élan and makes for a
bravura piece of reflexive filmmaking. But what is really remarkable is how
this elaborate game-playing enriches the integrity of the world, rather than
undermining it. This is because the *meneur* is both a director of the action *and*
a character in his own right. His hurrying along of the characters, the concerns
he expresses that things will run to time, give us a sense of him as 'as a guy who
is just doing his job' (White 1995: 240). If it had been handled differently, the
interposition of a 'master of ceremonies' could have been alienating (in both
its Brechtian and more basic meanings). However, in *La Ronde*, the *meneur*'s
structuring work instead undercuts the formal conceit of the Schnitzler text.

The rather closed play becomes a remarkably open film. This is, in a sense, paradoxical because, by adding the *meneur*, a voice is given to the text's requirement to close itself. Near the film's end, the *meneur* declares (resuming the position taken in the prologue, although not looking at the camera) '*La Ronde est fermé*' ('*La Ronde* is closed'), but this can only occur once he has compelled the soldier and the count to salute each other as they pass in the street. Thus, as so often in the film, the tenuousness of the *meneur*'s control of the space and the other characters belies the creation of anything like a 'closed' film world; indeterminacy is too much a factor.

The delicacy of Ophuls's handling matches that of the *meneur*. For example, in the latter's introduction to Mademoiselle Marie, Ophuls's camera movement reminds us that in the cinema a small adjustment of framing could reveal the technology of representation placed in the wings. As a dramatisation of directorial control, we might describe the *meneur*'s guiding of Marie as revealing both what White calls the 'perils of directorship' and what I would call the 'anxieties of orchestration'. The latter term seems more appropriate because of the links between the *meneur*'s task and the business of conducting an orchestra – indeed, the passage began with a modest gesture recalling the tapping of a conductor's baton and ends with him moving into an orchestra. With similar modesty, the *meneur*'s claims to see and, by implication, to be able to reveal *all* are presented in the prologue through the briefest of looks at camera (see Figure 6.1 again).

In the space that remains, I want to move towards saying something more of Ophuls's use of direct address as a part of his 'theatricalisation' of romantic desire. To clarify Ophuls's position, a brief recourse again to Brechtian approaches to drama will be instructive. One may then note those elements held in common, at least superficially, with Ophuls:

> The aesthetic which Eisenstein, Brecht and Godard hold in common is hostility to illusionism; illusionism being a mode of artistic experience that has at its most central characteristics: a desire to (psychologically) penetrate individual experience; its primary appeal is to the emotions rather than the intellect, desiring the audience's empathetic involvement with the events presented before them, in a passive manner suggested by Coleridge's 'willing suspension of disbelief'; it has a closed form which implies a certain artistic autonomy, a self-validation; it prefers to regard the medium of expression as somehow transparent. (Walsh 1981: 11)

Discussing the 'Brechtian Aspect of Radical Cinema', Martin Walsh here outlines the antagonistic relationship of certain avant-garde practitioners to cinematic illusionism. The above can be read as a list of characteristics of 'illusionist narrative film' to which Eisenstein, Godard, Brecht *and* Ophuls's 1950 film can be contrasted. Clearly, the *meneur*'s frequent signalling of the narrative representation *as* representation precludes any straightforward 'suspension of disbelief', as well as any narrational 'transparency'. Aligning himself with us as an involved and sophisticated observer of events (when he is not their orchestrator), the *meneur* also denies the possibility of 'passive' involvement with the fiction. However, Ophuls's fundamental difference from the mode of practice Walsh invokes turns on the term 'hostility'. If Ophuls uncovers some of the inner workings of 'illusionism', *La Ronde* seems to suggest that profound truths are available from within artifice. As we have seen, insouciant but self-deprecating mastery characterises the *meneur*'s relationship to the film's world.

To return to the above quotation, this can also be related to the film's position vis-à-vis 'psychological penetration' and our 'empathetic involvement' as audience members, a particularly complex issue in this film. The introduction of the *meneur* and the meta-fictional world he traverses is designed, precisely, to enable us to observe the behaviour of other characters at a degree of distance. However, the film manages, in its considerable generosity, to let this co-exist with an involvement with the characters. The co-presence of detachment and involvement can be illustrated with reference to V. F. Perkins's (1982) analysis of the scene between the wife and her husband (Fernand Gravey). The context of this scene is important. It follows Alfred's seduction of the wife, Emma (though the delicacy of the scene suggests she is perhaps the passive-active seducer), which is followed by Gélin / Alfred's acknowledgement of the camera (examined below); this then gives way to the shot of the *meneur* as a giant towering over the couple, which moves us into the scene between the wife and the husband. Perkins comments on the surface-level irony of the husband's words in this last sequence, 'One can really only love in truth and purity':

> In the play these words can scarcely be more than a joke against the
> husband's blindness and complacency (he has been cuckolded in the
> previous episode) and against his hypocrisy – the pattern of the play
> makes it sure that he will be unfaithful in the next. (Perkins 1982: 32)

However, in comparing the profound irony of *La Ronde* to the 'shallow sarcasm' (ibid.) of its source text, Perkins attends beautifully to the effect of this line's delivery:

> the line . . . [is allowed] an inwardness, a weight and a relevance that
> extend well beyond the immediate context of infidelity and negotiated

deceptions. There is an ambiguity in the husband's speaking. He is
not talking *to* his wife. He is in some sense talking *at* her – his words
are calculated to block her enquiries into his past. But he may also be
thinking aloud. And in so far as he is choosing the thoughts which may
most conveniently be spoken, we may wonder how deeply his memory
and imagination are stirred by the old passions whose significance
he wishes to deny. Ophuls makes it possible – not more – that the
husband's declaration may be sincere and may have validity, despite
the compromised position from which it is offered . . . Were there
not . . . moments of truth and purity *within* the delicate pretences and
calculations of that scene? (ibid.)

Perkins's stress on the possibility, 'not more', of the sincerity of the husband's
declaration should warn us against basing too much on it; his definition of
Ophuls's practice as having the quality of a 'constant Perhaps' (ibid.) resonates
with so much of what we have already found in the film. However, seen in
the context of this investigation, one might venture to say something broader
about the significance of the husband's delivery.

Perkins suggests the husband's talking 'at' rather than 'to' his wife is the
source of his statement's potential sincerity, authenticity or truth. Normally,
describing someone as talking 'at' another evokes only pomposity and a barrier
to communication; indeed, at times the husband pontificates to, rather than
engages with, his wife. However, the scene between the husband and the
wife (named Emma and Charles in likely reference to the lead characters of
Flaubert's *Madame Bovary* – Thomas 1982: 79) is extraordinary in the way it
allows the husband's performance to fluctuate between pompous outrage at his
wife's interest in his pre-marital affairs to moments of more considered introspection which hint at truths within his 'delicate pretences'.[9] Gravey's delivery
throughout the sequence contains many pauses in which he weighs his words.
He also repeats lines he considers particularly successful in communicating
some of the problems of romantic liaisons. Gravey's delivery is reminiscent
of the *meneur*'s at the start of the film, in which he searches for his words with
careful consideration of their impact. While the husband will be shown to be a
hypocrite in a way the *meneur* is incapable of being, his projection, outwards,
'at' rather than 'to' his wife suggests a momentary truth unavailable to his later
unreflective self, linking him, on some level, to the *meneur*.

In the subsequent scene with his young lover (Odette Joyeux), no such
insights emerge from the husband's discourse. This adds to a sense that the
film puts its faith in the theatricalisation of love and desire; that is, the mode
of delivery associated with the *meneur* (as, *almost*, the only figure to address the
film spectator) articulates truths unavailable to the non-theatrical performances within the film's discrete episodes – 'non-theatrical' in terms of their

I'm a married woman's lover!

Figure 6.6 Alfred (Daniel Gélin) reveals his motivations direct to us.

being unreflective, enclosed in on themselves, bound up in their duplicity towards the partner to whom they play. In this sense, I am aware that, controversially, I am divorcing 'theatricality' from the connotation of pretence. However, I am reminded of the ending of Jean Renoir's 1953 *The Golden Coach* (with which *La Ronde* has a number of things in common), where Anna Magnani's Camilla is addressed thus: 'Your only way to find happiness is on any stage . . . in those two little hours when you become a different person, your true self.'

This brings us, finally, to the brief instance of direct address by someone other than the *meneur*, where Alfred lets slip the true motivations for his conquest of Emma. After Emma has finally agreed to see Alfred again, he turns from her departing carriage and, while walking past the camera, he turns and declares to us: 'Here is the lover of a married woman' ('*Nous voilà l'amant d'une femme mariée*'; Figure 6.6). The theatrical flourish of the '*voilà*' is underlined by the theatrical flourish of direct address. Alfred skips off and ends the shot by literally jumping for joy. This moment breaks the usual register in which Gélin / Alfred's performance operates, and suggests that his happiness emerges more out of a triumphant sense of increase in socio–sexual status than out of genuine love. But, importantly, the impact of his delivery is not fully under his control. Whereas the older, more worldly-wise *meneur* and the husband strive carefully to weigh up their words (clearly, the *meneur* much more consistently than the husband, though the former's 'everywhere' – earlier cited – does lapse into hubris), the young, impetuous Alfred blurts out his admission. However, ultimately, his acknowledgement of the camera has revealed a truth generally unavailable to those stuck within the world's fictional (as opposed to meta-fictional) space. The film seems to say 'all the world's a stage' and the (sound) stage is the most revealing metaphor for the world.

NOTES

1. A '*reigen*' is a rural dance, which may use something like a maypole. Some dictionaries translate it as 'roundelay'. I am grateful to Bernd Rest for this explanation (as well as for other musical matters).
2. I can find no satisfactory translation for the word; it is arcane enough not to appear in bilingual dictionaries. It appears in my monolingual *Le Petit Robert* (1995) as 'Young girl of modest means, a worker in a fashion house, of free and easy morals' [my translation]. (It appears such girls dressed in grey [*gris*].) The point, primarily, is one of balance with the 'femme honnête' (it therefore appears more likely that *femme* means wife here); the young girl may be somewhat 'free and easy' but 'tender' is more alluring than 'honest'. This is characteristic of both a refusal to judge felt through-out the film (and a facet of Ophuls's œuvre more broadly) and a careful search for the words that is a part of this refusal. Later in the film, in a discussion between the *meneur* ('disguised' as a head waiter) and a junior colleague (uncredited), they debate whether to call the young lover of 'the husband' (Fernand Gravey) a 'cocotte' or a 'midinette' (the meaning of the latter is almost the same as that of 'grisette'). It should be remarked that the language would have been arcane, even for a French audience of 1950.
3. The most interesting instance of this is Masao Yamaguchi's essay on *Lola Montès*, which relates Ophuls's 'encounter' with Brecht via Karl Valentin.
4. See also Pye's 2002 essay, which takes many of these points further.
5. There is, of course, a wider range of scholarship on the notion of film worlds. Daniel Yacavone (2008) provides an account of much of this scholarship and an important intervention of his own. However, while my analysis of direct address as a facet of the worldhood of films is by no means incompat-ible with Yacavone's emphases, the notion of film worlds I prefer here is more in line with both Perkins's and Kendall Walton's (1990) complemen-tary (though admittedly much broader) line of enquiry – it is noteworthy

that neither scholar is referred to in Yacavone's essay. Yacavone very usefully stresses that film worlds are constituted of both diegetic and extradiegetic elements (2008: 84) and sees self-reflexivity as also constituting a film world rather than seeing these, reductively, as destroying immersion in that world (ibid.: 104), as was the case with many previous discussions of direct address that have stressed a narrowly 'Brechtian' function. However, I have found Yacavone's account less valuable for this book because of his overly sceptical attitude towards the significance of the ontology of film's photographic base (ibid.: 84) and it is notable that he rarely touches upon examples of films working within what would traditionally be discerned as broadly 'realist' practices (such as classical Hollywood) – his examples are primarily from 'alternative' filmmaking. As my recourse to Perkins shows, I do not see direct address as an issue principally of realism but my previous emphasis of the 'documentary' aspect of much filmmaking and the more overriding emphasis on performance in this study (demanded because of the material that direct address is made up of – the human doing the looking at the camera) find this ontology to be important. Moreover, I would contend that the world of every film is separate from the world of any other (though Perkins more than adequately acknowledges their capacity for overlap) while Yacavone is more interested in the 'inter-cinematic' relationships between the worlds of various directors' films.

6. Not being a physicist, I do not wish to debate the constitution of these dimensions further, nor enter into a debate over whether time is the 'fourth dimension'. What I will suggest is that, in the particular fourth dimension dominated by the *meneur*, time is adaptable to a degree it is not inside of the discrete episodes. There are still temporal ellipses within the narrative sections, but often these ellipses are drawn attention to by the *meneur*'s interventions.

7. For example, Sarah Kozloff's otherwise insightful book on voiceover, a device related to direct address, is hampered by a reliance on a personified implied narrator – Kozloff chooses the term 'image-maker' (1988: 44).

8. As a result of the over-enthusiasm of DVD producers to 'clean up' celluloid artefacts, the cue mark has disappeared from the new, digitally remastered *La Ronde* (which I have used to extract my images from, though not for any other purposes).

9. Other ironies not yet noted emerge out of the relationship of one of the husband's other statements to the placement and the performance of the scene in the film as a whole. He tells his wife, this time pompously, 'the principle of life is variation'; he says, in French, '*alternance*', which has the connotation of the passage of the seasons. This describes the cyclical repetitions-in-variation of the film's structure as a whole, but this emerges out of the most self-contained of scenes. The *mise-en-scène* is characterised

by insistent symmetry and the most measured, incremental camera move-ments in the whole film. Moreover, the scene begins almost exactly midway through the film, and conveys beautifully a staid marriage (while hinting at the relationship's potential to achieve something more).

CHAPTER 7

Conclusion

This study has not attempted to address *all* the meanings and effects that direct address may produce in movie fictions (let alone begin to account for its role within a wide range of genres of actuality, television news being only one example), nor to give a comprehensive account of its cinematic history. Indeed, it has become increasingly clear to me that such an account would be impossible. When one begins to look for it, one sees direct address in many more films than one would expect and with much more varied functions than has been acknowledged. The meanings of each instance of direct address are determined by the surrounding context, the details of its performance and the wider rhetoric of its placement. However, it is possible to make some broader conclusions, based first on what was encountered in the three case studies, and then to relate some of these issues (such as tone, point of view and the particularly vexed issue of irony) to developments in strands of more recent cinema.

A key discovery here has been the value of direct address as a particularly rich metaphor for the problems of vision experienced by film characters. Cabiria's status as victim at the hands of deceitful and exploitative men sits in tension with her extraordinary forcefulness as a performer. A systematically 'frontal' relationship to the camera comes to fruition in its final acknowledgement, which suggests a consciousness of things previously only hinted at unconsciously (the 'unconsciousness' of *Le Notti di Cabiria*'s music, Cabiria's hypnotic trance and so on). The ingenuousness of Rob's to-camera testimony in *High Fidelity*, on the other hand, expresses a failure of insight for much of the narrative, while *La Ronde* contrasts the duplicity of 'non-theatrical' exchanges between characters with the honesty of the theatrical presentation of the self – and here we saw, again, how delivery / performance is crucial, in the contrast, for instance, between the worldly-wise *meneur* and Alfred's 'inadvertent' revelation of his own motives. The 'truth' of these characters is available, as in the real world, only through performance; whether it is more social (we observe their often-duplicitous interactions) or directed more at us, it is always performance that shapes our understanding of the character's thoughts or feelings. Within this continuum, direct address seems to promise more vividly (or, alternatively, reflect ironically upon) the possibility of unmasking the 'inner essence' of character.

I suggested in Chapter 3 that direct address is more compatible with comedic films than with any other genre or mode of filmmaking but then proceeded to analyse three films at length that, according to Deborah Thomas's model, must be considered melodramatic; though the central performances are often comedic in Alex Clayton's (2010) sense (frequently, their intentions are clearly to amuse), the underlying structures of all three films (even of *High Fidelity*) tend towards a more 'realist' sense of danger, repression and hierarchical power (see Thomas's table [as presented on page 57 above]); moreover, *Le Notti di Cabiria* and *La Ronde* (the latter in its spiral-like structure) present clearly fated narratives. It would seem, then, that my close analysis has focused on films I have otherwise implied are non-representative. The reality is more complex. First of all, as stressed in Chapter 3, Thomas's melodrama–comedy distinction is no binary. Indeed, after first discussing melodrama versus comedy, I went on immediately to consider a film that makes use of direct address (*Make Way for Tomorrow*) but is undoubtedly a melodrama in Thomas's terms (though one in which characters often face their unforgiving fate with the best of humour). *Le Notti di Cabiria* is another film that helps both to illustrate and to qualify the distinction between these film modes, as it seems apt to say that Cabiria displays a confusion as to whether she is in a melodrama or a comedy. The tragic disparity is a feature of her performance through much of the narrative; the foreshadowing and presentiments encouraged by the film's *enchaînement dramatique* suggest, to the viewer, that she is in a melodrama, while Cabiria greets her world as if it possessed the safety of comedy. Seen in this light, Cabiria's final acknowledgement of the camera seems to be a reconciliation with the dangers of her world but where, paradoxically, the encounter with the young players enables a momentary lightness, a transformativity (qualities more in tune with the comedic) that can be expressed, perhaps can only be expressed, via direct address; for the first time, she reconciles herself with the melodramatic determinism of her world, but in a comedic spirit. Such a paradox is, again, perhaps something direct address is in a unique position to express (a position somehow both inside *and* outside the fiction). The self-consciousness / reflexivity that the above characterisations of *Le Notti di Cabiria* imply is appropriate, given the frequency of inter-cinematic references (to Chaplin and to other Fellini films certainly, perhaps also to *Singin' in the Rain*) and the sense of 'to-be-watched-ness' displayed by the character throughout. However, this self-consciousness is by no means limited to the obvious reflexivity of filmmaking such as Federico Fellini's.

The confusion described above may be another way of characterising the problems characters in other kinds of films encounter in facing their fictional world.[1] However, Cabiria's performativity as an individual character does sit apart from what 'to-be-watched-ness' might typify within more narrow generic strictures; it might more normally vivify the musical star's desire for connection with their audience, while, in comedy, 'to-be-watched-ness' seems tied to the common theme of social embarrassment, direct address acting often as the awakening from the obliviousness that often characterises comic performance.

Ophuls's *La Ronde* offers us an opportunity to underline further the expressive potential of direct address and its distinctiveness from other kinds of looking at the camera – for example, that found in optical point-of-view shots ('POV'):

> [Ophuls's] films rarely use POV; in fact its absence is almost as central a feature of Ophuls' work as its presence is in Hitchcock. A tendency to avoid POV filming is one aspect of the ways in which Ophuls' films require us to look *at* his characters, seeing them within the elaborate material constraints of their worlds. (Pye 2002: 22)

To contrast *La Ronde*'s use of direct address with *Lady in the Lake* (1947), a grotesque example of the (over)use of point-of-view shots (point of view in Hitchcock is complexly involving), one can see *La Ronde* as tacitly mocking the special claims the 1947 film makes for optical point of view; advertisements for *Lady in the Lake*, which is shot almost entirely from the visual perspective of the private eye hero, proclaimed, 'You and Robert Montgomery solve a murder mystery together'; it is implied that by 'seeing through his eyes', we 'identify' more strongly with his experience.[2] Elsewhere in the film:

> A mirror shot . . . shows off the ingenuity that puts the hero's image on screen while the camera is supposedly confined within his point of view. Through trickery, however, the shot is also making a display of the camera's absence. (Perkins 2005: 25)

The camera's erasure is technically impressive in Montgomery's film, but far more ingenious is *La Ronde*'s making of the camera present both to the actors *and* to some of the characters. This enables the film to reveal more by looking *at* characters and, on occasions, at characters who look back *at us*, than would likely be possible by having us look 'through their eyes'. *Le Notti di Cabiria* and *High Fidelity*, in very different registers (the latter, particularly, by its 'matter-of-factness'), demonstrate how much more flexible is the interface between audience and film fictions than some long-standing definitions of cinema as a medium of 'presence–absence', or of the spectator as unseen 'voyeur', have been capable of acknowledging.

The heritage such models have left to film studies is perhaps one reason that direct address is so rarely probed. Another reason is its 'obviousness'. In an essay on the look at the camera, Marc Vernet talks of the problems of the then-existing critical literature on the subject: 'they are either only based on a very small number of examples, or (but this may go hand in hand . . .) it is as if the figure of the look at the camera was too obvious [*évidente*] for precise definition to be necessary' (1983: 32; my translation). Vernet might object to the case studies approach that has been central here but my focus has been such precisely in order to counter the implication that the device may not reward close attention; the effect of direct address in the three films examined at length above has not been self-evident.

The 'obviousness' of direct address has another meaning for the more particular neglect of its 'mainstream' instances. The role the device took in Godard's 1970s filmmaking was valued in the engaged criticism of the decade – this is the period of the most extensive writing on direct address – but it was partly the strong sense, the 'obviousness' of the radical *filmmaker*'s appeal to us as individual subjects that was valued. In reality, I have suggested that Godard's use of direct address is much less assertive and / or unambiguous than this but, still, the prominent film writing continued to link the device to polemical and didactic models of film practice. The kind of direct address that can be grouped loosely under the banner of Pascal Bonitzer's 'counter-look' was, in the end, the much more valued; camera looks that desired union between character and spectator went largely unexplored, such romanticism, one assumes, being beyond the pale for much film scholarship. In contrast to the evaluative preoccupations of this previous critical orthodoxy, I chose the case studies films for the co-existence, interdependence and balance of character agency with the potentially extra-diegetic force of direct address, which enables it to point towards external frameworks – in the important role taken by music, the relationship between inside and outside the fiction has, in fact, been a recurrent concern. I have been attracted by the generosity each film displays in its varied handling of this balance.

Questions of balance and the very notion of inside and outside of the fiction inevitably bring to mind issues of proximity and distance in terms of characterisation and our 'identification' with a film's characters. *High Fidelity* illustrated that direct address enables a particular co-existence between a strong sense of intimacy, and allegiance with a character and a critical distance from them – not distance in any Brechtian sense but in the more banal sense that films might often warmly mock the attitudes and values of its heroes. The nature of this critical distance and the broader issue of a film's point of view on its characters (or the relationship of the film's wider rhetoric to the point of view *of* its characters) take us to the heart of debates about the tone of recent and contemporary (mainly American) 'independent' cinema, trends that have found a prominent place for direct address or other kinds of camera looks. I wish to say something of this issue principally with reference to an influential film from this cycle, Paul Thomas Anderson's *Magnolia* (1999). The film has been located at the nexus of developments in recent filmmaking identified as 'smart cinema' (Sconce 2006) and the 'quirky' (MacDowell 2010).

Magnolia follows the interweaving lives of multiple protagonists dealing with various personal and familial crises in modern-day Los Angeles. The film is often bleak in its portrayal of a range of damaged and dysfunctional individuals, and operatic in its scope (it is three hours long). It presents a number of highly stylised crescendos in which characters come close to achieving realisations about themselves and their situations. The ending is one such crescendo and it makes use of direct address's special claims as a metaphor for a character's realisation and vision. The final scene is preceded by a cop, Jim (John C. Reilly), talking to himself in his car. We have seen him do this at numerous earlier points, and these are initially presented as jokes at his expense – for example, he was shown earlier talking in his car, offering words of wisdom to some rookie cop, only for the film to reveal he is alone. However, at the end of *Magnolia*, context, what he says and its performance suggest Jim has undergone a change; he is certainly now less ridiculous. We then see a woman he has just begun dating, Claudia (Melora Walters), who, like Jim, is recovering from some trauma. During this, the final shot, Jim enters and sits on the edge of Claudia's bed. The dialogue is unclear because it competes with one of the Aimee Mann songs that punctuate the film, the words of which ('You're a girl in need of a tourniquet . . . save me from the ranks of the freaks who . . . could never love anyone') speak directly to the narrative situation and the camera's framing of Claudia's tearful face. Jim's speech is meant to be just about audible, and it is basically a plea to Claudia to give their relationship a chance.

The camera tracks in extremely slowly to frame Claudia's face ever closer. The soundtrack favours the song, though it allows us also to consider Claudia's reaction to Jim's words. Her tearful eyes are fixed on him almost constantly from his entrance to the room until he sits on her bed. He says to her, 'If you want to be with me, then be with me' and she looks down in a gesture that suggests she is looking inwards to consider this. His last words ask her 'You see?' She then nods barely perceptibly before looking up and at the camera. She then smiles at us (Figure 7.1). The film cuts to the closing credits. It is a moment reminiscent of the ending of *Le Notti di Cabiria* but somewhat more assertive of an 'editorial' rhetoric in the sudden cut on the look and on a crescendo of the soundtrack music (its execution reminds us more of other endings, such as *La Dolce Vita* and, more loosely, *Les Quatre cents coups*). Here, again, direct address can be said to vivify a breakthrough in vision. The weak nod answers

Figure 7.1 *Magnolia* (New Line Cinema et al., 1999): Claudia (Melora Walters) smiles through her tears in the film's final image.

Jim's question, but looking at us, a look that is 'impossible' according to the terms of most films, says more powerfully, 'Yes, I do see.' As we have seen, direct address is often an expression of a revelation of vision: vision in terms of the attainment of insight, knowledge of one's place in the film's world, or, more self-reflexively, apparent awareness of the filmic construct in which the actor and / or character is a part, though these things, importantly, are often linked. In the case of *Magnolia*, the importance of vision should not detract from the importance of audition. Claudia's look is timed to match precisely the crescendo of 'Save Me' and Aimee Mann's music is integral to the film and was crucial to its conception – indeed, in the liner notes to the soundtrack album, Paul Thomas Anderson calls *Magnolia* 'an adaptation of Mann's songs'. Another of the film's emotional crescendos shows again that film worlds that make use of direct address might often use music as a complementary blurring of the diegetic–extra-diegetic boundary.

Earlier, we saw all of the film's main characters, each in a different place, sing along to Mann's song, 'Wise Up'. In many cases, there is no possible source within the diegesis for the music and, in at least one case (a character who has just been rendered unconscious by a powerful dose of morphine), the character cannot 'really' be singing. In a way that echoes direct address itself, which can complicate the distinction between the world of the film and the world of the filming, there is a deliberate blurring of the diegetic versus extra-diegetic boundary – here, *characters* perform the narrational rhetoric that typically joins them in disparate spaces via soundtrack music. Moreover, the singing of 'Wise Up' anticipates the ending in its lyrics; the repeated line, 'It's not going to stop, until you wise up' could be said to look forward to the ending. At the end, Claudia seems to have 'wised up'. The 'it' of 'it's not going to stop' could thus be taken to be the film itself – a degree of self-referentiality not inconsistent with the text as a whole (inter-titles, pretend archive footage and voiceover commentary join events in other ways). However, the tone of the wider film, particularly its irony, demands that we consider how we are supposed to take the final moment of revelation / realisation.

Jeffrey Sconce situates *Magnolia* within a group of 1990s and 2000s American films he dubs 'smart cinema'. Smart cinema defines itself in contradistinction to 'big, dumb Hollywood blockbusters'. Though smart cinema is not fully 'art cinema', nor truly 'independent' filmmaking, '"smart" films nevertheless share an aura of "intelligence" (or at least ironic distance) that distinguished them (and their audiences) from the perceived "dross" (and "rabble") of the mainstream multiplex' (Sconce 2006: 430). (Incidentally, *High Fidelity* is mentioned by Sconce in passing – 2006: 437.) The 'smartness' of these films is tangibly felt in certain recurrent stylistic traits and *Magnolia* possesses many of these: a narrative emphasis on simultaneity, coincidence, multiple-strand narratives; marked symmetry in much of its framing, and tableau compositions; a 'blank', dampened comic style and often bleak subject matter. However, the film's irony is particularly important for considering its relationship to what Sconce identifies. As we have seen, irony is an immensely complex issue and is immensely difficult to discuss in precise terms. It has, however, by necessity entered into the discussion of various moments analysed in this book. It is perhaps best discussed here through the limited frame of 'knowingness'. A film may be 'knowing' in the way it conjoins or juxtaposes scenes or characters in order to articulate a point to the audience about the actions in those scenes or of those characters; characters may be performed in a knowing way, with 'tongue in cheek', for example (saying one thing but meaning another), or may even appear cognisant of the trajectory of the film narrative in which they participate – in the latter example, a character's knowingness conjoins to a significant extent with the rhetoric of the wider film, a conjunction suited, in many cases, to the performance of direct address. These issues of irony were broached in the earlier evaluation of *Le Notti di Cabiria* over *La Dolce Vita* – I suggested that the latter film displayed a knowing superiority over its characters while *Le Notti di Cabiria* evinces an extraordinary balance between exposing the frequent blindness of its protagonist (we see her throw herself into events we know will not end well) and suggesting that more profound understandings of her world are available from within the character, most notably in its moment of direct address. These are questions of point of view (a film's point of view on its characters and the extent to which we are encouraged as spectators to subscribe to or reject the point of view of these characters) and have been crucial to many critical reactions to art films, such as *La Dolce Vita*. For *Magnolia*, the question is more vexed because its narration's degree of superiority over its characters impacts on precisely *where* one situates it within trends of recent American cinema.

James MacDowell offers the category of the 'quirky' as an additional category to the 'smart', suggesting that the former may have superseded the latter (MacDowell relates the quirky's areas of concern to a broader interest in 'the new sincerity' of contemporary independent and quasi-independent US cinema – 2010: 14). However, MacDowell's distinguishing of the quirky from the smart turns principally on the role assumed by and for irony and this sees him situate *Magnolia* in a different tradition to Sconce (the film is discussed by Sconce at various points of his essay – 2006: 429, 435, 436, 438):

> One thing I want to take issue with, however, is Sconce's desire to define all the films he mentions in relation to the tone of the smart as he sets it out – in particular those of P. T. Anderson, Wes Anderson, Hal Hartley and Spike Jonze . . . All these directors seem to me to be firmly tied to the quirky, a sensibility that has a much more complicated relationship with the 'trope of irony' than does the smart, and which comes far closer to expressing precisely those attitudes – 'sincerity', 'positivity', 'passion' – to which the smart is contrasted. (MacDowell 2010: 11)

'Sincerity', 'positivity' and 'passion' are qualities that, for MacDowell distinguish the quirky tradition from the smart. Though quirky films are far from unironic, MacDowell's fine readings of films such as 2002's *Adaptation* (MacDowell 2010: 10–12) show that a kind of emotional and romantic sincerity is ultimately recuperated on behalf of the characters – MacDowell tentatively relates the quirky to the long tradition of 'romantic irony' in fiction (2010: 14). In contrast, the kind of irony Sconce finds (correctly, I would suggest) in many of the films he surveys is sometimes crude to the point that one might call it a *sarcastic* approach to characterisation. MacDowell wants to claim *Magnolia* for the quirky (2010: 9, 12–13; see also his reference to director Paul Thomas Anderson in the quotation above). However, here I must disagree and situate the film, in the main, with the tone Sconce identifies as the smart. This is, in fact, felt most vividly through the use of some of the film's music, most crudely with the recurrent accompaniment of 'Quiz Kid' Donnie Smith (William H. Macy) by the pop song, 'Dreams Can Come True' – at these moments, the screen positively drips with an irony that mocks Donnie's pathetic attempts to chase his dreams. However, pigeonholing is unhelpful and these competing categories (of the smart and the quirky) are principally useful for hitting on a tension felt within the film. It is the single moment of direct address that gives me the greatest hesitation over the ultimate sincerity of the film's attitudes to its characters.

To return to the final moment, we might wonder about the sincerity of its presentation of a personal realisation. As viewers, we may measure Jim's romantic declarations against the brevity of their relationship – they have been on only one date. Jim has been characterised by his romantic desperation (we first meet him using a dating service) as much as Claudia is characterised by a damaged family past. As a police officer, Jim has also shown himself to be spectacularly imperceptive in not realising that Claudia is a drug addict (though the suppressed dialogue in the final scene hints that he may have woken up to this). Lastly, the very fact of the competition between music and Jim's words represents an editorial mediation of our view of their exchange – perhaps we would accept the strength of their connection more fully if Jim's tender words were all we heard? The problem of understanding the ending can thus be posed as follows: is Claudia's direct address a sincere expression of her awakening or a final joke at the characters' expense? Myopia has characterised almost all the characters up to this point and the film's scope and breadth of vision contrast markedly with the characters. That the film narration offers us much greater knowledge than that possessed by any one character is perfectly common, but it is the degree of this disparity and the *tone* of its presentation that is crucial to the distinction between the 'smart' and the 'quirky'.

Ultimately, it is more appropriate to hesitate to come to a conclusion about this moment of *Magnolia* because, otherwise, one would negate its ambiguity. A wider ironic structure may have framed the characters in a particular way but, in the final moments, the space given to focusing solely on Melora Walters's very affecting performance, and the more unique space given to her character in having her look at us, perhaps escape that structure. (Also, perhaps rather than distance us from the emotionality of the moment, the affectivity of the music wins out over any other kind of meaning?) These are the sorts of responses, interpretations and evaluations that critics argue over. However, in my analysis of the 'meanings' of various looks at the camera, I wish not to lose sight of the essential mystery direct address proposes to offer:

> Aside from films that use this ambiguity in the service of the notion of the eternal ineffability of the face as window to the soul . . . most films do . . . narrow down the range of meanings that a facial expression considered in isolation may have. (Dyer 2001: 134)

Dyer is right to stress the way movies regularly narrow down the meanings a filmed face might have – my reading of Claudia's has hesitated over the film's attitude to what she expresses, but has found it perfectly in tune with the film's wider themes. However, its romanticism notwithstanding, direct address may indeed use the 'eternal ineffability of the face as window to the soul' as one of its most powerful effects.

The different kinds of ambiguity at which direct address is adept make it

Figure 7.2 *Submarine* (Film4 et al., 2010): the adolescent hero (Craig Roberts) welcomes us (sort of) into his world.

perhaps particularly suited to the quirky, 'a tone that exists on a knife-edge of judgment and empathy, detachment and engagement, irony and sincerity' (MacDowell 2010: 13). Future work on direct address could well take the quirky sensibility in recent cinema as a profitable focus. MacDowell devotes some space to considering quirky cinema's 'rhetoric of self-consciousness' evinced by presentational framing that is clearly arranged for the spectator (2010: 5–7) – this is perhaps part of its heritage from smart cinema, which Sconce characterises by an often symmetrical and frontal *mise-en-scène* (2006: 436). Such a stance (literally) vis-à-vis the audience makes direct address easily assimilable into the general style. As an example, a recent addition to the international quirky canon (according to MacDowell, at least – 2011), Richard Ayoade's *Submarine* (2010), has its young hero and narrator (Craig Roberts) look furtively at us in one of our first views of him (see Figure 7.2). However, in considering the wider trend, future work might be better served considering the camera look more broadly. For example, in Wes Anderson's films, whose frontality from *The Royal Tenenbaums* (2001) onwards self-consciously recalls the aesthetics of the family photo album, the question of whom the characters are looking at when they look at the camera is difficult to discern.

A trend in the use of direct address that has remained pretty constant is its greater frequency in the final shots of films than at any other point. As I suggested in the Introduction and elsewhere, this is because direct address as a cross-diegetic device fits with the way endings prepare to move us out of the fiction; a final moment of direct address also evinces a film's attitude towards the spectator and its aspirations (in some cases, pretensions) for us to take

Figure 7.3 *Eden Lake* (Rollercoaster Films & Aramid Entertainment, 2008): the monstrous Brett (Jack O'Connell) breaks the fourth wall in the final frames.

away with us from the viewing space a more 'active' sense of reflection on what we have just seen. For example, the final frames of *Eden Lake* (2008; Figure 7.3) seem consciously to ape Michael Haneke's *Funny Games* in suggesting audience complicity in the on-screen horrors. However, in this more recent film, it is experienced as a disruption of previous patterns of characterisation and, in line with Marc Vernet's reading of Pascal Bonitzer's account of direct address (1983: 35), can be seen to 'strip the actor of his character', making him a conduit for an externally imposed authorial message. The film up to that point has been *relatively* discrete about the allegorical-political level of its story but its respectable achievements in the characterisation of the horrific Brett (Jack O'Connell) are undercut by his final look at us. *Funny Games* is much more consistent and ruthlessly rigorous in its use of direct address. Nevertheless, we experience direct address as an assertion of a particular meaning or message – the device in this context might be called 'director's address'. This kind of 'counter-look' is primarily a rhetorical gesture and is suited to the signalling of some message, some 'issue'. Another example might be *4 Months, 3 Weeks and 2 Days* (2007), where Otilia (Anamaria Marinca) turns from Gabita (Laura Vasiliu) in the final shot to look out through the window of the hotel restaurant and at us (see Figure 7.4). However, in this case, didactic confrontation does not overshadow the human drama (they work, rather, in unison) as the length of the shot, its framing and Marinca's pacing of her response to our looking make active a sense of our intruding on the wordless aftermath of a horrific experience the characters have shared (a backstreet abortion). In a way reminiscent of a moment from *Make Way for Tomorrow*, the film activates our sense of the 'privacy' of this moment by momentarily puncturing the fourth wall.

The above rests upon an almost spatial sense of the inside and outside of the

Figure 7.4 *4 Months, 3 Weeks and 2 Days* (Mobra Films et al., 2007): another concluding image – Otilia (Anamaria Marinca) acknowledges our intruding presence.

film world and future work might also expand the sense of our sometime 'presence' to characters through the framework of phenomenological film theory – this is particularly invested in considering the relationship of our bodies to the bodies on the screen. That has been beyond my purview here. In terms of what I have focused upon in this study, it seems clear that the examination of direct address can expand our understanding of the 'worldhood' of film fictions in other ways, not only in the specific sense examined in Chapter 6 but in the fluidity of the diegetic–extra-diegetic boundary seen in all three case studies films. Direct address occurs on this and other related boundaries, which makes it especially apt for the kind of enquiry represented here – that is, looking close up at the detail of films and the effects of their choices. Response to these moments occurs neither inside nor outside the film world but in a non-spatial in-between, in which we are encouraged to enter into a kind of dialogue with characters who strive to communicate 'to' us. Direct address is, of course, one of a great many narrational choices available to filmmakers but we have seen that assigning such force to a human agent within the fiction is an enormously significant one. This is not to overstate its importance for film narration more broadly, but the value of attending to direct address has been underestimated and its significance undertheorised. In demanding that we enter into a dialogue with fictional characters, direct address also demands that theory works in harmony with close attention to the details of filmcraft.

NOTES

1. For example, discussing one of film studies' most written-about and most valued films, James Zborowski offers the following:

Vertigo [1958] is one of Hitchcock's least humorous films. Whilst it is the case that the introduction of humour would probably disrupt the movie's tone and its intended effect upon the viewer, this scene can be read as the movie's acknowledgement that an inability to laugh at the situation one finds oneself in – and to attain, even if only momentarily, the distanced perspective, the stepping-out of the situation to look in, the release of psychic energy, that laughter entails – can have fatal consequences. (2008: 80)

Zborowski does not suggest here that *Vertigo* is anything other than melodramatic in its underlying structures. However, he does suggest that the film makes active the question of the appropriateness of humour to its fictional world and suggests, if only for a moment (and in a manner that some might describe as 'Brechtian'), an alternative, more comedic way of playing the scene and, indeed, perhaps then the film as a whole.

2. The relationship of point-of-view shots to 'identification' has been discussed in a number of places (see, for example, Pye 2000 and Wilson 2006).

Bibliography

Altman, Rick (2004), *Silent Film Sound*, New York: Columbia University Press.

Andrew, Dudley (1978), *André Bazin*, New York: Oxford University Press.

Andrew, Geoff (2008), 'The Quiet American: Clint Eastwood', *Sight and Sound*, 18, 9, 14–23.

Aristarco, Guido (1978a), '*La Strada* and the Crisis of Neo-Realism', in Peter Bondanella (ed.), *Federico Fellini: Essays in Criticism*, Oxford: Oxford University Press, 60–1.

Aristarco, Guido (1978b), 'Guido Aristarco Answers Fellini', in Peter Bondanella (ed.), *Federico Fellini: Essays in Criticism*, Oxford: Oxford University Press, 63–6.

Bacher, Lutz (1996), *Max Ophuls in the Hollywood Studios*, New Brunswick, NJ: Rutgers University Press.

Bazin, André (1999), *Qu'est-ce que le cinéma* (11th edn), Paris: Éditions du cerf.

Bondanella, Peter (1992), *The Cinema of Federico Fellini*, Princeton: Princeton University Press.

Bonitzer, Pascal (1977), 'Les Deux regards', *Cahiers du cinéma*, 275, 40–6.

Bordwell, David, Janet Staiger and Kristin Thompson (1985), *The Classical Hollywood Cinema: Film Style & Mode of Production to 1960*, London: Routledge.

Bordwell, David and Kristin Thompson (2010), *Film Art: An Introduction* (9th edn), New York: McGraw-Hill.

Brecht, Bertolt (1978), *Brecht on Theatre: The Development of an Aesthetic*, ed. and trans. by John Willett, London: Eyre Methuen.

Britton, Andrew (1982), 'Metaphor and Mimesis: *Madame De . . .*', *Movie*, 29/30, 91–107.

Britton, Andrew (1978 / 1979), 'The Ideology of *Screen*', *Movie*, 26, 2–28.

Brown, Tom (2008), 'Spectacle / Gender / History: The Case of *Gone with the Wind*', *Screen*, 49:2 (Summer), 157–78.

Brown, Tom (2011), 'Valuing Film Spectacle', in Laura Hubner (ed.), *Valuing Films*, London: Palgrave Macmillan, 49–66.

Brown, Tom and James Walters (eds) (2010), *Film Moments: Criticism, History, Theory*, Houndmills: Palgrave Macmillan / BFI.

Burke, Frank (1984), *Federico Fellini:* Variety Lights *to* La Dolce Vita, Boston: Twayne.

Clayton, Alex (2007), *The Body in Hollywood Slapstick*, London: McFarland.

Clayton, Alex (2010), 'Play-acting: A Theory of Comedic Performance', 62–80.

Clayton, Alex and Andrew Klevan (2011), *The Language and Style of Film Criticism*, Abingdon: Routledge.

Cohan, Steven (2002), '"Feminizing" the Song-and-Dance Man: Fred Astaire and the Spectacle of Masculinity in the Hollywood Musical', in Steven Cohan (ed.), *Hollywood Musicals, The Film Reader*, London: Routledge, 87–101.

Collins, Jim (1981), 'Toward Defining a Matrix of the Musical Comedy: The Place of the Spectator Within the Textual Mechanisms', in Rick Altman (ed.), *Genre: The Musical*, London: Routledge, 134–46.

Costantini, Costanzo (1995), *Fellini on Fellini*, trans. by Sohrab Sorooshian, London: Faber & Faber.

Crafton, Donald (1995), 'Pie and Chase: Gag, Spectacle and Narrative in Slapstick Comedy', in Kristine Brunovska Karnick and Henry Jenkins (eds), *Classical Hollywood Comedy*, London: Routledge, 106–19.

Deleuze, Gilles (1989), *Cinema. Volume 2: The Time-image*, trans. by Hugh Tomlinson and Robert Galeta, London: Athlone.

Dixon, Wheeler Winston (1995), *It Looks at You: The Returned Gaze of the Cinema*, Albany: State University of New York.

Dyer, Richard (1992), *Only Entertainment*, London: Routledge.

Dyer, Richard (2001), *Stars*, London: BFI.

Dyer, Richard (2007), 'Side by Side: Nino Rota, Music, and Film', in Daniel Goldmark, Lawrence Kramer and Richard Leppert (eds), *Beyond the Soundtrack: Representing Music in Cinema*, London: University of California Press, 246–59.

Dyer, Richard (2010), *Nino Rota: Music, Film and Feeling*, London: British Film Institute / Palgrave Macmillan.

Eitzen, Dirk (1997), 'Comedy and Classicism', in Richard Allen and Murray Smith (eds), *Film Theory and Philosophy*, Oxford: Clarendon, 394–411.

Falcon, Richard (1998), 'The Discreet Harm of the Bourgeoisie', *Sight and Sound*, 8, 4, 10–12.

Feuer, Jane (1993), *The Hollywood Musical* (2nd edn), Bloomington: Indiana University Press.

Gibbs, John (2006), 'Filmmakers' Choices', in John Gibbs and Douglas Pye (eds), *Close Up 01*, London: Wallflower.

Gledhill, Christine (ed.) (1987), *Home is Where the Heart is: Studies in Melodrama and the Woman's Film*, London: BFI.

Gorbman, Claudia (1978), 'Music as Salvation: Notes on Fellini and Rota', in Peter Bondanella (ed.), *Federico Fellini: Essays in Criticism*, Oxford: Oxford University Press, 80–94.

Gorbman, Claudia (1987), *Unheard Melodies: Narrative Film Music*, London: BFI.

Gunning, Tom (1990), 'The Cinema of Attractions: Early Film, its Spectator and the Avant-Garde', in Thomas Elsaesser (ed.), *Early Cinema: Space, Frame, Narrative*, London: BFI, 56–62.

Gunning, Tom (1991), *D. W. Griffith and the Origins of American Narrative Film: The Early Years at Biograph*, Urbana: University of Illinois Press.

Gunning, Tom (1995), 'Crazy Machines in the Garden of Forking Paths: Mischief Gags and the Origins of American Film Comedy', in Kristine Brunovska Karnick and Henry Jenkins (eds), *Classical Hollywood Comedy*, London: Routledge, 87–105.

Gunning, Tom (1999), 'An Aesthetic of Astonishment: Early Film and the (In)credulous Spectator', in Leo Braudy and Marshall Cohen (eds), *Film Theory and Criticism: Introductory Readings* (5th edn), Oxford: Oxford University Press, 818–32.

Heath, Stephen (1974), 'Lessons from Brecht', *Screen*, 15, 2 (Summer), 103–28.

Heath, Stephen (1978), 'The Question Oshima', in Paul Willemen (ed.), *Ophuls*, London: BFI, 75–87.

Heath, Stephen (1981), *Questions of Cinema*, London: Macmillan.

Hornby, Nick (1995), *High Fidelity*, London: Penguin.

Kaplan, E. Ann (1998), 'Classical Hollywood Film and Melodrama', in John Hill and Pamela Church Gibson (eds), *The Oxford Guide to Film Studies*, Oxford: Oxford University Press, 272–82.

Keel, Anna and Christian Strich (eds) (1976), *Fellini on Fellini*, trans. by Isabel Quigly, London: Eyre Methuen.

Kemp, Phillip (1999), sleeve notes to the BFI VHS release of *Le Notti di Cabiria*.

Kezich, Tullio (2007), *Federico Fellini: His Life and Works*, London: I. B. Tauris.

Klevan, Andrew (2005), *Film Performance: From Achievement to Appreciation*, London: Wallflower.

Kozloff, Sarah (1988), *Invisible Storytellers: Voice-over Narration in American Fiction Film*, London: University of California Press.

Kristeva, Julia (1982), *Powers of Horror: An Essay on Abjection*, New York: Columbia University Press.

Landy, Marcia (2000), *Italian Film*, Cambridge: Cambridge University Press.

Lellis, George (1982), *Bertolt Brecht: Cahiers du cinéma and Contemporary Film Theory*, Ann Arbor: UMI Research Press.

Levinson, Jerrold (1996), 'Film Music and Narrative Agency', in David Bordwell and Noël Carroll (eds), *Post Theory. Reconstructing Film Studies*, Wisconsin: University of Wisconsin Press, 248–82.

MacCabe, Colin (1974), 'Realism and the Cinema: Notes on Some Brechtian Theses', *Screen*, 15, 2, 7–27.

MacCabe, Colin (1975 / 1976), 'The Politics of Separation', *Screen*, 16, 4, 46–58.

MacDowell, James (2010), 'Notes on Quirky', *Movie: A Journal of Film Criticism*, 1, http://www2.warwick.ac.uk/fac/arts/film/movie/contents/notes_on_quirky.pdf, last accessed 15 September 2011.

MacDowell, James (2011), 'Defining "Quirky"', *Alternate Takes*, http://www.alternatetakes.co.uk/?2011,3,250, last accessed 15 September 2011.

Marcus, Millicent (1993), 'Fellini's *La Strada*: Transcending Neo-realism', in Peter Bondanella and Cristina Degli-Espositi (eds), *Perspectives on Federico Fellini*, New York: G. K. Hall, 87–99.

Marks, Laura (2000), *The Skin of the Film: Intercultural Cinema, Embodiment, and the Senses*, Durham, NC: Duke University Press.

Metz, Christian (1975), 'The Imaginary Signifier', *Screen*, 16, 2, 14–76.

Mulvey, Laura (1992), 'Visual Pleasure and Narrative Cinema', in John Caughie and Annette Kuhn (eds), *The Sexual Subject: A Screen Reader in Sexuality*, London: Routledge, 22–34.

Naremore, James (1988), *Acting in the Cinema*, London: University of California Press.

Perez, Gilberto (1998), *The Material Ghost: Films and their Medium*, Baltimore: Johns Hopkins University Press.

Perez, Gilberto (2008), 'Looking at the Camera', keynote paper delivered at 'Continuity and Innovation: Contemporary Film Form and Film Criticism' conference, University of Reading, 5–7 September.

Perez, Gilberto (2009), 'Building with Wood', *London Review of Books*, 31, 4, 27–9.

Perkins, V. F. (1982), '*La Ronde*', Ophuls season programme notes, Birmingham Arts Lab, July–October, 32–3.

Perkins, V. F. (1993), *Film as Film: Understanding and Judging Movies*, New York: Da Capo.

Perkins, V. F. (2005), 'Where is the World? The Horizon of Events in Movie Fiction', in John Gibbs and Douglas Pye (eds), *Style and Meaning: Studies in the Detailed Analysis of Film*, Manchester: Manchester University Press, 16–41.

Polan, Dana (1985), 'A Brechtian Cinema? Towards a Politics of Self-reflexive Film', in Bill Nichols (ed.), *Movies and Methods: An Anthology, Volume II*, Berkeley: University of California Press, 661–72.

Pratt, George C. (ed.) (1973), *Spellbound in Darkness: A History of Silent Film*, New York: New York Graphic Society.

Pye, Douglas (1982), '*Le Plaisir*', *Movie*, 29 / 30, 80–9.

Pye, Douglas (2000), 'Movies and Point of View', *Movie*, 36, 2–34.

Pye, Douglas (2002), 'Falling Women and Fallible Narrators', *CineAction*, 59, 20–9.

Robinson, David (date not shown), 'Chaplin at Keystone: The Tramp is Born', *Charliechaplin.com*, http://www.charliechaplin.com/en/filming/articles/212–Chaplin-at-Keystone-The-Tramp-is-Born, last accessed 18 September 2011.

Rohdie, Sam (2002), *Fellini Lexicon*, London: BFI.

Romney, Jonathan (1998), 'Screen: If You Can Survive This Film Without Walking Out, You Must Be Seriously Disturbed' [on *Funny Games*], *The Guardian* (23 October), 6.

Rubin, Martin (1993), *Showstoppers: Busby Berkeley and the Tradition of Spectacle*, New York: Columbia University Press.

Salt, Barry (1992), *Film Style and Technology: History and Analysis*, London: Starword.

Schnitzler, Arthur (1982), *La Ronde*, trans. by Frank and Jacqueline Marcus, London: Eyre Methuen.

Sconce, Jeffrey (2006), 'Smart Cinema', in Linda Ruth Williams and Mike Hammond (eds), *Contemporary American Cinema*, Oxford: Oxford University Press.

Smith, Murray (1995), *Engaging Characters: Fiction, Emotion, and the Cinema*, Oxford: Clarendon.

Sobchack, Vivian (1992), *The Address of the Eye: A Phenomenology of Film Experience*, Princeton: Princeton University Press.

Thomas, Deborah (1982), '*La Ronde*', *Movie*, 29 / 30, 73–9.

Thomas, Deborah (2000), *Beyond Genre: Melodrama, Comedy and Romance in Hollywood Films*, Moffat: Cameron & Hollis.

Vernet, Marc (1983), 'Le Regard à la caméra: figures de l'absence', *Iris*, 1, 2, 31–45.

Walsh, Martin (1981), *The Brechtian Aspect of Radical Cinema*, London: BFI.

Walters, James (2008), *Alternative Worlds in Hollywood Cinema: Resonance Between Realms*, Bristol: Intellect.

Walton, Kendall L. (1990), *Mimesis as Make-believe: On the Foundations of the Representational Arts*, London: Harvard University Press.

Wells, Steven (2008), 'List-making Fans are 1) Trainspotters 2) Sad 3) the Antithesis of Rock'n'roll 4) . . .', *The Guardian*, http://blogs.guar dian.co.uk/music/2008/08/listmaking_music_fans_are_1_tr.html, last accessed 15 September 2011.

Wheatley, Catherine (2009), *Michael Haneke's Cinema: The Ethic of the Image*, Oxford: Berghahn.

White, Susan M. (1995), *The Cinema of Max Ophuls: Magisterial Vision and the Figure of Woman*, New York: Columbia University Press.

Willemen, Paul (1976), 'Voyeurism, the Look and Dwoskin', *Afterimage*, 6, 40–51.

Willemen, Paul (ed.) (1978), *Ophuls*, London: BFI.

Williams, Alan Larson (1980), *Max Ophuls and the Cinema of Desire*, New Hampshire: Ayer.

Wilson, George M. (1986), *Narration in Light: Studies in Cinematic Point of View*, Baltimore: Johns Hopkins University Press.

Wilson, George M. (2006), 'Transparency and Twist in Narrative Fiction Film', *Journal of Aesthetics and Art Criticism*, 64, 1, 81–95.

Wolfe, Charles (1987), 'Direct Address in the Social Documentary Photograph: "Annie Mae Gudger" as Negative Subject', *Wide Angle*, 9, 1, 59–70.

Wollen, Peter (1985), 'Godard and Counter Cinema: *Vent d'est*', in Bill Nichols (ed.), *Movies and Methods: An Anthology, Volume II*, Berkeley: University of California Press, 500–9.

Wood, Robin (2006), *Personal Views: Explorations in Film* (revised edition), Detroit: Wayne State University Press.

Yacavone, Daniel (2008), 'Towards a Theory of Film Worlds', *Film-Philosophy*, 12, 2, 83–108.

Yamaguchi, Masao (1978), 'For an Archaeology of *Lola Montès*', in Paul Willemen (ed.), *Ophuls*, London: BFI, 61–9.

Zborowski, James (2008), '"Between Sympathy and Detachment": Point of View and Distance in Movies Directed by Alfred Hitchcock, Otto Preminger and Max Ophuls', unpublished PhD thesis, University of Warwick.

OTHER TEXTS CITED

(1975 / 1976) 'Brecht Event', *Screen*, 16, 4.

(1995) *Le Nouveau Petit Robert: dictionnaire alphabétique et analogique de la langue française*, Paris: Dictionnaires le Robert.

Index